AF334405

Gender Violence in Poverty Contexts

This book is concerned with understanding the complex ways in which gender violence and poverty impact on young people's lives, and the potential for education to challenge violence.

Although there has been a recent expansion of research on gender violence and schooling, the field of research that brings together thinking on gender violence, poverty and education is in its infancy. This book sets out to establish this new field by offering innovative research insights into the nature of violence affecting children and young people; the sources of violence, including the relationship with poverty and inequality, the effects of violence on young subjectivities; and the educational challenge of how to counter violence.

Authors address three interrelated aims in their chapters:

- to identify theoretical and methodological framings for understanding the relationship between gender, violence, poverty and education
- to demonstrate how young people living in varying contexts of poverty in the Global South learn about, engage in, respond to and resist gender violence
- to investigate how institutions, including schools, families, communities, governments, international and non-governmental organisations and the media constrain or expand possibilities to challenge gender violence in the Global South.

Describing a range of innovative research projects, the chapters display what scholarly work can offer to help meet the educational challenge, and to find ways to help young people and those around them to understand, resist and rupture the many faces of violence.

Gender Violence in Poverty Contexts will appeal to an international audience of postgraduate students, academics and researchers in the fields of international and comparative education, gender and women's studies, teacher education, poverty, development and conflict studies, African and Asian studies and related disciplines. It will also be of interest to professionals in NGOs and other organisations, and policy makers, keen to develop research-informed practice.

Jenny Parkes is a Reader in Education at the Institute of Education, University College London (UCL Institute of Education), UK.

Education, Poverty and International Development Series
Series Editors
Madeleine Arnot and Christopher Colclough
Centre for Education and International Development, University of Cambridge, UK

This series of research-based monographs contributes to global debates about how to achieve education for all. A major set of questions faced by national governments and education providers concerns how the contributions made by education to reducing global poverty, encouraging greater social stability and equity, and ensuring the development of individual capability and wellbeing can be strengthened. Focusing on the contributions that research can make to these global agendas, this series aims to provide new knowledge and new perspectives on the relationships between education, poverty and international development. It offers alternative theoretical and methodological frameworks for the study of developing-country education systems, in the context of national cultures and ambitious global agendas. It aims to identify the key policy challenges associated with addressing social inequalities, uneven social and economic development, and the opportunities to promote democratic and effective educational change.

The series brings together researchers from the fields of anthropology, economics, development studies, educational studies, politics, international relations and sociology. It includes work by some of the most distinguished writers in the fields of education and development, along with new authors working on important empirical projects. The series contributes significant insights on the linkages between education, economy and society, based on interdisciplinary, international and national studies.

Selected volumes will include critical syntheses of existing research and policy, work using innovative research methodologies, and in-depth evaluations of major policy developments. Some studies will address topics relevant to poverty alleviation, national and international policy-making and aid, while others will be anthropological or sociological investigations of how education functions within local communities, for households living in poverty or for particular socially marginalised groups. In particular, the series will feature sharp, critical studies that are intended to have a strategic influence on the thinking of academics and policy-makers.

Education Outcomes and Poverty
A reassessment
Edited by Christopher Colclough

Teacher Education and the Challenge of Development
A global analysis
Edited by Bob Moon

Education Quality and Social Justice in the Global South
Challenges for policy, practice and research
Edited by Leon Tikly and Angeline Barrett

Learner-centred Education in International Perspective
Whose pedagogy for whose development?
Michele Schweisfurth

Professional Education, Capabilities and the Public Good
The role of universities in promoting human development
Melanie Walker and Monica McLean

Livelihoods and Learning
Education For All and the marginalisation of mobile pastoralists
Caroline Dyer

Gender Violence in Poverty Contexts
The educational challenge
Edited by Jenny Parkes

Forthcoming titles:

The 'Poor Child'
The cultural politics of education, development and childhood
Edited by Lucy Hopkins and Arathi Sriprakash

Gender, Education and Poverty
The politics of policy implementation
Edited by Elaine Unterhalter, Jenni Karlsson and Amy North

Gender Violence in Poverty Contexts

The educational challenge

Edited by Jenny Parkes

Routledge
Taylor & Francis Group

LONDON AND NEW YORK

First published 2015
by Routledge
2 Park Square, Milton Park, Abingdon, Oxon OX14 4RN

and by Routledge
711 Third Avenue, New York, NY 10017

Routledge is an imprint of the Taylor & Francis Group, an informa business

British Library Cataloguing in Publication Data
A catalogue record for this book is available from the British Library

Library of Congress Cataloging in Publication Data
Gender violence in poverty context: the educational challenge /
edited by Jenny Parkes.
pages cm. — (Education, poverty and international development)
Includes bibliographical references and index.
1. School violence—Social aspects. 2. School violence—Prevention.
3. Sexual harassment in education—Prevention. 4. Women—Violence
against—Prevention. 5. Violence in adolescence—Social aspects.
6. Children and violence. 7. Poor children—Education.
8. Education—Social aspects. I. Parkes, Jenny, editor of compilation.
LB3013.3.G46 2015
371.'82—dc23
2014039400

ISBN: 978-0-415-71249-1 (hbk)
ISBN: 978-1-315-88396-0 (ebk)

Typeset in Galliard
by Swales & Willis, Exeter, Devon, UK

Contents

List of illustrations   ix
Notes on contributors   x
Acknowledgements   xiv

PART I
Theory and diagnostics   1

1 Introduction   3
   JENNY PARKES

2 Hope and history: education engagements with poverty,
   inequality and gender violence   11
   JENNY PARKES AND ELAINE UNTERHALTER

3 Researching gender violence in schools in poverty contexts:
   conceptual and methodological challenges   30
   FIONA LEACH

PART II
Experiencing violence in the home and the school   49

4 Gender violence in the home and childhoods in Vietnam   51
   KIRRILY PELLS, EMMA WILSON AND NGUYEN THI THU HANG

5 Children's perceptions of punishment in schools in
   Andhra Pradesh, India   67
   VIRGINIA MORROW AND RENU SINGH

6 Corporal punishment, capabilities and well-being: Tanzanian
   primary school teachers' perspectives   84
   SHARON TAO

viii   *Contents*

PART III
Negotiating gender violence　　　101

7　'You don't want to die. You want to reach your goals':
　　alternative voices among young Black men in urban
　　South Africa　　　103
　　ARIANE DE LANNOY AND SHARLENE SWARTZ

8　Young men and structural, symbolic and everyday violence
　　in Lima, Peru　　　118
　　ANA MARIA BULLER

9　Sexuality, sexual norms and schooling: choice–coercion
　　dilemmas　　　135
　　JO HESLOP, JENNY PARKES, FRANCISCO JANUARIO,
　　SUSAN SABAA, SAMWEL OANDO AND TIM HESS

PART IV
Policy and interventions　　　151

10　From assets to actors: reassessing the integration of girls
　　in anti-gang initiatives in Rio de Janeiro　　　153
　　POLLY WILDING

11　Violent lives and peaceful schools: NGO constructions of
　　modern childhood and the role of the state　　　168
　　KAREN WELLS

12　Gender violence, teenage pregnancy and gender equity
　　policy in South Africa: privileging the voices of women
　　and girls through participatory visual methods　　　183
　　RELEBOHILE MOLETSANE, CLAUDIA MITCHELL AND
　　THANDI LEWIN

13　Conclusion: emerging themes for the field of gender,
　　violence, poverty and education　　　197
　　JENNY PARKES

Index　　　207

Illustrations

Figures

5.1   Children's experiences of physical punishment in last
typical week by cohort   73

5.2   Children experiencing physical punishment in last
typical week of school, aged 14–15 years   73

5.3   Children experiencing physical punishment in last
typical week of school, aged 7–8 years   74

13.1   The production and perpetuation of violence   198

13.2   Mediators/mechanisms for countering violence   200

Tables

2.1   Global declarations on violence: contested definitions   13

3.1   Some key ethical considerations in research involving children   39

Contributors

Ana Maria Buller is a lecturer at the Gender Violence and Health Centre, within the Department of Health & Development at the London School of Hygiene and Tropical Medicine (LSHTM). Ana Maria holds an MSc in Social Research Methods from the London School of Economics and a PhD in Public Health from LSHTM. Her main research interests lay on the intersection of gender based violence (including interpersonal and domestic violence, as well as labour and sexual exploitation), health and development with a focus on developing countries, in particular the Latin American region. Her teaching includes social research methods and supervising doctoral students with an interest on qualitative or mixed methods approaches.

Ariane De Lannoy is a sociologist and senior researcher with the Poverty and Inequality Initiative, Southern Africa Labour Development Research Unit, at the University of Cape Town. She holds masters degrees in languages and international politics from the Universities of Ghent and Antwerp (Belgium) and a PhD from the University of Cape Town (South Africa). Her research focuses on youth in rapidly changing urban environments. She is especially interested in youth transitions and decision-making in the complex context of post-apartheid South Africa.

Nguyen Thi Thu Hang is policy coordinator for the Young Lives project in Vietnam. She leads the Young Lives policy work and engagement with policy-makers and government bodies, both at central and sub-national levels, and the National Assembly. Hang has been a researcher at the Centre for Analysis and Forecasting (CAF), within the Vietnam Academy of Social Sciences (VASS) since CAF was first established in 2005. She has expertise and strong policy engagement experience, especially in trade liberalisation, poverty and governance. Hang holds an MSc in Development Economics from SOAS, University of London, UK.

Jo Heslop is a lecturer at the Institute of Education, University College London. She works in the field of gender, education and international development, with particular interests in gender violence in schools, sexuality, identities and the research–policy–practice interface. Her current research is located in Nigeria, Tanzania, Kenya, Mozambique and Ghana.

Tim Hess is currently working with the International Rescue Committee in March, coordinating a research project looking at violence against women and girls in conflicts and emergencies funded from DFID's research and innovation fund. Formerly, he was the International Project Manager for ActionAid's Stop Violence Against Girls in School project in Mozambique, Kenya and Ghana.

Francisco Januario is Deputy Dean for Research and Extension and Course Director for the Masters in Science and Mathematics Education at Eduardo Mondlane University, Maputo, Mozambique. He works in the field of educational assessment, research methods, and gender in education and was the coordinator of the research in Mozambique for ActionAid's Stop Violence Against Girls in School project.

Fiona Leach is Emeritus Professor of Education at University of Sussex. Her research interests are: gender and education, the history of girls' education, training for women's empowerment and participatory research methodologies. She is best known for her research and awareness raising in the field of gender violence in schools.

Thandi Lewin is Executive Manager: Monitoring and Evaluation at JET Education Services in Johannesburg. She is former Chief Director of University Policy at the Department of Higher Education and Training, and between 2007 and 2010, Chief Director of Equity at the Department of Education, Government of South Africa.

Claudia Mitchell is James McGill Professor in the Faculty of Education, McGill University, Canada and Honorary Professor in the Faculty of Education, University of KwaZulu Natal, South Africa. Her research interests include visual arts based research methodologies, youth, gender violence and HIV/AIDS.

Relebohile Moletsane is currently a professor and the John Langalibalele Dube Chair in Rural Education in the School of Education, University of KwaZulu-Natal in Durban, South Africa. Her areas of expertise include curriculum studies, rural education, gender and education, HIV and AIDS education and girlhood studies in Southern African contexts. She is the co-author (with Claudia Mitchell, Ann Smith and Linda Chisholm) of the book: *Methodologies for Mapping a Southern African Girlhood in the Age of Aids* (Sense Publishers). She was the 2012 winner of the Distinguished Women in Science: Social Sciences and Humanities Award (awarded by the South African National Department of Science and Technology).

Virginia Morrow is Associate Professor and Senior Research Officer, Department of International Development, University of Oxford, and is Deputy Director of Young Lives. Her research interests include methods and ethics of research with children, history and sociology of child labour/children's work, and children's rights. She has published extensively on these themes, including her recent book *The Ethics of Research with Children and Young People: A Practical Handbook* (with P. Alderson, 2011, Sage).

Samwel Oando is currently writing a thesis on the relationship between family incomes and sexual violence against children in Kenya for a Master of Arts degree at Egerton University, Kenya. He is a data analyst at the Directorate of Quality Assurance of Catholic University of Eastern Africa. He coordinated the research in Kenya for ActionAid's Stop Violence Against Girls in School project.

Jenny Parkes is Reader in Education at the Institute of Education, University College London. Her specialist interests are in the relationships between violence, intersecting inequalities, subjectivity and education. She has led research projects on girls' and boys' engagements with urban violence in South Africa and the UK; violence against girls in mainly rural contexts of Kenya, Ghana and Mozambique; and is currently researching corporal punishment in Uganda. Her teaching includes coordinating the MA in Education, Gender and International Development, and supervising doctoral students whose research focuses on Asia, Latin America and Africa.

Kirrily Pells is Policy Officer for the Young Lives study based at the University of Oxford. She completed a PhD (London) focusing on rights-based approaches with children and young people in post-conflict situations with a case study on Rwanda. Her current role focuses on gender, inequality, child protection and violence.

Susan Sabaa is Executive Director of CRRECENT, the Child Research and Resource Centre in Ghana. She is a children's rights activist, researcher and a consultant with GNECC (Ghana National Education Campaign Coalition), and she coordinates the research in Ghana for ActionAid's Stop Violence Against Girls in School project.

Renu Singh is Country Director for Young Lives, and is based in New Delhi. With over 20 years of teaching experience in general and in special education in India and abroad, Renu has worked as Director at the School of Rehabilitation Sciences, University of Delhi and was Director of a USAID research project on 'whole school development'. She has been a Governing Body member of the Central Board of Secondary Education and served on various expert committees of the Rehabilitation Council of India, Jamia Millia Islamia University, Ministry of Women and Child Development and Indira Gandhi Open University.

Sharlene Swartz is Research Director in the Human and Social Development research programme of the Human Sciences Research Council and an adjunct Associate Professor of Sociology at the University of Cape Town, South Africa. Her research interest lies in the area of youth marginalisation, inequalities and social values. She is author of *The Moral Ecology of South Africa's Township Youth* and *Teenage Tata: Voices of Young Fathers in South Africa*.

Sharon Tao is an education adviser at Cambridge Education currently working on the DFID-funded Education Quality Improvement Programme in Tanzania (EQUIP-T). Her work as a volunteer teacher in primary schools in Tanzania and Rwanda prompted her PhD entitled: 'Rethinking teacher quality: using the capability approach and critical realism to provide causal explanations for teacher practice in Tanzania', which recently won the Institute of Education's Director's Thesis Prize. Her research and programme activities currently focus on improving teacher well-being and practice, and reducing gender-based violence in schools.

Elaine Unterhalter is a professor in Education and International Development at the Institute of Education, University College London. She was one of the coordinators of the Beyond Access project, a collaboration between Oxfam and the Institute of Education, and led the team conducting the rigorous literature review on girls' education and gender equality commissioned by DFID in 2013. Her specialist interests are in the capability approach and human development and education. Recent research has focused on gender, education, poverty and global social justice with country studies in a number of countries in Africa.

Karen Wells is Senior Lecturer in International Childhood Studies and Development Studies at Birkbeck College, University of London. Her research focuses on how global processes and structures interact with practices of childhood in local contexts and how this dialectic between the global and the local impacts on children's lives and on practices of childhood. She has published widely on visual representations and global/local dynamics of childhood. A specific focus of her research is on representations of violence and suffering.

Polly Wilding is a lecturer of Gender and Development at the University of Leeds, where she is also the Director of the Centre for Global Development. Her research has focused on bringing a gender analysis to urban violence, with a focus on young people in Rio de Janeiro. She is the author of *Negotiating Boundaries: Gender, Violence and Transformation in Brazil* (2012). Her teaching includes Gender and Development modules at MA and UG level, and a module on Gender and Violence.

Emma Wilson recently started her PhD in the faculty of Epidemiology and Population Health at the London School of Hygiene and Tropical Medicine. Her research involves conducting a mixed method evaluation of Internet-based sexual health services in London. Prior to this, she worked for two years as a research assistant for the Young Lives study, based at the University of Oxford.

Acknowledgements

My first thanks go to my co-authors, for their enthusiasm to participate in this book project, their continuing goodwill and efficiency throughout the process of writing and re-writing, and most of all for their brave, inspiring work. A few of them were present when the idea for this book germinated in Dakar at the UNGEI E4 conference on *Engendering Empowerment: Education and Equality* (2010), when activists, practitioners, policy-makers and scholars grappled with the most pressing obstacles faced by girls in pursuit of education, including violence, poverty and educational quality. Also there was Madeleine Arnot, who later invited me to submit the proposal for this book. I am very grateful to Madeleine and to Christopher Colclough, the editors for the book series on *Education, Poverty and International Development*, for their detailed, insightful feedback on the book. My gratitude extends to Anna Clarkson at Routledge for her support for the book.

Many other people have helped this book come to fruition. Colleagues and doctoral students at the Institute of Education, including Jo Heslop, Claudia Lapping, Annette Braun, Emily Henderson, Charley Nussey and Gary McCulloch, have provided encouragement and insight. Discussions with students on the MA in Education, Gender and International Development and the 'Gender, Education and Development' module have also helped crystallise ideas. I am grateful for the study leave awarded by the Institute of Education, which gave me the space to revise the manuscript, to ActionAid, the Big Lottery Fund and the Economic and Social Research Council for funding some of the research discussed in the book, and to the Young Lives project on Childhood Poverty that generated two of the chapters.

Some of my harshest and kindest critiques come from my own family, and especial thanks go to John, Sam and Tom Hughes, and to my dad, Colin Parkes.

Finally, I'd like to dedicate this book to three women who over the years have been such sources of inspiration to me: Patricia, Carol and Elaine. And to the girls and boys who have generously and courageously shared with researchers their 'troublous wringing of hands' (so beautifully evoked in Sylvia Plath's poem) as they struggle against the odds to live lives free from violence. All [12] lines from "CHILD" FROM WINTER TREES by SYLVIA PLATH. Copyright © 1963 by Ted Hughes. Reprinted by permission of HarperCollins Publishers and Faber and Faber Ltd.

Child

Sylvia Plath

Your clear eye is the one absolutely beautiful thing.
I want to fill it with color and ducks,
The zoo of the new

Whose names you meditate —-
April snowdrop, Indian pipe,
Little

Stalk without wrinkle,
Pool in which images
Should be grand and classical

Not this troublous
Wringing of hands, this dark
Ceiling without a star.

Part I
Theory and diagnostics

1 Introduction

Jenny Parkes

Gender violence evokes in us strong emotions. In the course of working on this book, we have been enraged by a girl shot in the head merely for claiming her right to education in Pakistan. We have been horrified by a young woman gang-raped on a Delhi bus, an act so brutal that she died of her injuries. We have been incredulous at a Kenyan judge's decision to pass a sentence of lawnmowing on the men who raped a young woman.[1] These events seem inexplicable in their horror. Our instinctive response is to clamour for justice – for punishments that fit the crime, for protection systems that keep girls and women safe from the perpetrators. While these responses are laudable, we need to beware of our instinctive emotional reactions and to reflect on why these extreme events captivate us. Could it be that the focus on extreme acts at the tip of the iceberg allows us to ignore the murkier waters below where our own more banal, everyday fears are located, at the same time deflecting attention away from the roots of violence in which we may ourselves be uncomfortably implicated? Or alternatively, do these events remind us about our own vulnerabilities? Most of us have memories of bullying, harassment or humiliation (inflicted by us or against us, or witnessed by others), which we may prefer to forget. Individually and collectively we are positioned within regimes of power that discriminate, exclude and violate. Violence is a tool for struggles over power, a means of communication that attempts to impose through force or coercion. It can be subtle and hidden, or banal and commonplace, and mostly it is not particularly newsworthy. As researchers, we are tasked with trying to explain the dynamics of power at the heart of violence.

Research on gender violence and schooling has been accumulating fast since the start of the twenty first century, propelled by movements for women's and children's rights, and with the HIV/AIDS pandemic and the massive growth in primary schooling drawing attention to multiple forms of violence in and around schools (see Chapters 2 and 3). But this new field of research that brings together thinking on gender violence, poverty and education is in its infancy and we are only just beginning to address key concerns around: (1) the nature of violence involving children and young people; (2) the sources of violence, including the relationship with poverty and inequality; (3) the effects of violence on young subjectivities; and (4) the educational challenge of how to counter violence. This book sets out to establish this new field of research through offering innovative research insights into the parameters of the field, its definitional problems, the types of social theory that can be adapted and employed, and the power of contextual case studies to help explore gender violence and the many ways in which violence is embedded in ordinary everyday lives.

In planning the book, I invited the authors to address three different aims for their chapters. Each responded in their own way and brought their expertise into the frame by describing a range of different types of research projects. The three interrelated aims given to authors were to help:

1   Identify theoretical and methodological framings for understanding the relationship between gender, violence, poverty and education.
2   Demonstrate how young people living in varying contexts of poverty in the Global South learn about, engage in, respond to and resist gender violence.
3   Illustrate how to investigate the ways institutions, including schools, families, communities, governments, international and non-governmental organisations and the media constrain or expand possibilities to challenge gender violence in the Global South.

In identifying potential authors, I searched for innovative researchers whose work engaged with multi-dimensional themes and concepts.

Cross-cutting themes and concepts

The book has three cross-cutting themes. Each chapter in their own way explores not a single dimension of gender violence and its relation to poverty, but the complex intersections between *violence, inequality, marginalisation* and *poverty*. Gender violence is a global phenomenon, but its contours are shaped by economic, political and socio-cultural contexts. Our definition of violence is multi-dimensional, and refers not just to acts of physical, sexual and emotional force, but to the everyday interactions that surround these acts, and to their roots in *structural violence* of inequitable and unjust socio-economic and political systems and institutions. Poverty too is multi-dimensional. Understanding poverty only in economic terms omits the social and political processes through which intersecting structural boundaries are set (Stewart 2008; Unterhalter 2012). At these boundaries, where social, political and economic hardship and marginalisation collide, violence may take many guises. Economic distress, generated through the structural violence of the uneven distribution of power and resources, for example, may aggravate sharply delineated gender regimes in which girls' bodies are commodified in various ways – as labour in the family, or as collateral to be exchanged in marriage, or in sexual exchange in which girls are coerced into sex with older men in order to pay costs of schooling or to provide food for the family. Boys and men are expected to be providers, and the impossibility of fulfilling this expectation may create pressure, which is displaced into acts of physical violence (Moore 1994; Barker 2005). The structural violence of multi-dimensional poverty may thus impact differently on the lives of young men and young women. For both, violence may sometimes be a survival strategy.

In schools, underpaid, ill-trained teachers working in overcrowded, poorly resourced classrooms may be unable to provide safe spaces for learning and challenging violence. Instead, there is ample evidence that through their curricula, pedagogies and management structures, schools may reinforce rather than disrupt violence (Kenway and Fitzclarence 1997; Davies 2004; Harber 2004). But the dynamics of violence vary from one context to another, with particular cultural manifestations shaped by distinct political, social and economic histories. With chapters offering case studies from Asia, Latin America and Africa, and from rural and urban settings, we trace the diverse manifestations of violence in specific contexts, and explore the social relations that underlie acts of violence.

The second cross-cutting theme can be described as the relationship between *violence, subjectivity* and *agency*. Chapters focus less on the extreme or exceptional acts that we read about in the headlines than on *everyday violence*: the mundane, corrosive and often hidden practices that imprint their mark on gendered bodies and subjectivities. Through violating bodily integrity, physical violence attempts to wield control, over-determining relations of power seen as under threat. Psychic wounds can be inflicted through humiliation, denigration and exclusion. These forms of violence are frequently institutionalised, taken for granted and no longer recognised as acts of violation by their protagonists. Practices like corporal punishment, exchange sex, forced marriage or beatings by an intimate partner may be accepted because no other possibilities can be envisaged. Young people living in poverty may have aspirations that are unattainable, yet, in not recognising the structural constraints, they may face disillusion and self-blame (Swartz *et al.* 2012). This non-recognition of forms of domination and injustice constitutes *symbolic violence* (Bourdieu and Wacquant 2004). Because they are not recognised as violent, these forms of violation do not make the crime statistics, and yet it is precisely because they are not recognised that they are (symbolically) violent. While this relationship between violence and subjectivity is examined by many of our contributors, we actively avoid the reinscription of victimhood by focusing on the perspectives of young people as subjects, actively negotiating their social worlds. Through close attention to these negotiations, we set out to shed light on the processes through which young people learn about and resist violence and begin to develop critical consciousness.

The third theme, that of *gender violence*, echoes the multi-dimensionality of poverty and violence. *Gender*, in our framing, is not just about differences between boys and girls, but is a conceptual lens for examining intersecting structural power inequalities, as well as a way of understanding how subjectivities are constituted through repeated practice in classrooms, playgrounds and communities where the rules of masculinities and femininities are learned in everyday interactions, and where transgressions are policed by denigration and exclusion (Thorne 1993, Butler 1999; Humphreys *et al.* 2008). Gender violence includes overt acts, including sexual harassment or homophobic bullying, and also those hidden, implicit practices which reproduce inequality and injustice. Following Leach and Mitchell (2006: 7), we use the term 'gender violence' in preference to 'gender-based' or 'gender-related' violence, since the latter seem to imply that some forms of violence are not gendered. However, we take the view that violence is always linked in some way to norms, structures and subjectivities associated with gender, as well as other dimensions like ethnicity, religion, physical appearance, sexuality and ability. Various chapters explore gender violence enacted between same sex and other sex peers, and across generations within school classrooms and playgrounds, in families and communities. This multi-dimensional framing of gender departs from over-simplified dichotomous views of men/boys as perpetrators and women/girls as victims, instead attempting to understand how gendered norms, practices and subjectivities may reproduce and amplify violence, and may also offer spaces for negotiation, subversion and resistance.

Organisation of the book

The book draws together established and new authors to develop the emerging field of gender violence studies in education in poverty contexts. This is a particularly difficult field to research (replete as it is with risks, taboos and sensitivities) but there is a growing range of theoretical and methodological tools, and empirical evidence to learn from, as discussed in Part I, 'Theory and diagnostics'. Bringing together work on gender, violence, poverty and education entails the challenge of working across disciplines: gender studies, childhood studies, sociology, anthropology, development studies and post-conflict studies. As discussed above, the meanings of 'violence', 'gender' and 'poverty' are contested, within and between disciplines. In Chapter 2, Jenny Parkes and Elaine Unterhalter start to map out this terrain, exploring different ways in which poverty, inequality and gender violence have been discussed in theoretical and empirical writings on education in diverse contexts, and developing the multi-dimensional conceptualisation begun above in this chapter. Whilst critical of over-simplified claims that poverty causes violence (or violence causes poverty), they start to unravel some of the complex connections between gender violence, poverty and inequality. In Chapter 3, Fiona Leach considers why this is such a difficult field of research. Drawing on a wide range of studies of gender violence in schools, including her own extensive research with young people in poverty contexts, she discusses how differing understandings of terms, concepts and research approaches, along with methodological difficulties, have stymied the potential of research to provide clear, robust evidence. She also offers concrete suggestions for carrying out sensitive, ethical and rigorous research with children.

Through their wide-ranging review of theoretical, methodological and empirical work around the globe, and particularly from southern contexts, these opening chapters start to map out the emerging field. The case studies presented in the rest of the book build on this body of work to offer new insights and nuanced elaborations of the multi-dimensional framework in research practice.

Part II, 'Experiencing violence in the home and the school' reveals the commonplace nature of violence in families and schools, and some of the effects on girls, boys and teachers of witnessing and experiencing first hand violence in these settings. Two chapters use data from Young Lives, a longitudinal study of childhood poverty in four countries.[2] In the first of these (Chapter 4) Kirrily Pells, Emma Wilson and Nguyen Thi Thu Hang analyse Young Lives data from Vietnam to explore the under-researched theme of children's responses to violence in the home. Their analysis draws out how children's responses to witnessing violence between parents are shaped by old and new structural forces, including cultural ideals of family harmony and rapid socio-economic change. Their subtle discussion of children's reflections on their own family dynamics illuminates the complex, varied and active ways in which children struggle to cope with violence, and how their responses are influenced by age, gender, economic resources and social networks. In Chapter 5, Virginia Morrow and Renu Singh, also working with Young Lives data, consider violence in schools in Andhra Pradesh, India. Drawing on quantitative as well as qualitative evidence, they reveal the high prevalence of corporal punishment experienced by girls and even higher prevalence experienced by boys in this context, alongside an analysis of children's and parents' perspectives. They paint a disturbing picture of how poverty as well as norms about childhood, schooling and gender influence disciplinary practices at school, and of how parents and children collude with these practices, often through fear and helplessness. In contrast, Sharon Tao's research (Chapter 6) examines corporal punishment from the perspectives of teachers in Tanzania. She draws on Amartya Sen's Capability Approach to shift the blame away from teachers, to view corporal punishment as a product of the ways in which teachers are constrained from achieving the capabilities they value. Environmental factors linked to poverty and social conditions mediated by gender relations, and the conflicting capabilities valued by students result in conflicts that are commonly resolved through beating. Through shifting the focus from children's rights to teachers' capabilities the analysis opens up avenues for direct interventions with teachers.

Part III, 'Negotiating gender violence', delves into the relationship between violence and the subjectivity and agency of young people in poverty contexts. Two chapters engage with issues of masculinity, youth and risk. In Chapter 7, Ariane De Lannoy and Sharlene Swartz trace how the structural violence of social and economic inequality, an inadequate education system, and personal experiences of violence and loss, create for some young men in an urban township of South Africa a strong attraction to gang affiliation. However, a central concern of this chapter is to explore the varying hopes, doubts, anxieties and aspirations of the young men as they strive to perform alternative masculinities. Moving continents, Ana Maria Buller (Chapter 8) traces some similar themes in her analysis of young men and structural, symbolic and everyday violence in Peru. Her analysis examines how young men attempt to challenge the contexts in which they experience oppression and discrimination, sometimes through using violence, but also through avoiding and sublimating violence. Buller shows how violence can be a means of asserting social hierarchies and belonging, and at the same time associated with complex emotions of anger, revenge, frustration and shame. Both chapters problematise the dichotomy between perpetrator and victim. Chapter 9, by Jo Heslop *et al.*, also critiques this dichotomy, through exploring how young women negotiate the blurred boundaries between coerced and consensual sex. Drawing on data from a longitudinal study in Kenya, Ghana and Mozambique, they examine how normative discourses about adolescent sexuality, masculinity and femininity are in themselves coercive, through constraining girls' choices about sex. They reflect on the challenges for an NGO project attempting to address these issues, signalling how difficult it can be to achieve meaningful change where structural, symbolic and everyday violence combine. These chapters vividly show the workings of symbolic violence. They trace the complex negotiations and strategies used by young people to navigate violence within schools, families and neighbourhoods, beginning to map out possibilities for young people themselves to challenge violence.

Part IV, 'Policy and interventions', considers strategies to counter gender violence, and how these are constrained or expanded by institutions, including schools, governments, international organisations, NGOs and the media. In Chapter 10, Polly Wilding laments the invisibility of young women in interventions on youth violence in urban Brazil. Through an analysis of two NGO projects that offer a 'holistic' range of interventions, she argues that the emphasis on addressing the more visible, public forms of violence associated with practices of young men means that women's concerns and the multiple ways in which gang violence affects their lives are neglected. NGOs are also the object of Karen Wells' critique in Chapter 11. Through a Foucauldian discourse analysis of NGO campaign material, she shows how NGO campaigns on gender and education in conflict and poverty contexts construct an image of schools as modernity's solution to the 'problem' of communities or societies seen as violent and dangerous. This legitimises the NGO 'right to govern', with childhood, and particularly girlhood, becoming the site for inscribing new attitudes and practices. In Chapter 12 Relebohile Moletsane *et al.* shift the gaze from NGOs to governments. They consider why it is that, despite the South African government's commitment to gender equality, this lauded policy framework has not effectively addressed gender inequality and its manifestations in violence against girls and women and teenage pregnancy. Drawing on participatory research using visual methodologies, they discuss how the films made by female teachers and schoolgirls both echo and challenge norms, arguing that these approaches have much potential for 'from the ground up' policy dialogue.

In the concluding chapter, I reflect on the contribution of the rich body of research discussed in the collection to the new field of gender violence, poverty and education. Drawing on the book's theoretical and empirical insights, I construct a multi-dimensional theory of change, which sets out how violence is produced, perpetuated and countered, and discuss the future direction for scholarship and policy-making in this field. I hope that readers will be inspired to reflect on, adapt and improve this framework, and to create new studies building on the research agenda set out in this chapter, and throughout the book.

The chapters display what scholarly work (not just policy-making and initiatives) can offer to countering gender violence. The field needs more scholarship of the sort in this book. It needs anthropological studies of communities and youth cultures; it needs sociological studies of schools, classrooms, teachers and students' experiences and relations; it needs critical policy research on even well-meaning initiatives and their assumptions, international declarations and agendas and national prioritisations of anti-violence as a means of poverty alleviation. Poverty and inequality are deeply implicated in violence, and violence associated with poverty can lead to children and women finding themselves outcast, marginalised, silenced and damaged by violence. Established gender relations are not always comfortable or safe. Through building on this scholarship, we may be better able to meet the educational challenge, and find ways to help young people and those around them to understand, resist and rupture the many faces of violence.

Notes

1 See extensive coverage of the case of Malala Yousafzai shot in October 2012 following activism for girls' education in the Swat Valley, Pakistan, where the Taliban had banned girls from attending school (Husain 2013); and of the young student in Delhi in December of the same year (Majunder 2012); and reactions to the rape of 16-year-old 'Liz' in Kenya (BBC 2013).
2 Young Lives is an ongoing longitudinal study investigating the changing nature of childhood poverty in four countries: Ethiopia, India (Andhra Pradesh), Peru and Vietnam. The study follows two cohorts of children (born in 1994/5 and 2000/1), their households and communities over 15 years (2001–16). Led by a team in the Department for International Development at the University of Oxford, it is funded by DfID, UK (2002–17) (www.younglives.org.uk).

References

Barker, G. (2005), *Dying to be Men: Youth, Masculinity and Social Exclusion*. Abingdon: Routledge.
BBC (2013), 'Kenyans demand gang-rape justice in police petition'. Available at: www.bbc.co.uk/news/world-africa-24755318 (accessed 31 October 2013).
Bourdieu, P. and Wacquant, L. (2004), 'Symbolic violence'. In N. Scheper-Hughes and P. Bourgois (eds), *Violence in War and Peace: An Anthology* (pp. 202–4). Oxford: Blackwell.
Butler, J. (1999), *Gender Trouble: Feminism and the Subversion of Identity*. London and New York: Routledge.
Davies, L. (2004), *Education and Conflict: Complexity and Chaos*. London: RoutledgeFalmer.
Harber, C. (2004), *Schooling as Violence. How Schools Harm Pupils and Societies*. London: RoutledgeFalmer.
Humphreys, S., Undie, C. and Dunne, M. (2008), 'Gender, sexuality and development: key issues in education and society in Sub-Saharan Africa'. In M. Dunne (ed.), *Gender, Sexuality and Development: Education and Society in Sub-Saharan Africa* (pp. 7–40). Rotterdam: Sense.
Husain, M. (2013) 'Malala: the girl who was shot for going to school'. *BBC News Magazine*, 7 October. Available at: www.bbc.co.uk/news/magazine-24379018 (accessed 29 June 2014).
Kenway, J. and Fitzclarence, L. (1997), 'Masculinity, violence and schooling: challenging "poisonous pedagogies"'. *Gender and Education*, 9 (1), 117–33.

Leach, F. and Mitchell, C. (eds) (2006), *Combating Gender Violence In and Around Schools*. Stoke on Trent: Trentham.

Majunder, S. (2012), 'Protests in India after Delhi gang-rape victim dies'. *BBC News India*, 29 December. Available at: www.bbc.co.uk/news/world-asia-india-20863707 (accessed 29 May 2014).

Moore, H. (1994), 'The problem of explaining violence in the social sciences'. In P. Harvey and P. Gow (eds), *Sex and Violence: Issues in Representation and Experience* (pp. 138–55). London: Routledge.

Stewart, F. (2008), *Horizontal Inequalities and Conflict: Understanding Group Violence in Multiethnic Societies*. Basingstoke: Palgrave Macmillan.

Swartz, S., Harding, J. and De Lannoy, A. (2012), 'Ikasi style and the quiet violence of dreams: a critique of youth belonging in post-Apartheid South Africa'. *Comparative Education*, 48 (1), 27–40.

Thorne, B. (1993), *Gender Play: Girls and Boys in School*. New Brunswick: Rutgers University Press.

Unterhalter, E. (2012), 'Poverty, education, gender and the Millennium Development Goals: reflections on boundaries and intersectionality'. *Theory and Research in Education*, 10 (3), 253–74.

2 Hope and history

Education engagements with poverty, inequality and gender violence

Jenny Parkes and Elaine Unterhalter

Incidents of violence against women and girls currently feature frequently in international news and, since 2010, have ignited a global policy discussion. The role of education in perpetuating and challenging gender violence has been a key theme of these discussions, but recent reviews have questioned whether we are any nearer to tackling and reducing violence (United Nations 2011; Leach *et al.* 2014). The purpose of this chapter is to look critically at the sorts of assumptions being made about violence – how it is defined, what causes it, with what consequences. We focus in particular on assumptions in academic literature about how violence has intensified, dropped or transformed over time and across space, including its links with poverty. The epidemiological studies reviewed in *The Spirit Level* (Wilkinson and Pickett 2010) suggested that violence was linked with inequalities, eliciting considerable controversy[1] (e.g. Saunders 2010). This chapter aims to investigate the interface between poverty, inequality and violence, and shows how there is no simple story. It maps a wide range of links between poverty, inequality and the levels of violence experienced by young people and reflects on the implications for thinking about education interventions.

Here, we offer a particular multi-dimensional definition of gender violence and link this with some of the ways in which poverty and inequality have been analysed. Drawing on these definitional refinements, we argue that the contours of gender violence do indeed ebb and flow across time, space and place. However, we consider that generalised claims about global rises or reductions in violence are misguided, since they neglect the multi-dimensionality of violence and complex ways in which violence is embedded and produced differently in diverse moments, contexts, spaces and places associated with particular forms of inequality. Gender violence is indeed associated with poverty and inequality but these links are not causal in a simple direction. Considerable work remains to be done to understand and explain some of these connections, associations and the possibilities for change. In this, education has much to contribute, but much work remains ahead to develop research and relevant programmes in this area. Our account therefore offers, we hope, a valuable platform on which to build the field.

Defining violence, inequality and poverty

Table 2.1 provides a time line of global declarations on eliminating violence against women and children. This shows how since the 1980s, violence has been framed in terms of children's rights and women's rights, with the two strands tending to operate largely independently of each other. Key definitions, including the UN Declaration on the Elimination of Violence Against Women's (DEVAW) definition of gender based violence (1993) and the definition of violence against children in the UN Report on Violence Against Children (2006) speak to a view of violence that is addressed in terms of its effects rather than its causes. Violence is largely associated with particular kinds of violent *acts* perpetrated under particular kind of conditions. Such perspectives have been a major feature of the engagement of UN agencies and large NGOs in relation to policy-making and legal protection on gender based violence, notably in conflict areas. They have been influential in how data are collected and analysed, and have affected programmes on violence in schools, sexual and reproductive health, and work with boys and men.[2] While we acknowledge the achievement of the definition in the context of widespread silence and denial regarding these forms of violence, these perspectives close off analysis of how the association with poverty and inequality might be explored. For example, in considering causes, DEVAW acknowledges that violence against women and girls is:

> a manifestation of historically unequal power relations between men and women, which have led to domination over and discrimination against women by men and to the prevention of the full advancement of women, and that violence against women is one of the crucial social mechanisms by which women are forced into a subordinate position.

While there is an acknowledgement here of the origins of violence in unequal power relations and gender discrimination, it is so broadly stated that the space to understand links with poverty and nuanced forms of inequality is not apparent. This analysis suggests that the primary social division is between women and men, and that other forms of inequality are not explicit or implicit in these relationships. In the case of the UN Report on Violence Against Children, by contrast, the definitional emphasis is on some of the special features of childhood, and elements of the abuse of care across the generations. However, again the stress is on consequences, particular acts of violence, and one form of social division – between adults and children – rather than the complexity of the situations causing violence.

By contrast, some of the academic conceptualisations on violence, and specifically gender violence, draw out its connections with multiple sites of inequality and that it cannot just be confined to particular kinds of actions, although these are important. For example, Philippe Bourgois' definition of violence includes structural, symbolic and everyday strands. Structural violence is 'chronic, historically entrenched political-economic oppression and social inequality, ranging

Table 2.1 Global declarations on violence: contested definitions

Women's rights	Children's rights
1981 Convention on the Elimination of All Forms of Discrimination Against Women (CEDAW) Obliged countries to pledge to take measures to eliminate discrimination against women	
	1989 UN Convention on the Rights of the Child (CRC) Education as a fundamental human right; states required to take all appropriate measures to ensure that school discipline is administered in manner consistent with child's human dignity
1993 Vienna Declaration Called for elimination of violence in public and private life as a human rights obligation **1993 UN Declaration on the Elimination of Violence Against Women (DEVAW)** Gender-based violence defined as any act 'that results in, or is likely to result in, physical, sexual or psychological harm or suffering to women, including threats of such acts, coercion or arbitrary deprivation of liberty, whether occurring in public or in private life' UN appointed Special Rapporteur on Violence Against Women (SRVAW) **1995 Beijing Declaration and Platform for Action** Opposition to violence against women recognised as integral to realisation of equality, development and peace	
	2000 Dakar Framework for Action on Education For All Goals on education for all children (EFA), especially girls, to have access to and complete basic education cycle by 2015

(continued)

Table 2.1 (continued)

Women's rights	Children's rights
	2000 Millennium Development Goals Goal 2: Achieve universal primary education, ensuring that by 2015, children everywhere, boys and girls alike, will be able to complete a full course of primary schooling Goal 3: Promote gender equality and empower women, eliminating gender disparity in primary and secondary education, preferably by 2005 and at all levels of education by 2015
United Nations Security Council Resolution 1325 (2000) on Women, Peace and Security Mandates protection of women and girls during and after conflict and greater involvement of women in conflict resolution, peace building and peace keeping.	**2000 Optional protocols to CRC** Provided more detailed protection for children from forms of violence, including sale of children, child prostitution and pornography, and involvement and rehabilitation of children in armed conflict
2006 Ending Violence Against Women: From Words to Action Report commissioned by UN Secretary General	**2006 UN Report of Violence Against Children** Violence against children defined as 'All forms of physical and mental violence, injury and abuse, neglect or negligent treatment, maltreatment or exploitation, including sexual abuse' Established Office of the Special Representative of the Secretary General on Violence Against Children (SRSG) to assist governments, international organisations and civil society to work towards ending violence
2008, United Nations Security Council Resolution 1820 Explicitly recognises sexual violence as a security issue and weapon of war and emphasise the importance of women's participation in peace processes	

from exploitative international terms of trade to abusive local working conditions and high infant mortality rates' (Bourgois 2004a: 426). His emphasis on social and political inequalities as well as economic inequalities addresses the critiques of the concept of structural violence as implying an association exclusively with the poor (Kleinman 2000: 228). Drawing on Bourdieu's work, Bourgois views symbolic violence as the ways in which hierarchy and inequality become taken for granted, internalised and 'misrecognised' within subjectivities. At the interface of structural and symbolic violence is everyday violence, which includes not just extreme acts of force but also mundane 'daily practices and expressions of violence on a micro-interactional level' (Bourgois 2004a: 426).

The multi-dimensionality of inequalities associated with violence can help illuminate some of its connections with poverty. Iris Marion Young (1990) links a number of specific oppressions associated with vulnerability and disadvantage as features of poverty, some of which are structural, some symbolic, and some which mix the two. Her list comprises: exploitation; marginalisation; violence; powerlessness; cultural imperialism; and, exclusion from decision-making. By implication gender violence in its association with poverty and inequality may be linked with any of these. Frances Stewart has written about inequality indicating that it concerns not just inequality of *what* (opportunities, outcomes or capabilities), but inequality amongst *whom* (Stewart 2002, 2008, 2009). She illuminates how it is important to understand the significance of inequalities and how they operate vertically (for example, as socially constructed and maintained networks for the distribution and consumption of resources defined in terms of socio-economic groups or classes). In addition, inequalities operate horizontally in relation to ideas such as religious beliefs, cultural or political values. They are also embedded in aspirations, bodies, feelings and emotions associated with valued or reviled identities, material and symbolic exchanges between socially constructed groups defined in terms of race, ethnicity or location.

Elaine Unterhalter (2012) has drawn on three metaphors to indicate different ways of understanding poverty, which we have extended to help us think further about the connections that need investigating between poverty, inequality and gendered violence. In one guise, Unterhalter suggests poverty is seen as a *line* of income, expenditures or education level; inequalities are captured either by the numbers of men or women from different groups who do or do not cross this line or the amount of resources distributed above or below this line. From this perspective, when delineating violence the presence or absence of acts of violence by groups, who are described as situated above or below the poverty line, is investigated. Education programmes to address violence perpetrated or experienced tend to take on particular notions of recasting the behaviours associated with these groups, who are often portrayed in essentialised forms. For example, boys living in poor neighbourhoods can be portrayed in uniform terms as tough members of gangs, while girls from these neighbourhoods can be portrayed as particularly vulnerable because of where they live and the assumptions young men make about them. Education projects that aim to work with these communities aim to shape behaviours of perpetrators or victims to try to insure against violent acts.

In a second approach to thinking about poverty, Unterhalter uses the metaphor of the *trap* or the *net* in which structures of exclusion, exploitation and denigration associated with denial of economic, political, social and cultural resources shape the vulnerability of the poor. From this perspective, violence is structural and symbolic and particular acts of violence are indications of these structures at work. Approaches to education which draw on this type of analysis are concerned with a reshaping of structures and symbols and will work over lifetimes with teachers, learners, education and information systems to build alternative relationships based on class, gender, race or ethnicity.

Unterhalter's third metaphor for thinking about poverty concerns a *fuel* which can drive action against poverty or inequality, but this might take positive or negative directions. Thus, engaging with violence and poverty can take a positive route, as exemplified by Gandhi, Martin Luther King and Mandela, who all thought, wrote and worked to formulate particular words, strategies and social movements to confront the violence of structural inequalities with actions that did not share the violence of this oppression, but instead sought to change it.[3] These processes and social movements were themselves explicitly educational. However, other active engagements with violence may be 'bad education' entailing crime, risk and harm.

Drawing on these writers, we consider that poverty and violence may be understood as both an effect and a cause of vertical and horizontal inequalities, linked both with structural and symbolic manifestations of oppression. Thus gender violence is structural and symbolic, derived from and implicated in inequalities and associated forms of exclusion and oppression. The implications are that, in seeking to document its features and bring about the social change that can transform both the deep forces that maintain gender violence and the particular acts which are its most evident form, education projects and programmes need to work on many levels and with many partners.

In the discussion that follows, we look at a range of writers on violence in different settings and draw out the ways in which their analyses tend to focus on certain aspects of poverty or gender, while underplaying others. We begin by considering different perspectives on whether gender violence is on the increase. The analysis we wish to develop suggests that a multi-dimensional definition of poverty and inequality is needed to make such an assessment. This will throw forms of violence into sharper relief and help to clarify the forms of educational engagement required to address such forms.

Violence on the rise?

We live in turbulent times, with the start of the twenty-first century scarred by global crises. Devastating wars and long-standing conflicts in parts of Africa and the Middle East, natural disasters including hurricanes and extended periods of drought, and financial crises and food shortages have particular repercussions for the lives of women (Unterhalter *et al.* 2010). Global inequality is staggering, with the wealthiest 1 per cent of the world's adult population owning 40 per cent of global assets, while the poorest 50 per cent own barely 1 per cent (Davies *et al.* 2006). Research is beginning to uncover the extent not just of single, brutal acts but also everyday, taken-for-granted violence, with a recent World Health Organization (WHO) study claiming that globally a third of women have experienced intimate partner violence (WHO 2013), and another study estimating that 150 million girls and 73 million boys have been forced to have sex or experienced sexual violence by people known to them (Jones *et al.* 2008). Such statistics beg the question has gender violence intensified in recent times and are forms of poverty and inequality implicated?

Explanations for rises in violence are sometimes associated with inequalities. Wilkinson and Pickett (2010) use statistical evidence to demonstrate that levels of violence are highest in more economically unequal countries, though their analysis has been criticised for over-generalising from a limited evidence base, mainly drawn from high income countries (see endnote 1). The World Health Organization study on intimate partner violence (IPV) found that prevalence was higher in poorer regions, with 37 per cent of women in Africa, the Eastern Mediterranean and South-East Asia experiencing IPV, and lower in high income countries, though still 23 per cent of women in these countries reported such experiences (WHO 2013). Another study in ten sites around the world found considerable variability, with between 15 per cent and 71 per cent of women reporting violence by their intimate partners, and violence more prevalent and more severe in rural settings than in more industrialised sites (Garcia-Moreno *et al.* 2006). A review of 41 studies of economic empowerment and IPV found that household assets and women's education were protective, though sometimes women's engagement in income generation was associated with increases in violence in the home (Vyas and Watts 2009). Sylvia Walby (2013) claims that a number of features of modernity are generating new forms of violence, including violence associated with inequalities produced by neoliberalism, increasingly coercive criminal justice systems, and changing patterns of warfare. These forms of violence associated with interconnected modernities, she argues, reveal how violence is perpetrated by the powerful against the disadvantaged.

However, in contrast to the line of discussion on violence rising, other writers claim that we are living in more peaceful times, and that modernity brings a civilising influence (Elias 1994; Pinker 2011). Steven Pinker stresses the influence since the Universal Declaration of Human Rights in 1948 of human rights discourse: 'the decline of violence against women in the West is pushed along by a humanist mindset that elevates the rights of individual people over the traditions of the community, and that increasingly embraces the vantage point of women' (Pinker 2011: 499). Walby (2013), however, criticises such perspectives for associating contemporary violence with poorer countries and disadvantaged people, and neglecting the inequalities and injustices in countries in the north. For many women and girls, life has never been better, with huge strides towards gender equality in education, health and participation in political, social and economic life since the 1990s, although there is still a considerable way to go (World Economic Forum 2013). In the USA and UK, although it remains difficult for women who are victims of rape or other sexual assault to have these crimes investigated, prosecuted, and perpetrators punished, feminist activism has led to legislative change, provision of domestic violence shelters and rape crisis centres. Pinker claims that the world today 'is blessed by unprecedented levels of peaceful coexistence' (Pinker 2011: xix). Could it be that, as women become more central to the political, social and economic stage, there is a shift away from militaristic, 'masculinised' norms towards more democratic, 'feminised' norms? Perhaps we should not be so quick to dismiss the 'civilising' dimensions of modernity, which include the influence of movements for the rights of women, children and other marginalised groups. We might allow the possibility that feminism has had a positive influence on gender regimes, perhaps leading to reductions in gender violence through shifting attitudes, changing inequitable norms and improving institutional practices for violence prevention and response.

Given the multi-dimensionality of our definition of gender violence, it appears to us that both processes may be happening simultaneously. Thus failures to address entrenched inequalities and forms of poverty within and between countries may continue to perpetuate gender violence while, at the same time, the education, peace and tolerance dividend will deliver improved quality of life with reduced threats of violence for those who live in particular locales. An important aspect of global policy-making with regard to gender and education is to try to ensure that the benefits for the few are extended to the many. This point is brought into sharp focus when we consider gender violence in zones of war and conflict.

Gender and youth in war and conflict

War and armed conflicts associated with insurrections, revolutions, terrorism and crime are a key index of conflict, and gender is very often deployed in inciting support for and sustaining armed conflict (Enloe 2000; Al-Ali and Pratt 2009). Poverty and inequalities often form part of the rationale for armed conflicts. Since the end of the Cold War, there has been a general decline in global armed conflict, but this has been much more marked in richer countries. There have been protracted smaller scale and more diverse conflicts in some of the poorest regions, particularly in Sub-Saharan Africa and Central and South Asia, as well as in the Middle East (Lacina and Gleditsch 2005; OECD 2012).

War and conflict are highly gendered, with men, women, boys and girls affected differently by fragility and conflict. Men, who make up the majority of soldiers and those taking an active combat role, are more likely to suffer from direct violence, injury and killing through combat. Women do serve in some armies, but not always on the front line. In addition a key feature of armed conflict from the end of the nineteenth century has been the extension of the field of combat to include civilian populations. Feminist activism has resulted in key UN Resolutions (1325 and 1820 – see Table 2.1) that recognise the extent of systematic rape and sexual violence and sexual exploitation as well as women's involvement in conflict resolution and peace-building. As Graca Machel's seminal work documented, rape can be used to torture, humiliate and terrorise the enemy (Machel 1996). Men and boys too suffer from sexual violence in war and conflict, though the evidence on this is sparse, in part because disclosure risks further shame of humiliation and emasculation (Trenholm *et al.* 2013).

The gendered effects of conflicts do not end with a cessation of armed attacks. In fragile states, weak public services, lack of access to justice and physical insecurity affect women, and particularly poor women, disproportionately. In the aftermath of conflict, violence and sexual assault against girls has been found to persist in and around schools (McKay 2004; Sharkey 2008). A study of refugee camps in Guinea and Sierra Leone, for example, found that girls were exploited for sex by humanitarian workers and teachers and that, although employing classroom assistants offered some protection, these assistants tended to reinforce rather than challenge unequal gender norms (Kirk 2007). Further, a number of studies attest to the deprivations refugees experience, even in the richest countries (Pinson *et al.* 2010; Hyndman and Giles 2011).

Overwhelmingly it is and always has been men who commit most acts of violence. Social scientists have struggled to account for this 'truth' without resorting to essentialising biological explanations about male aggression or testosterone levels. Raewyn Connell's concept of hegemonic masculinity has generated a rich scholarship which goes some way to explain the association of masculinity and violence. Connell conceives hegemonic masculinity to be 'the configuration of gender practice which embodies the currently accepted answer to the problem of legitimacy of patriarchy, which guarantees (or is taken to guarantee) the dominant position of men and the subordination of women' (Connell 1995: 77). While there has been a lack of conceptual clarity about whether hegemonic masculinities describe norms, aspirations or ideals (Hearn 2012), and while features vary from context to context, there tends to be a confluence around particular constellations of characteristics, including 'heterosexuality, toughness, power and authority, competitiveness and the subordination of gay men' (Frosh *et al.* 2002: 76). Within this framing, violence may be a strategy to maintain the gender order and, while not all men practise violence, the fact that some men do enables men in general to 'reap the patriarchal dividend', often leading to complicity.

In an attempt to theorise the link between violence and masculinity, Henrietta Moore argues that hegemonic masculinities are idealised discourses, invested with fantasies of power and agency, and that the failure to sustain or achieve subject positions in the dominant gender discourse can generate a crisis of identity: 'the inability to maintain the fantasy of power triggers a crisis in the fantasy of identity and violence is a means of resolving this crisis because it acts to reconfirm the nature of a masculinity otherwise denied' (Moore 1994: 154). In other words, violence may both be performative, projecting an idealised masculine identity of control over women and weaker, or feminised men, and it may arise from frustration or thwarting at the impossibility of attaining the ideal.

The scholarship on war, gender and the difficulties of peace-building (Cockburn 1996; Jacobs *et al.* 2000) illustrates the importance of using multidimensional concepts to think about gender in relation to why particular forms of violence are incited. Narratives of women and girls about their wartime experiences illuminate how the reverberations extend far beyond the explosive moments of violence. For example, in an ethnographic study in the highlands of Peru with communities affected by the armed conflict of the 1980s and 1990s, women spoke sometimes about rape and sexual violations, but more often about how they suffered legal and socio-economic injustice and ethnic discrimination (Theidon 2007). In the aftermath of conflicts, women's experiences of war may be silenced or distorted. In Rwanda, for example, the government project of rebuilding the nation post-genocide has led to the creation of forms of cultural memory that remember the dead but fail to recognise the experiences of vast numbers of women survivors' of violence – both as victims and perpetrators (Burnet 2012; Andrews 2013).

However, there are studies that reveal women's memories of war, and how conflict can be both destructive and transformatory for young women. Joanne de Berry's study of young women living in settlement camps during the war in Uganda documents their horrific experiences of rape and sexual abuse by soldiers, often resulting in pregnancy, the threat of HIV/AIDS, and depression and anxiety (de Berry 2004). Yet after the war, their liminal position as single mothers forced them to labour (often brewing beer and working on the land) which enabled them to maintain positions of comparative social and economic advantage, and relative autonomy in a traditionally patriarchal context. In another study, women recalling their engagement as members of the female detachment of FRELIMO in the military conflict in Mozambique in the 1960s, recalled how the socialist ideology of the insurgency had invited them to overturn gender- and age-based hierarchies (West 2005). In retrospect, this time was viewed as a 'golden age', while the post-independence period was viewed with resentment and disappointment, as FRELIMO's commitment to gender equality flagged. Atreyee Sen's study of women in India traces how joining the aggressive right-wing Shiv Sena movement derived from harsh socio-economic conditions combined with displacement and alienation, as well as sexual exploitation in the jobs they took following migration to Bombay slums. In a context where girls and women were expected to be gentle and compliant, for these women, although violence transgressed gender boundaries, they viewed it as functional since it enabled them to gain a sense of control and solidarity in their lives (Sen 2006: 8).

These studies show how war and conflict may sometimes expand women's autonomy, increasing their mobility, resources and leadership opportunities, and disrupting social codes and gender regimes. The material changes to their lives can enable women to recognise inequalities and injustices previously taken for granted through processes of symbolic violence, and to realise their own resourcefulness and resilience. But often these disruptions are momentary, and multiple political, social, cultural and economic forces combine in working against long-term transformations. Education seems to have the potential to support these struggles against intersecting inequalities, but there is little evidence of this happening. Indeed some writers have argued that a global tendency to merge security and development is leading to resources re-directed towards the military and away from areas like education, thus deflecting attention away from the structural inequalities at the root of conflict (Novelli 2013). Since Dakar (see Table 2.1) and the growing awareness that at least half of children out of school live in conflict affected areas, there has been increasing emphasis on provision of education in emergencies and education for peace-building; however, inequalities, including gender, are frequently not taken on board in programming (UNICEF 2010; UNESCO 2011; Corrie 2013).

Girlhood, masculinity, modernity and risk

The evident forms of violence implicated in armed conflicts and their aftermath highlight extreme conditions. However, more taken-for-granted forms of inequality are persistent features of experiences of everyday violence, with its mixture of the structural and the symbolic, under conditions of modernity and risk. Indeed, it may be that the very conditions that help fuel modernity and market liberalisation, such as physical, financial and social mobility, entrepreneurialism, risk and the power of symbols, often associated with gendered bodies conferred by ICT, both erode some forms of inequality and entrench others. A number of writers have argued that increasing economic insecurity, inequalities and destabilisation of gender norms that sustain male privilege combine to make the attainment of hegemonic masculine ideals even more impossible, increasing the potential for violence (Wilkinson and Pickett 2010; Decoteau 2013). Indeed, some of the insights regarding the connection between the ideal and the real noted in the debate about hegemonic masculinities discussed above, may be useful in explaining the ways in which particular configurations of gender are evident in forms of violence associated with inequalities in the global north and south.

Recent sociological studies of girlhood in the global north have traced some of the dilemmas faced by girls today, bombarded as they are by mixed messages about what it means to be a girl. Judith Butler's theory of gender performativity has informed much of this work, generating rich insights into how masculine and feminine identities become 'fixed' through repeated acts (Butler 1990). According to Butler, the fragility of gender categories is revealed by the forms of violence, denigration and exclusion that are used to 'police' those who transgress gender codes. Other writers have stressed how the erosion of structures of class, community and family in 'risk societies' and the shift towards reflexive individualism can create uncertainty, anxiety and risk for young people constructing identities (Mitchell *et al.* 2004). New technology can aggravate these anxieties, as illustrated in UK studies, in which a third of 11–16-year-olds admitted that they had been targeted, threatened or humiliated through cyber-bullying (Livingstone and Palmer 2012), and one in six girls reported having been forced to have sex by their boyfriends, with mobile phones and the Internet used by boys to humiliate and threaten girlfriends (Barter *et al.* 2009). 'Sexting', in which young people exchange sexual messages and images through mobile phones and the Internet, is increasingly commonplace and, in a context where consumer oriented, popular culture sexualises female bodies, often young people, and particularly girls, feel pressurised to engage in these practices (Ringrose *et al.* 2012).

Alongside this body of work which stresses girls' increasing vulnerability is another strand that views girls as becoming increasingly violent in contemporary societies. McRobbie (2009) asserts that shifting technologies associated with fashion and beauty, education and work, sexuality and reproduction, and commercialism are producing new femininities, resulting in, for example the 'phallic girl', who mimics masculine norms, like swearing, drinking and fighting. Other studies lend some support to the notion that girls in the UK are increasingly adopting masculine practices, but see this not as mimicry but as a form of resistance or rupture (Renold and Ringrose 2012). Girls are expected to display contradictory characteristics, including hyper-feminine embodiments as nice, nurturing, passive and sexually desirable as well as those ascribed to masculinity (rational, competitive, sexually assertive). These contradictory characteristics were clearly evident in an account given by Lauren, a 15-year-old girl who participated in a study of risk in a gang affected neighbourhood in London. Her frequent movement between glamorous femininity embodied in the piercings on her face and elaborately crafted hairstyles, together with frequent violent conflicts that had resulted in exclusion from school were summed up in her self-description: 'Put it this way, I'm a fighter, that's how I am. I take out my piercings and I fight' (Parkes and Conolly 2011). While for many girls movement between these contradictory subject positions may be managed successfully, for Lauren, and for the working-class, urban girls on the fringes of school exclusion in another London based study, these moves could bring them into conflict with school authorities and with their families (Archer *et al.* 2010). Indeed, Archer *et al.* argue that these findings challenge claims of the erosion of social structures, but that the effects of social class, gender and ethnicity/race are becoming more obscure, hidden within a discourse of individualism in a meritocratic society.

At the same time, claims about increasing levels of female violence are frequently exaggerated, with young women accounting for a tiny amount of violent crime in the UK (Eagle and Arnull 2009). A number of studies reveal that girls' reasons for committing crime and violence are far more complex than a straightforward mimicking of boys' aggression, including histories of physical, sexual and emotional abuse, of self-harm and drug abuse, and of coercive sexual relationships in which they may be expected to carry weapons or drugs for their boyfriends (Burman *et al.* 2003; ROTA 2010).

Studies with boys in schools have illustrated the processes through which hierarchies of masculinity are struggled over. Emma Renold traced how boys in UK primary schools attempted to demonstrate 'doing tough, being hard', through games that involved physical power, domination and endurance (Renold 2005). Studies in schools have examined how violence sustains masculine privilege through disciplinary systems, misogynist acts towards female pupils and teachers, and through boys denigrating male peers who transgress gender codes (Mills 2012). A number of studies have examined how homophobic practices in school are central to the constitution of heterosexual masculinity for boys (Frosh *et al.* 2002; Davies and McInnes 2012). The fragile, conflicted subject positions of boys and the elusiveness of hegemonic masculine ideals may produce violence, as the borders of 'acceptable' heterosexuality are policed in classrooms and playgrounds (Phoenix *et al.* 2003). Some boys, however, refuse to take up the denigrated identities ascribed to them, remaking their own identities in ways that defy the heterosexual matrix (Youdell 2004).

While these studies help to show how violent practices are learned in schools and how they may become inscribed in masculine subjectivities, studies drawing on postcolonial gender theory have been particularly effective in illuminating how the contours of violent masculinities may change over time and place. For example, Robert Morrell's ethnography of a white boarding school in Natal, South Africa, traced how colonialism, gender order, racial hierarchies and black resistance influenced punishment practices and the formation of masculinities that oppressed women and subordinated men (Morrell 1998). A further school-based ethnography examined the violent practices of young 'tsotsi boys' in an economically deprived school in Durban, showing how oppositional street masculinities became hegemonic, fuelled by competition for food, and enacted through misogyny, jostling for power between boys, and denigrating weaker 'yimvu' boys (Bhana 2005). These analyses reveal how masculinities are shaped by colonial histories, conflictual transitions and modernising processes.

A further strand of research has focused on the self-destructive dimensions of contemporary youth masculinities. Globally, fuelled by the commercial interests of the tobacco and alcohol industries, men face greater health burdens than women because of masculinity norms that involve risk-taking, including consumption of alcohol, smoking, unsafe sex, driving injuries and violence (Hawkes and Buse 2013). Much of the work on masculinity and risk focuses on how precarious socio-economic conditions create uncertainty and insecurity for young men (Barker 2005; Connell 2008). In the USA, for example, Philippe Bourgois studied Puerto Rican young men in crack joints in an East Harlem barrio, for whom crack dealing, and associated violence, offered 'respect' in a context where legitimate opportunities were denied, in part through institutionalised racism. He describes hearing graphic accounts of rapes by those he had befriended during his field work: 'ultimately the violence against women . . . reflected itself back on a sense of internalised worthlessness that the misogyny of their frustrated patriarchal dreams was not able to placate' (Bourgois 2004b: 346).

In the UK, John Pitts traces the proliferation of gangs from the end of the twentieth century to a political economy which created neighbourhoods of acute deprivation and crime (Pitts 2008: 7). While gang crime has been influenced by the global drugs trade, Jamaican 'yardies', and Americanisation of popular youth culture, for most young men who join gangs, he argues that popular culture is much less influential than socio-cultural factors. And for many young men, whom he terms 'reluctant gangsters', joining gangs is a way to try to keep themselves safe in a highly dangerous situation. Similarly, studies of young people living in gang affected neighbourhoods in the UK and in South Africa identified a complex range of emotions influencing boys' risk engagements (Parkes 2008; Parkes and Conolly 2013). Boys were both attracted to the hegemonic ideals of toughness, control and affluence displayed by gang members, and critical of their extreme violent practices. Boys in London spoke of how they felt it necessary to fight back if attacked with a knife, because they perceived humiliation by their peers if they were seen to display signs of cowardice as a greater risk to their identities (Parkes and Conolly 2013). Negotiating masculinities for boys growing up in communities blighted by high levels of gang crime and unemployment can be fraught, with violence of the neighbourhood reverberating in peer relationships in school.

Transforming forms of violence and gender associated with hyper-modernities requires multi-layered engagements with young people, and with the institutions – schools, media and technology, commerce and advertising – that foster these paradoxical youth subjectivities. Education may have an important role in bringing into view the continuing political, social and economic divisions and inequalities that are obscured in consumerist, individualistic cultures, so that girls and boys are able to reflect on processes of subjectification and the configurations of gender that produce everyday violence.

Conclusion

These examples indicate a complex set of relations in which, depending on particular social relations, locations and conditions of conflict or post-conflict, some forms of violence are increasing and others, decreasing. Sometimes the structural features of violence are particularly salient, sometimes its symbolic features are more evident, and sometimes both are apparent. Poverty construed as a line, a trap or as fuel and violence are implicated with each other and, as we have shown, may be read both as an effect and a cause of reproducing vertical and horizontal inequalities. These in turn support structural and symbolic manifestations of oppression.

However, detailed contextualization of these processes shows up the many different forms of violence and poverty associated with gender inequalities. In our view, it is a mistake therefore to think about direct, simple causal links between gender, poverty and violence. To do this directs analysis towards a single meaning of poverty, possibly based on income, or a single form of violence, say a physical act, and a single notion of gender implicating men or women. As we have shown, gender, poverty and violence are multi-dimensional, dynamic and associational in more complex ways. For example, particular networks of relationships, like horizontal and vertical inequalities and hegemonic masculinities, are nested in each other. Clusters of structural and symbolic violence tend to be seen together under particular kinds of conditions.

This more detailed form of associational mapping of relationships appears to us a crucial accompaniment to work on the ways in which formal and informal education can be used to undo the structural and symbolic manifestations of violence by offering alternative explanations and enactments of different social relationships. Some schools and educational encounters reproduce the rage and exclusion documented in work on gender, poverty and violence. But education is also a key component of efforts at peace-building, reforming gender relationships, and reducing inequalities. In order for this process to be more effective the details of the multi-dimensional associational relationships entailed in poverty, gender inequality and violence need to be better understood.

Thus gender violence is structural and symbolic, derived from and implicated in vertical and horizontal inequalities and associated forms of exclusion and oppression, and the many different ways in which poverty can be understood. In seeking to document its features and bring about the social change that can transform both the deep forces that maintain gender violence and the particular acts which are its most evident form, education projects and programmes need to work on many levels and with many partners. There is much to understand in order to effect the change so movingly invoked in Seamus Heaney's poem as the moment when 'hope and history rhyme'.[4]

Notes

1 The Spirit Level draws on statistical evidence to claim that more unequal states suffer from a range of social and health problems, including higher levels of crime and violence, concluding that all would benefit from more egalitarian distribution of income. Critical discussion includes Saunders (2010), who comments they draw selectively from data on homicides in the USA, with no evidence from low-income countries. Other responses make the point that reporting crime is not the same as levels of crime, thus there are methodological problems with the approach.
2 For example in programmes in South Africa working with boys through sport to examine the consequences of violence, if a boy, practising ball control, kicks a ball into a cone, he personally has to do 20 press-ups. In another moment in the programme where his action has negative consequences for the team they all have to do press-ups (Dringus 2013). This kind of programme aims to change personal behaviour by indicating the consequences for individuals and groups.
3 All three are notable for leading struggles that opposed violence and inequality based on race or caste. While these leaders did not themselves articulate a politics that directly challenged gender inequalities, women were prominent members of their movements, and in the process began to articulate ideas about how gender intersected with other inequalities.
4 From 'The Cure at Troy: A Version of Sophocles' Philoctetes' by Seamus Heaney (1991):

> History says, don't hope
> On this side of the grave.
> But then, once in a lifetime
> The longed-for tidal wave
> Of justice can rise up,
> And hope and history rhyme.

References

Al-Ali, N. and Pratt, N. (2009), *What Kind of Liberation? Women and the Occupation in Iraq*. Berkeley: University of California Press.

Andrews, K. (2013), 'Fragmented memories: women, experience and place in Rwanda's genocide memorialisation'. Unpublished MA thesis, Institute of Education, London.

Archer, L., Hollingworth, S. and Mendick, H. (2010), *Urban Youth and Schooling*. Maidenhead: Open University Press.

Barker, G. (2005), *Dying to be Men: Youth, Masculinity and Social Exclusion*. Abingdon: Routledge.

Barter, C., McCarry, M., Berridge, D. and Evans, K. (2009), *Partner Exploitation and Violence in Teenage Intimate Relationships*. London: NSPCC.

Bhana, D. (2005), 'Violence and the gendered negotiation of young masculinities in South African schools'. In R. Morrell and L. Ouzgane (eds), *African Masculinities* (pp. 205–20). New York: Palgrave.

Bourgois, P. (2004a), 'The continuum of violence in war and peace: post-Cold war lessons from El Salvador'. In N. Scheper-Hughes and P. Bourgois (eds), *Violence in War and Peace: An Anthology* (pp. 425–34). Oxford: Blackwell.

Bourgois, P. (2004b), 'The everyday violence of gang rape'. In N. Scheper-Hughes and P. Bourgois (eds), *Violence in War and Peace: An Anthology* (pp. 343–7). Oxford: Blackwell.

Burman, M., Brown, J. and Batchelor, S. (2003), '"Taking it to heart": girls and the meanings of violence'. In E. Stanko (ed.), *The Meanings of Violence* (pp. 71–89). London: Routledge.

Burnet, J. (2012), *Genocide Lives in Us: Women, Memory and Silence in Rwanda*. Madison: University of Wisconsin Press.

Butler, J. (1990), *Gender Trouble*. New York: Routledge.

Cockburn, C. (1996), *The Space Between Us: Negotiating Gender and National Identities in Conflict*. London: Zed Books.

Connell, R. (2008), 'A thousand miles from kind: men, masculinities and modern institutions'. *The Journal of Men's Studies*, 16 (3), 237–52.

Connell, R. (1995), *Masculinities*. Berkeley and Los Angeles: University of California Press.

Corrie, L. (2013), 'Designing a gender module for teachers working in emergency contexts'. Unpublished MA dissertation, Institute of Education, London.

Davies, C. and McInnes, D. (2012), 'Speaking violence: homophobia and the production of injurious speech in schooling cultures'. In S. Saltmarsh, K. Robinson and C. Davies (eds), *Rethinking School Violence: Theory, Gender, Context* (pp. 131–48). Basingstoke: Palgrave Macmillan.

Davies, J., Sandstrom, S., Shorrocks, A. and Wolff, E. (2006), 'The world distribution of household wealth'. University of California Santa Cruz, Center for Global, International and Regional Studies. [Online], available at: www.escholarship.org/uc/item/3jv048hx (accessed 13 January 2014).

de Berry, J. (2004), 'Sexual vulnerability of adolescent girls during civil war in Teso, Uganda'. In J. Boyden and J. de Berry (eds), *Children and Youth on the Front Line: Ethnography, Armed Conflict and Displacement* (pp. 45–62). Oxford: Berghahn Books.

Decoteau, C.L. (2013), 'The crisis of liberation: masculinity, neoliberalism, and HIV/AIDS in postapartheid South Africa'. *Men and Masculinities*, 16 (2), 139–59.

Dringus, S. (2013) 'Process evaluation and qualitative impact assessment of a sports-based HIV prevention intervention in South African high schools'. Unpublished report.

Eagle, S. and Arnull, E. (2009), *Girls and Offending: Patterns, Perceptions and Interventions*. Youth Justice Board.

Elias, N. (1994), *The Civilizing Process*. Oxford: Blackwell.

Enloe, C. (2000), *Maneuvers: The International Politics of Militarizing Women's Lives*. Berkeley: University of California Press.

Frosh, S., Phoenix, A. and Pattman, R. (2002), *Young Masculinities*. Basingstoke: Palgrave.

Garcia-Moreno, C., Jansen, H., Ellsberg, M., Heise, L. and Watts, C. (2006), 'Prevalence of intimate partner violence: findings from the WHO multi-country study on women's health and domestic violence'. *The Lancet*, 368, 1260–9.

Hawkes, S. and Buse, K. (2013), 'Gender and global health: evidence, policy, and inconvenient truths'. *The Lancet*, 381, 1783–7.

Heaney, S. (1991), *The Cure at Troy: A Version of Sophocles' Philoctetes*. New York: Farrar, Straus and Giroux.

Hearn, J. (2012), 'A multi-faceted power analysis of men's violence to known women: from hegemonic masculinity to the hegemony of men'. *The Sociological Review*, 60, 589–610.

Hyndman, J. and Giles, W. (2011), 'Waiting for what? The feminization of refugees in protracted situations'. *Gender, Place and Culture*, 18 (3), 361–79.

Jacobs, S., Jacobson, R. and Marchbank, J. (2000), *States of Conflict: Gender, Violence and Resistance*. London: Palgrave Macmillan.

Jones, N., Moore, K., Villar-Marquez, E. and Broadbent, E. (2008), *Painful Lessons: The Politics of Preventing Sexual Violence and Bullying at School, Working Paper 295*. London: Overseas Development Institute.

Kirk, J. (2007), 'Gender-based violence in and around schools in conflict and humanitarian contexts'. In G. Terry and J. Hoare (eds), *Gender-Based Violence* (pp. 121–32). Oxford: Oxfam.

Kleinman, A. (2000), 'The violences of everyday life: the multiple forms and dynamics of social violence'. In V. Das, A. Kleinman, M. Ramphele and P. Reynolds (eds), *Violence and Subjectivity* (pp. 226–41). Berkeley: University of California Press.

Lacina, B. and Gleditsch, N. (2005), 'Monitoring trends in global combat: a new dataset of battle deaths'. *European Journal of Population*, 21, 145–66.

Leach, F., Dunne, M. and Salvi, F. (2014), *School-Related Gender-Based Violence: A Global Review of Current Issues and Approaches in Policy, Programming and Implementation Responses to School-Related Gender-Based Violence (SRGBV) for the Education Sector*. Paris: UNESCO Education Sector.

Livingstone, S. and Palmer, T. (2012), *Identifying Vulnerable Children Online and What Strategies Can Help Them*. London: UK Safer Internet Centre.

Machel, G. (1996), *Impact of Armed Conflict on Children*. New York: United Nations, UNICEF.

McKay, S. (2004), 'Reconstructing fragile lives: girls' social reintegration in northern Uganda and Sierra Leone'. *Gender and Development*, 12 (3), 19–30.

McRobbie, A. (2009), *The Aftermath of Feminism: Gender, Culture and Social Change*. London: Sage.

Mills, M. (2012), 'Schools, violence, masculinities and privilege'. In S. Saltmarsh, K. Robinson and C. Davies (eds), *Rethinking School Violence: Theory, Gender, Context* (pp. 94–110). Basingstoke: Palgrave Macmillan.

Mitchell, W., Bunton, R. and Green, E. (eds) (2004), *Young People, Risk and Leisure: Constructing Identities in Everyday Life*. Basingstoke: Palgrave Macmillan.

Moore, H. (1994), 'The problem of explaining violence in the social sciences'. In P. Harvey and P. Gow (eds), *Sex and Violence: Issues in Representation and Experience* (pp. 138–55). London: Routledge.

Morrell, R. (1998), 'Of boys and men: masculinity and gender in South African studies'. *Journal of South African Studies*, 24 (4), 605–30.

Novelli, M. (2013), 'The merging of security and development in the education sector: discourses, programmes and effects'. *Educação & Sociedade*, 43 (123), 345–70.

OECD (2012), *Fragile States 2013: Resource Flows and Trends in a Shifting World*. Paris: Organisation for Economic Cooperation and Development.

Parkes, J. (2008), 'Resisting the magnet: a study of South African children's engagements with neighbourhood violence'. In R. Stevenson and G. Cox (eds), *Perspectives on Violence and Violent Death* (pp. 97–106). Amityville: Baywood.

Parkes, J. and Conolly, A. (2011), Young people and neighbourhood risk project: the girls' perspectives. Paper presented at the conference 'Negotiating risk: gender, youth and urban neighbourhoods'. Institute of Education.

Parkes, J. and Conolly, A. (2013), 'Dangerous encounters? Boys' peer dynamics and neighbourhood risk'. *Discourse: Studies in the Cultural Politics of Education*, 34 (1), 94–106.

Phoenix, A., Frosh, S. and Pattman, R. (2003), 'Producing contradictory masculine subject positions: narratives of threat, homophobia and bullying in 11–14 year old boys'. *Journal of Social Issues*, 59 (1), 179–95.

Pinker, S. (2011), *The Better Angels of Our Nature*. London: Penguin.

Pinson, H., Arnot, M. and Candappa, M. (2010), *Education, Asylum and the 'Non-Citizen' Child: The Politics of Compassion and Belonging*. London: Palgrave Macmillan.

Pitts, J. (2008), *Reluctant Gangsters: The Changing Face of Youth Crime*. Cullompton: Willan Publishing.

Renold, E. (2005), *Girls, Boys and Junior Sexualities: Exploring Children's Gender and Sexual Relations in the Primary School*. London: RoutledgeFalmer.

Renold, E. and Ringrose, J. (2012), 'Phallic girls? Girls' negotiating phallogecentric power'. In N. Rodriguez and J. Landreau (eds), *Queer Masculinities: A Critical Reader in Education* (pp. 47–68). New York: Springer Publishing.

Ringrose, J., Gill, R., Livingstone, S. and Harvey, L. (2012), *A Qualitative Study of Children, Young People and 'Sexting': A Report Prepared for the NSPCC*. London: National Society for the Prevention of Cruelty to Children.

ROTA (2010), *Female Voice in Violence Project: A Study into the Impact of Serious Youth and Gang Violence on Women and Girls*. London: Race on the Agenda (ROTA).

Saunders, P. (2010), *Beware False Prophets: Equality, the Good Society and The Spirit Level*. London: The Policy Exchange.

Sen, A. (2006), 'Reflecting on resistance: Hindu women "soldiers" and the birth of female militancy'. *Indian Journal of Gender Studies*, 13 (1), 1–36.

Sharkey, D. (2008), 'Contradictions in girls' education in a post-conflict setting'. *Compare*, 38 (5), 569–79.

Stewart, F. (2002), *Horizontal Inequalities: A Neglected Dimension of Development*. QEH Working Paper Series 81, Oxford.

Stewart, F. (2008), *Horizontal Inequalities and Conflict: Understanding Group Violence in Multiethnic Societies*. Basingstoke: Palgrave Macmillan.

Stewart, F. (2009), *A Global View of Horizontal Inequalities: Inequalities Experienced by Muslims Worldwide*. MICROCON Research Working Paper 13, Brighton, MICROCON.

Theidon, K. (2007), 'Gender in transition: common sense, women, and war'. *Journal of Human Rights*, 6, 453–78.

Trenholm, J., Olsson, P., Blomqvist, M. and Ahlberg, B. (2013), 'Constructing soldiers from boys in Eastern Democratic Republic of Congo'. *Men and Masculinities*, 16 (2), 203–27.

UNESCO (2011), *The Hidden Crisis: Armed Conflict and Education. Education for All Global Monitoring Report 2011*. Paris: UNESCO.

UNICEF (2010), *Progress Evaluation of the UNICEF Education in Emergencies and Post-Crisis Transition Programme*.

United Nations (2011), *Five Years On: A Global Update on Violence against Children. Report from the NGO Advisory Council for Follow-up to the UN Secretary-General's Study on Violence Against Children*. New York: United Nations.

Unterhalter, E. (2012), 'Poverty, education, gender and the Millennium Development Goals: reflections on boundaries and intersectionality'. *Theory and Research in Education*, 10 (3), 253–74.

Unterhalter, E., North, A. and Parkes, J. (2010), *Gender Equality and Women and Girls' Education, 1995–2010: How Much is There a Space for Hope?* Paris: UNESCO.

Vyas, S. and Watts, C. (2009), 'How does economic empowerment affect women's risk of intimate partner violence in low and middle income countries? A systematic review of published evidence'. *Journal of International Development*, 21 (5), 577–602.

Walby, S. (2013), 'Violence and society: introduction to an emerging field of sociology'. *Current Sociology*, 61 (2), 95–111.

West, H. (2005), 'Girls with guns: narrating the experience of war of FRELIMO's "female detachment"'. In J. Boyden and J. de Berry (eds), *Children and Youth on the Front Line* (pp. 105–29). Oxford: Berghahn.

WHO (World Health Organisation), Department of Reproductive Health and Research, London School of Hygiene and Tropical Medicine and South African Medical Research Council (2013), *Global and Regional Estimates of Violence against Women: Prevalence and Health Effects of Intimate Partner Violence and Non-Partner Sexual Violence*.

Wilkinson, R. and Pickett, K. (2010), *The Spirit Level: Why Equality is Better for Everyone*. London: Penguin.

World Economic Forum (2013), 'The global gender gap report 2013'. Online. Available at: www.weforum.org/reports/global-gender-gap-report-2013 (accessed 14 January 2014).

Youdell, D. (2004), 'Wounds and reinscriptions: schools, sexualities and performative subjects'. *Discourse: Studies in the Cultural Politics of Educations*, 25 (4), 477–93.

Young, I. (1990), *Justice and the Politics of Difference*. Princeton: Princeton University Press.

3 Researching gender violence in schools in poverty contexts

Conceptual and methodological challenges

Fiona Leach

Introduction

There is now a relatively large body of research on violence in schools. Although much of it originates in the global North, there is sufficient evidence to assert that schools across the world are not always the sites of safety and security that parents and educators expect them to be. However, little of this research has engaged in a gender analysis of school violence. Much of it has been framed as either corporal punishment (teachers as perpetrators) or bullying (students as perpetrators), with gender-neutral data collected through large-scale surveys (e.g. Akiba *et al.* 2002; Smith 2003), which are unable to illuminate the links between violence, institutional structures and gender inequality. A small number of in-depth ethnographic studies, most of them from Sub-Saharan Africa, have produced rich case study descriptions but they are too small-scale to provide reliable data about the prevalence and patterns of gender violence across societies. Research studies which *combine* large-scale gender-disaggregated quantitative data on school violence with in-depth qualitative insights into the underlying gender-based causes and consequences are lacking.

Despite global concern about the high incidence of sexual violence against women, research into gender violence in schools is surprisingly limited. There are some exceptions, for example a few surveys of sexual harassment in the USA and Western Europe (e.g. Timmermann 2003; AAUW 2011) and some qualitative studies which have raised the issue of violent behaviours in exploring gender and sexuality issues in education (Mac an Ghaill 1994; Kehily 2002). More recently, studies of dating violence, cyber-bullying, homophobic and girl-on-girl violence, as well as heightened concerns over gang violence (and, in the USA, school shootings), have turned attention towards a broader understanding of schools as sites of violence (e.g. Shariff 2008; Bhana and Pillay 2011; UNESCO 2012).

The one regional exception is Sub-Saharan Africa, where there already exists a considerable body of research evidence on the nature and scale of gender violence in schools (Leach *et al.* 2012). This attention to Sub-Saharan Africa is due in large part to international concern over the high level of young people's exposure to HIV, high rates of teenage pregnancy, the prevalence of sexual violence in conflict settings, and the interest in girls' education among bilateral donors anxious to close the gender gap. These studies show that girls are at much greater risk of gender violence than boys, especially when it is of a sexual nature. Sexual abuse by male teachers is a particularly disturbing feature: compelling evidence from several research studies (USAID 2003; Leach and Mitchell 2006; UNICEF *et al.* 2010; Devers *et al.* 2012), supplemented by police statistics on rape and sexual assault, district education office records and media coverage of individual cases, confirms that teachers across the region regularly demand sex from girls in their school. From very limited research evidence, it also appears to be prevalent in Latin America and the Caribbean. Girls living with high levels of poverty and gender inequality are most vulnerable, as are those who attend schools within poorly resourced educational systems with low levels of accountability or who live in conflict zones and in refugee camps (Kirk and Winthrop 2006). In addition, boys as well as girls with disabilities, those from ethnic and religious minorities, orphans and children affected by AIDS are vulnerable to a wide range of gender-based forms of violence and discrimination (UNICEF 2005; Deacon and Stephney 2007).[1]

In this chapter, I pick up on the earlier discussion (Chapters 1 and 2) of the multi-dimensional nature of gender violence in educational settings and its intersection with poverty to explore some of the challenges posed by its complex conceptualisation and diverse manifestations. I consider the particular difficulties of carrying out research in poverty contexts, drawing on my own experience of researching gender violence in schools in Sub-Saharan Africa (and to a lesser extent in India). I start by outlining some common challenges faced by researchers of gender violence in schools and then focus on some of the methodological and ethical issues of relevance to research in the global South, in particular in relation to children.

Challenges to researching gender violence in schools

Researchers face multiple challenges, including differing perspectives on the meaning of violence and associated terminology, uneven evidence from different regions, gaps in knowledge about many forms of violence, and continuing silences and denial.

Differing conceptualisations of gender violence

Early research on gender violence in schools was usually framed in terms of the sexual abuse of girls (Leach and Machakanja 2000; Shumba 2001; Brown 2002; Leach *et al.* 2003), which presented males as aggressors and perpetrators of violence and girls as passive victims. These stereotypical notions of gender based on the binary categories of male and female have now given way in at least some studies to more contextualised understandings of gender as a social construct, which intersects with other social markers such as class, ethnicity, race, caste, sexuality and religion to create multi-faceted and shifting identities and multi-layered forms of discrimination. These more nuanced studies acknowledge that the school, along with the home and the community, is an important site for the construction of gender identities and gender relations built on socially sanctioned inequalities. Those who contest or fail to abide by the dominant (heterosexual) norms of behaviour promoted by the 'gender regime' of school risk discrimination, victimisation and exclusion.

The intersection of gender inequalities with these other categories of social and economic disadvantage creates complex and deeply rooted patterns of poverty, violence and discrimination which are difficult both to map out and to address. Poverty is most often recognised as economic (lack of assets, paid employment, etc.) but it is also social (lack of social capital, disadvantage inherent in class hierarchies) and political (discrimination on the grounds of caste, religion or ethnicity). Poverty complicates definitions of gender violence – where, for example, the boundaries between consensual and coercive sexual relations are blurred by the need for survival or where girls' bodies are treated as a commodity, e.g. as family labour or as a marriage asset, or where, in our increasingly materialistic world, some girls enter multiple-partner sexual relationships with older well-off men to secure gifts or cash to spend on clothing, cosmetics and mobile phones (Hunter 2002).

Once we accept the inadequacies of essentialised notions of gender, it is necessary to recognise the significance of local context to the production of gender identities. To date, much of the research and public knowledge about the global South is cast in theoretical and ethical terms that emanate from dominant perspectives in the North, whose citizens tend to regard themselves as more gender equal (Oyěwùmi 2005). Chilisa and Ntseane (2010) criticise the dominance of Western feminist language, concepts, theories and worldviews in explaining, and usually devaluing, the experiences of non-Western women and men. The need to avoid making assumptions about social rules, norms or behaviours, or assuming common meanings and terminology, presents a challenging environment for researchers working across cultures: for example, local support for corporal punishment as a necessary and justifiable form of discipline may be at odds with the internationally accepted view that it is a human rights violation and a cruel practice; the local acceptance of transactional sex between an older man and a young girl as part of 'traditional' culture may conflict with the researcher's view that it is sexual exploitation or prostitution (Luke and Kurz 2002).

Differing terminology

The lack of awareness of (and agreement over) the gendered nature of violence has resulted in a range of terms to describe various types of violent behaviour in schools, compounding the difficulty of obtaining reliable comparative data. There is evidence that the incidence of violence reported in interviews and surveys depends heavily on the terms used, on how they are interpreted and whether the questions relate to perceptions of violence or personal experience. For example, *sexual abuse* is generally defined as the sexual exploitation of children by adults, which, under the majority of jurisdictions, is a criminal offence; by contrast, *sexual harassment* is usually regarded as a 'lesser' violation of human rights and interpreted more widely as any unwelcome conduct of a sexual nature intended to offend, humiliate or intimidate, and it usually involves adolescents and adults rather than children. However, this distinction is not always made. In turn, *sexual violence* may be interpreted narrowly as referring only to serious assault and rape, or more widely to include verbal abuse, gossip or threats of a sexual nature. And questions about bullying are likely to receive very different responses to those asked about sexual abuse or violence.

Because of the differences in terminology, sample sizes, age cohorts, questions asked and data collection methods used, the research findings vary widely. This can be the case even where the research designs are comparable. For example, Rivers (2000) reported 40 per cent of girls in 12 secondary schools in remote areas of Botswana having experienced sexual harassment at school but only 0.24 per cent admitting that a teacher had asked them for sex; the following year Rossetti (2001), in another study with a similar cohort and location in Botswana, claimed that 67 per cent had experienced sexual harassment by a teacher and that 20 per cent had been asked for sex by a teacher (of whom 42 per cent had accepted). Also, when the term 'abuse' is used rather than 'harassment', figures tend to be lower (e.g. Brown 2002).

Regional focus

The predominance of research from a single region, namely Sub-Saharan Africa, has complicated the search for a balanced and reliable global picture. Research studies conducted in Asia, Latin America and the Caribbean have, until recently, viewed violence in schools in largely gender-neutral terms as either bullying or corporal punishment (UNICEF ROSA 2001; Akiba *et al.* 2002; Abramovay and Rua 2005), with sexual harassment largely confined to universities. There has been little understanding of the complex ways in which a school culture which promotes hyper-masculinity and gender inequality can encourage and perpetuate violence. Moreover, the broad social tolerance of high levels of violence against women and girls in these regions has discouraged national evidence-gathering and policy and legislative reform, and allowed perpetrators to act with impunity.

It is tempting to conclude that gender violence in schools is less of a problem in socially conservative societies where strict sex segregation is practised, as in much of South Asia, North Africa and the Middle East. However, the cultural taboo about discussing sexual matters, the fierce control of female sexuality and the intense fear of scandal as a stain on family honour makes this a particularly challenging environment for research, resulting in the problem being left largely unexplored (Leach and Sitaram 2007). The level of secrecy and denial around any incident of sexual abuse, or even mild harassment, involving a girl is likely to be high and the consequences for her and her family possibly devastating. Any sexual abuse is likely, therefore, to take subtle and secretive forms and to be rarely exposed. Nevertheless, research evidence of sexual violence within schools is gradually emerging (UNICEF ROSA 2005; Save the Children Sweden 2011).

Focus on heterosexual violence

The studies from Sub-Saharan Africa broadly concur in reporting consistent patterns of violence in the form of sexual abuse and harassment, in which girls are most often the target and older male students the perpetrators. Alongside these are regular reports of male teachers demanding sexual favours from girls, often in exchange for goods or preferential treatment in class, with threats of exam failure, punishment or public ridicule if their demands are not met (Leach and Mitchell 2006; Dunne *et al.* 2006; Jones *et al.* 2008). This narrow focus on heterosexual violence has impeded consideration of other less recognised forms of gender violence, including homophobic violence towards lesbian, gay, bisexual and transgender students (and teachers), and new forms which confound the usual authority/age hierarchy, e.g. sexual violence perpetrated by students (usually male) on teachers (usually young and female) or female teachers procuring sex from male students. In South Asia, the strict policing of girls' movements has meant that boys are at greater risk of sexual abuse in schools than in other regions, although this is rarely discussed openly. One exception, however, came in 2004 when Pakistan's Minister of State for Religious Affairs stunned the nation by admitting that they had received more than 2,500 complaints of sexual assault against young boys by clerics in religious schools in the past two years (*Daily Times*, 9 December 2004, *Frontpagemag*, 21 December 2005, cited in United Nations 2006). While acknowledging that girls are overwhelmingly the target of much gender violence in schools, the research agenda needs to be cognisant of the vulnerability of other groups, especially young boys.

Silence and denial

Adults, whether government officials, education personnel, community members or (even) parents, may deny that gender violence in schools is widespread or try to downplay its scale. They may trivialise it as natural sex-related characteristics, such as 'boys will be boys' or 'schoolgirl gossip' (Dunne *et al.* 2005) or resort to the 'not in my school' refrain in response to questions about teacher sexual misconduct (Clacherty and Donald 2007). Female teachers in patriarchal societies, where women are expected to show deference to men, find it especially difficult to comment negatively on male colleagues' behaviour and most prefer to remain silent on the issue in interviews (De Lange *et al.* 2012). This culture of denial is reinforced by teachers' unions, which tend to protect teachers found guilty of sexual abuse and accuse the authorities of witch hunts when cases are investigated.

The extreme reluctance to speak about children's sexuality and sexual activities, and the silence around child sexual abuse, complicates data collection and makes it very difficult to establish a true picture of the scale of the problem. Researchers who are unable to gather supporting evidence from documents or observations may need to decide whether what is reported in interviews and questionnaires is sexual rumour (a mainstay of school culture) or the tip of an iceberg of unreported violence.

Methodological challenges

We turn now to the methodological challenges facing researchers in this field. It has been recognised for some time that standard interviewing and survey methods are generally less reliable with children and adolescents, especially when the research concerns matters around sex and sexuality. Questions of an intimate nature around teenage sexuality and around teachers' relations with pupils may not generate meaningful answers, if any answers at all. This is especially complex when primary-school-age children or vulnerable children are involved.

Interviews are first and foremost adult forms of enquiry, with which children may not feel at ease. They may be inhibited by the formal nature of most interviewing styles, the unnaturalness of the interview process, with the researcher ticking boxes on a form or recording on tape or disc, the location (interviews are often held on school premises) and the constraints on time. The power relations between researcher and researched (in terms of age, authority and gender), social conventions which discourage talking about sexual matters and fear of victimisation or opprobrium may all influence a child's responses. Children may find it difficult to speak frankly to adult researchers in societies where age carries considerable authority and children are not usually asked for their opinion (or, indeed, where the interview is not being conducted in the child's first language). They may feel compelled to participate in the research, even when given a choice. In turn, the desire for children to comply may lead them to interpret the researcher's questioning as 'a search for the right answer' (Pryor 1995: 26), to say what they believe the researcher wants to hear rather than what they themselves believe. This will be especially the case if the interview is being conducted in a location bounded by authority relations and prescribed behaviour such as a school. At the same time, even if children feel compelled to agree to be interviewed, they still have some freedom to decide the extent of their collaboration: as with adults, they can resist or divert the questioning, invent or deny facts and be generally uncommunicative. For example, studies in Botswana, Ghana and Zimbabwe have shown that girls are anxious to downplay their involvement in sexual activity, being aware that they are expected to remain 'pure' outside of marriage, while boys are more frank and informative and enjoy talking about male sexual prowess and exploits. Boys also tend to over-report the extent of sexual activity in the school (Leach and Machakanja 2000; Dunne *et al.* 2005), a tendency which is noted elsewhere (e.g. Mensch *et al.* 2003; Parkes and Heslop 2011).

An additional set of methodological challenges arises when the research involves children and adults living in poor or marginalised communities. The multi-country longitudinal study called Young Lives (2002–17) that is discussed in detail in Chapters 4 and 5 illuminates some of these challenges (Morrow 2009). Using a combination of quantitative and qualitative methods, this study is tracing the changing lives of 12,000 children in four countries over 15 years, gathering evidence on the causes and consequences of childhood poverty and inequality. The Young Lives research teams found that poor, remote and marginalised communities often had no understanding of what 'research' entailed or else confused it with 'aid project' (Morrow 2009), with the expectation that participation would lead to some improvement in their, or their children's, lives. It was not usually understood or accepted that the data collected through the research could be used to inform interventions intended in the longer term to improve their lives. Payment for participation was often expected and any outsiders who were not strictly government representatives providing government services became the object of speculation.

In very poor communities, many parents and community members are illiterate and the children may have only basic literacy. Many adults have a deep-seated suspicion of officialdom and may refuse to sign a consent form (if literate) or give voice-recorded consent. This highlights the need for local responses and adaptation, with researchers who are sensitive to cultural and other differences, and who are ready to invest time in explaining the research in locally relevant ways which reassures parents concerned about why their children have been selected to participate.

Alternatives to standard interviews and surveys

Most of the alternatives offered to semi-structured interviewing with children take the form of what are grouped together as 'participatory methods', i.e. involving people as active agents in the research process. This approach suggests not the usual separation of subject (researcher) and object (researched) but a more equal partnership, one in which both have knowledge to contribute and both can learn from the research process (Hart 1997).

Participatory research with children is a relatively new but increasingly popular method of research in the global South, encouraged by the UN Convention on the Rights of the Child (UNCRC) (1989), which recognises children's right to participate and be heard. Engaging children as researchers or co-researchers involves them in designing the research and collecting and interpreting data, thereby building on their own abilities and capabilities and allowing their agenda to take precedence. It can be an empowering experience for them, while providing adults with a clearer understanding of how children construct their world. It may bring to the fore factors that are important to children which might otherwise be overlooked, e.g. toilets identified as a place of danger for girls, where boys might assault them, and, for boys, the staffroom as they fear being summoned there for a beating. For girls in particular, who are used to being silenced and disadvantaged in relation to boys, this engagement in the research process and the possibility of talking through solutions to their problems provides them with valuable skills of communication and increased self-confidence for use with both adults and peers. For boys, it may develop a greater awareness of how their behaviour can be distressing, humiliating and unwelcome to girls.

Participatory research is an overtly political process when it transforms participants' lives. Its use in developing countries has emerged out of the methodology of Participatory Rural Appraisal (PRA), developed by Robert Chambers in the 1970s to provide a voice to rural communities (Chambers 2002). PRA methodology is now used in very diverse settings, in the process acquiring new labels such as Participatory Action Research (PAR) and Participatory Learning and Action (PLA). The emphasis on visual representation such as diagrams and maps rather than verbal communication makes it particularly suited to children and those with limited literacy. Hart (1997) believes that collective drawing is empowering for children as it shows both to themselves and to others that they have knowledge, and provides a forum for sharing it. Drawing activities with children in participatory workshops have been used in a number of research studies on gender violence in schools (Leach 2003; USAID/DevTech 2008; Chapter 12, this volume) and have proved effective in creating a relaxed climate in which sensitive issues can be discussed with children and adolescents and suggestions gathered on how to combat violence (Leach and Mitchell 2006). PRA is most appropriate when it supplements findings already gathered through other methods such as interviews or stimulates early discussion of issues which can be explored subsequently through interviews.

Other participatory methods which have been tried with the specific aim of facilitating discussion of sensitive issues with children and adolescents include diary and narrative essay writing (Pattman and Chege 2003), discussion of hypothetical stories (Van Eerdewijk 2004), and arts-based visual work which goes beyond drawings to include photography and photo-voice (see Chapter 12) and participatory video (de Lange and Geldenhuys 2012). Pupil-scripted role play and drama are also seen as helpful methods of exploring difficult and sensitive issues with children and adolescents (DramAidE 2000; Nyanzi *et al.* 2000).

Chilisa and Ntseane (2010) see participatory research as an appropriate form of indigenous research that has empowering potential for promoting social justice and helping to fight gender oppression, in a way which challenges standard Western research methods. They cite an example of where women in Botswana insisted on singing songs and telling their own stories about their struggle with patriarchy rather than being interviewed in a conventional format, and where they replaced the moderator in focus group discussions with objects of symbolic importance, a spoon in one case and a basket in another. They also insisted on dissemination of the research findings through the local public parliament. In this way they drew the researcher/moderator into the research process as a participant, an equal and, by implication, an activist who can use his/her research experience to make a difference in the lives of those researched.

There are, however, drawbacks: participatory research is unable to provide an accurate picture of the scale of any particular problem and does not easily allow for the recording of individual views or incidents, and so cannot generate the hard data usually required by policy-makers before they can be persuaded to take action. These methods have mostly been used in small qualitative studies and it is difficult to know how transferable they are to new settings, how reliable their findings are or which activities are the most effective. The facilitation of participatory workshops also requires skill, which can only be acquired through training and experience, and badly managed events can be detrimental to children's wellbeing and even dangerous.

Designing reliable instruments for collecting quantitative data on gender violence for use with children and adolescents is also challenging. Questionnaires and structured interviews usually rely on self-reporting, i.e. subjective opinions and assertions, rather than sustained and objective observations or documentary evidence. These data lack reliability and validity. One alternative which has been trialled by the Population Council with adolescents in Brazil and a number of African countries is audio computer-assisted self-interviewing (ACASI), a technique in which the respondent uses a hand-held computer to listen to prerecorded questions through audio headphones and presses numbers on a numeric keypad to answer them. When researchers trialled the technique on a project investigating sexual behaviour and HIV/AIDS among 6,000 adolescents aged 15–21 in Kenya in 2000 and 2002, they found that it elicited a higher percentage of positive responses to questions about more stigmatising behaviours than other methods, suggesting that the increased privacy and confidentiality can produce more reliable and valid data (Mensch *et al.* 2003).

Ethical issues

As noted above, there has been increased recognition of the importance of giving a voice to children; recognising their right to express their views is contained in the UNCRC. However, the ethics surrounding children's involvement in research have been widely debated over recent years. Participatory research, for example, can be exploitative, given the imbalance in power between (adult) researcher and (child) researched; it can be seen as a quick route to extract information, or as providing findings that are relatively easy to manipulate, without the necessity of formal dissemination at a later date.

There is a vast literature on the ethics of research, although most of it originates in the global North (e.g. Hallett and Prout 2003; Tisdall *et al.* 2009; Alderson and Morrow 2011). Works with an international remit, or relating to research in the global South include Morrow (2009), Powell *et al.* (2012), Farrell (2005), Hart and Tyrer (2006) and Clacherty and Donald (2007). These authors stress how ethical issues are understood in varying ways across different contexts. Morrow (2009) notes the dissonance that characterises the application of ethical guidelines developed in the North to contexts in the global South while Gallagher (2009) repudiates the view that ethics can be reduced to codified sets of principles, and that following these systematically will make research more ethically sound. The continuing weak guidance and monitoring of research projects in the South, however, is worrying, given that research into gender violence may hold a higher risk of harm to both adult women and children than other kinds of study, unless carefully managed (Sikweyiya and Jewkes 2011).

Powell *et al.* (2012) have identified four core ethical issues which are common to the literature on the subject of research with children: *informed consent, protection of participants, anonymity and confidentiality*, and the *payment of participants*. Each of these will be discussed here, with Table 3.1 providing some useful guidelines from Save the Children on ethical research with children which are specifically adapted for research in the global South.

Table 3.1 Some key ethical considerations in research involving children

- Assess the risks of harm to participants through your research, and plan to minimise these.
- Ensure that all participants give informed consent to their involvement.
- Seek the informed consent of children, ensuring that children know that they can withdraw their consent at any point.
- Be prepared to deal with any distress children may express during the research process.
- Make arrangements for further ongoing support to individual children who need it.
- Consider child protection issues in daily practice and in the recruitment of research staff.
- Seek consent from parents and carers.
- Seek the support of community organisations, people who are important in the lives of children locally.
- Ensure that information about the research is given in such a way that it is understandable and attractive to children, and includes information about their rights as respondents, and about how the data they provide will be handled.
- Make practical arrangements to protect the confidentiality of respondents.
- Discuss how you would handle situations where risk of serious harm to respondents is disclosed.
- Make sure that your methods maximise the chances of girls and boys to participate fully.
- Consider how to include the voices of children who face discrimination.
- Consider whether there is a need to offer recompense to those helping you with your research, and what form this should best take.
- Assess possible risks to the safety of research staff and take steps to prevent these.
- Ensure that you properly consult with communities in planning your research, and contribute where possible to capacity building.
- Give feedback to respondents' communities on the findings of the research, in an appropriate form.

Source: Save the Children (2004: 40–1).

Informed consent

Obtaining informed consent has for some time been an important requirement of research in countries with well developed systems of research regulation. It is starting to become a required procedure for researchers in the global South, especially those working in partnership with Northern academics whose research is governed by an institutional research ethics committee. Parents, carers and children who are old enough to have the capacity to consent may be asked to give written (or, if illiterate, verbal) consent before any interview is conducted or other activity engaged in. Previously, permission from the relevant national Ministry of Education, or equivalent body, usually sufficed; head teachers of selected schools were not expected to refuse access and their staff were expected to cooperate unquestioningly. Clearly the concept of informed consent has less meaning in a context where neither teachers, parents nor children are perceived as needing to be consulted. At the same time, in some poverty contexts, especially where populations have been displaced or where the research involves street children, there may be considerable difficulty in tracing parents or guardians and researchers will need to decide whether their consent is crucial. Despite these problems, the existence of clear ethical guidelines and the requirement to obtain informed consent releases researchers from the burden of deciding themselves how to behave ethically, how to avoid distressing participants unduly or engaging in potentially harmful behaviour.

Protection of participants

In researching gender violence in educational settings, the greatest risk of harm for children stems from the need to ask them to recount their experiences of violence at the hands of adults (and to a lesser extent older children), especially where there is limited institutional accountability and varying levels of professionalism. When exploring the sensitive and potentially dangerous topic of adults' abuse of children, the child respondent may be constrained by fear of retaliation or victimisation by adults who suspect that their behaviour is being reported. In societies which subscribe to a particular concept of childhood which marginalises children and renders them powerless, or where children are displaced or affected by war, there is a heightened risk of harm (Boyden 2000; Clacherty and Donald 2007; Tisdall *et al.* 2009). However, a desire to protect children from harm may also deny them the right to express their views on matters that concern them; a balance needs to be struck between the two considerations.

Despite the obvious strengths of participatory research with children, there are numerous ethical pitfalls. Alderson and Morrow (2011) remind us that children's participation is not always in their best interests and any anticipated benefits should not allow researchers to disregard possible risks to the individual children who take part. The approach may also smack of tokenism, e.g. officials merely subscribing to the 'rhetorical orthodoxy' of children's participation (Hallett and Prout 2003), or researchers and/or development agency staff using it as a strategy to attract sponsorship for projects. The 'cosy' and relaxed nature of participatory workshops, with eye-catching visual aids, may also serve to lull the child (and indeed the adult) into divulging more information than they otherwise would. Because children are more trusting and open than adults, they can be more easily manipulated for data collection purposes and may not understand the ramifications of what they are saying. In turn, if the researchers have not thought through the consequences of some of the activities engaged in with children and put appropriate safeguards in place, children may be at risk.

The dilemmas faced by researchers who uncover cases of abuse are obvious, especially in countries with weak or under-developed systems of social welfare and child protection. This remains a contentious issue in the literature on research with children (Powell *et al.* 2012) as their protection can look different in different world contexts (Clacherty and Donald 2007). The World Health Organization's guidelines on research into domestic violence against women (WHO 2001) are useful in this respect. Several projects to address violence against girls have acted in anticipation of such disclosures and the possible distress caused to children by putting mechanisms in place to deal with cases, either through identified agencies or through engaging social workers or child protection officers as co-researchers (Leach and Machakanja 2000; Parkes and Heslop 2011). Protocols are usually prepared to guide researchers in dealing with difficult situations but they may not fit the circumstances; for example requiring evidence of a child being sexually abused, or at risk of being abused, to be passed to the relevant authorities may not help the child if no reliable reporting and follow-up mechanisms exist. Indeed, it may make the situation worse.

As many research studies are carried out against a backdrop of weak enforcement of legislation designed to protect children against sexual abuse and a disregard of teachers' codes of conduct which make sexual relationships with students a prosecutable offence, the risks to children who divulge information about sexual violence are very real. Chilisa and Ntseane (2010) recount one such dilemma when the universal application of anonymity and confidentiality, which they felt obliged to subscribe to, prevented them from reporting several accounts by girls of the headmaster in their school sexually harassing them, and they had no ethical guidelines to advise them as to what action to take. They argue that a researcher who was informed by an African perspective would have engaged with the community as a 'healer', to assist others and build harmony and social transformation, rather than being kept at a distance by the 'dominant Western discourse on methodology that uses EuroWestern standards as universal truths' (p. 625).

They cite the example of a Ghanaian researcher who discovered that one of the school sites chosen at random for her research was headed by a man who molested and demanded sex of girls in his school; she decided to move 'off script' to organise a traditional community event at which the issue of abuse of schoolgirls was discussed generally and students performed a play on the theme of a head teacher asking girls for sexual favours (Leach *et al.* 2003).' To a Western researcher, this move from researcher to activist would generate unease about role conflict but Chilisa and Ntseane (2010) regard it as culturally appropriate. Nevertheless, the incident raises issues around the safety of children and researchers who are involved in uncovering malpractices that threaten the interests of powerful individuals, and around what constitutes an appropriate response.

Anonymity and confidentiality

The promise of confidentiality also presents problems. Researchers are usually expected to guarantee confidentiality to everyone who agrees to take part in a study on a sensitive topic such as gender violence, to not name schools and communities, and to disguise their location. Children are most likely to be interviewed at school or at home, and in both locations confidentiality may be compromised by lack of a suitable private space and/or adult curiosity.

There are also differing understandings of the meaning of confidentiality; for example, researchers and officials may consider that this only applies to the identity of those involved in the selected schools rather than to the identity of the schools themselves. Parents may expect to be present when their children are being interviewed in order to ensure the 'correct' answers (Clacherty and Donald 2007). In small communities, the identities of individuals and schools might be guessed at, even with anonymity maintained and efforts made to disguise physical details of the schools.

Even with the commitment to confidentiality, there are likely to be different views as to how ethical it is to probe and to ask sensitive questions which may upset children, especially when the person asking the questions has limited scope to help solve their problems. On the Young Lives project certain sensitive and intrusive questions were dropped or refocused in case they caused distress or difficulties (Morrow 2009).

Payment of participants

People living in poverty may understandably take every opportunity to ask for help and money, and want to use their very limited time and resources on activities that will bring direct benefits to themselves or their children. The term 'project' has become loaded with expectations for material and financial benefits in countries with significant aid transfers. A research project without direct material benefits like Young Lives requires significant efforts to explain itself against the grain. Indeed, the researchers found in some cases that officials, teachers, education administrators and village cadres were more likely to insist on some form of compensation than ordinary people (Morrow 2009). Clacherty and Donald (2007) found that, in contexts of extreme poverty, there could be resentment against children who gained some material benefit from participating in the research.

The issue of payment for participation is difficult. It is generally accepted that compensation can, or should, be paid to reimburse expenses and sometimes for loss of earnings but that it should not be used as an incentive to participate as this can distort the findings. Nor should it be used to serve as pressure or persuasion (Morrow 2009). Practices vary according to circumstances; often small gifts or payments are made, or a collective compensation in the form of supplies for the local school. Some would argue that not making a payment to respondents living in deprivation is exploitative, especially where the research takes children away from reproductive or productive work (Powell *et al.* 2012). A more appropriate form of recognition may be reporting back to the community on issues relevant to them, without compromising the confidentiality promised to respondents; requests to provide advice, e.g. to teachers, however could be seen as encroaching on the territory of the intervention.

Recommendations and conclusion

The difficulty of conducting research into gender violence in schools in poverty contexts has been discussed in this chapter. There is a clear need for the design of rigorous research instruments that will gather consistent and comparable qualitative and quantitative data, while being sensitive to local understandings and manifestations of gender violence. I have highlighted some of the methodological challenges and ethical dilemmas faced by researchers, especially when collecting information from children and in poverty contexts. The problems of using interviews and questionnaires with children and the appeal of participatory research and computer-assisted interviews as alternatives have also been highlighted, along with key ethical issues that dominate the literature on research with children.

Recent literature on the ethics of research in the global South stresses the importance of understanding local context, circumstances and meanings, while acknowledging that there are some universal principles of ethical practice that must be adhered to, such as respect for autonomy, justice and avoiding harm. Research protocols developed by institutions in the global North may have little meaning elsewhere, as the ethical and moral dilemmas that arise during the research process are shaped by the context in which the activity took place. Powell *et al.* (2012) suggest that the UNCRC can provide a universal framework for outlining the principles of research with children but that these principles need to be applied with some flexibility according to each situation that arises, provided that they safeguard the respondents' interests and well-being. The Save the Children (2004) guidelines offer a useful checklist of procedures and potential risks which are broadly applicable to differing contexts; the Population Council (Schenk and Williamson 2005) has a similar set. Researchers should be trained to recognise and meet these ethical standards.

The need for sensitivity and flexibility is also important when outside researchers are carrying out research either alone or with indigenous colleagues (Morrow 2009; Powell *et al.* 2012). The power disparities between adults and children noted above apply equally to the relationship between researchers as outsiders and insiders, especially where the former control the funding. While social research may well involve compromise and uncertainty, the need to avoid harm and to ensure that consent is freely given and voluntary, is paramount.

It may be feasible to engage students as co-researchers, where they themselves determine the focus of the research and the methods used, and decide to some extent what to do with the findings. In other cases, they may take on the role of peer interviewer or participant observer. If handled well (avoiding the risk that they are viewed as spying by teachers or their peers), either approach can produce very rich and reliable data (e.g. Boyden 2000; Save the Children 2000; Hart and Tyrer 2006; Plan Togo 2006). However, this is a particularly challenging methodology in school cultures where children are expected to be deferential towards, and look for guidance from, adults.

In recognising the potential risks of involving children directly in the research process and acknowledging that the onus should not be on children alone to provide information about the scale of violence in their school, alternative avenues for addressing the issue might be considered. For example, little research has been carried out into teachers' (as opposed to students') attitudes and experiences relating to gender violence, in a way that might encourage them to take a stand against violence, including corporal punishment, in their own schools. One particularly interesting approach is provided by Chege (2005), who carried out research with trainee teachers in Kenya into their own experiences of school violence as children based on the construction of retrospective diaries, and Teni-Atinga (2005), who did similar memory work with newly trained teachers in Ghana.

To meet the risks and challenges of the growing interest in research on gender violence in schools, it is important that the appropriate national authorities and research sponsors put in place their own code of research ethics and a transparent and rigorous system of approval of research proposals. Much research is carried out in the global South, often by outsiders, which the authorities know nothing about. Research findings also need to inform public policy. This requires government bodies to commit themselves to learning from the findings and taking children's perspectives seriously (Clacherty and Donald 2007). The link between research and action is one that could also be explored fruitfully, although as pointed out it carries some dangers, not least role conflict for the researcher turned activist. Nevertheless, the potential for community action through involvement in research and increased access to information generated by the research process is important.

Notes

1 We now know that sexual exploitation by those with a duty of care for children and the vulnerable is not exclusively a problem for the poor and disadvantaged, as the recent scandal of widespread sexual abuse by Catholic priests and the regular trials of paedophile teachers in Europe, the United States and Australia make clear.
2 The head teacher finally admitted his guilt after a two-year investigation by the district education office and under pressure from local elders – his sole punishment being to be transferred to a boys' school.

References

AAUW (2011) *Crossing the Line: Sexual Harassment at School*. Washington, DC: American Association of University Women (AAUW) Educational Foundation.

Abramovay, M. and Rua, M. (2005) *Violences in Schools*. Brasilia: UNESCO.

Akiba, M., LeTendre, G.K., Baker, D.P. and Goesling, B. (2002) 'School victimization: national and school system effects on school violence in 37 nations', *American Educational Research Journal*, 39 (4), 829–53.

Alderson, P. and Morrow, V. (2011) *The Ethics of Research with Children and Young People*. London: Sage Publications.

Bhana, D. and Pillay, N. (2011) 'Beyond passivity: constructions of femininities in a single sex South African school', *Educational Review*, 63 (1), 65–78.

Boyden, J. (2000) 'Conducting research with war-affected and displaced children', in *Cultural Survival Quarterly*, 24 (2). Available at: www.culturalsurvival.org/publications/cultural-survival-quarterly/united-states/conducting-research-war-affected-and-displace.

Brown, C.K. (2002) 'A study of sexual abuse in schools in Ghana', University of Cape Coast.

Chambers, R. (2002) *Participatory Workshops: A Sourcebook of 21 Sets of Ideas and Activities*. London: Earthscan.

Chege, F. (2005) 'Memories of childhood violence', unpublished report, Nairobi: UNICEF ESARO.

Chilisa, B. and Ntseane, G. (2010) 'Resisting dominant discourses: implications of indigenous, African feminist theory and methods for gender and education research', *Gender and Education*, 22 (6), 617–32.

Clacherty, G. and Donald, D. (2007) 'Child participation in research: reflections on ethical challenges in the southern African context', *African Journal of AIDS Research*, 6, 147–56.

De Lange, N. and Geldenhuys, M. (2012) 'Youth envisioning safe schools: a participatory video approach', *South African Journal of Education*, 32 (4), 494–511.

De Lange, N., Mitchell, C. and Bhana, D. (2012) 'Voices of women teachers about gender inequalities and gender-based violence in rural South Africa', *Gender and Education*, 24 (5), 499–514.

Deacon, H. and Stephney, I. (2007) *HIV/AIDS, Stigma and Children: A Literature Review*. Cape Town: Human Sciences Research Council.

Devers, M., Henry, E., Hoffmann, E. with Benadballah, H. (2012) *Les Violence de genre en Milieu Scolaire en Afrique Subsaharienne Francophone*. ADEA/Ministère des Affairs étrangères et européeennes.

DramAidE (2000) *'See You at 7': Mobilising Young Men to Care*. Durban: Atlas.

Dunne, M., Humphreys, S. and Leach, F. (2006) 'Gender violence in schools in the developing world', *Gender and Education*, 18 (1), 75–98.

Dunne, M. and Leach, F., with Chilisa, B., Maundeni, T., Tabulawa, R., Kutor, N., Forde, L.D. and Asamoah, A. (2005) *Gendered School Experiences: The Impacts on Retention and Achievement in Botswana and Ghana*. London: DFID.

Farrell, A. (2005) *Ethical Research with Children*. Berkshire: Open University Press.

Gallagher, M. (2009) 'Ethics'. In E.K. Tisdall, J. Davis and M. Gallagher (eds), *Researching with Children and Young People: Research Design, Method and Analysis* (pp. 11–28). London: Sage Publications.

Hallett, C. and Prout, A. (eds) (2003) *Hearing the Voices of Children: Social Policy for a New Century*. London and New York: RoutledgeFalmer.

Hart, R.A. (1997) *Children's Participation: The Theory and Practice of Involving Young Citizens in Community Development and Environmental Care*. London: Earthscan.

Hart, J. and Tyrer, B. (2006) 'Research with children living in situations of armed conflict: concepts, ethics and methods', Refugee Studies Centre, Oxford. Available at: www.rsc.ox.ac.uk/publications/working-papers-folder_contents/RSCworkingpaper30.pdf/view?searchterm=research%20with%20children.

Hunter, M. (2002) 'The materiality of everyday sex: thinking beyond "prostitution"', *African Studies*, 61 (1), 101–20.

Jones, N., Moore, K., Villar-Marquez, E. and Broadbent, E. (2008) *Painful Lessons: The Politics of Preventing Sexual Violence and Bullying at School*. London: Overseas Development Institute.

Kehily, M.J. (2002) *Sexuality, Gender and Schooling: Shifting Agendas in Social Learning*. London: RoutledgeFalmer.

Kirk, J. and Winthrop, R. (2006) 'Eliminating the sexual exploitation of girls in refugee schools on West Africa: what classroom assistants can do'. In F. Leach and C. Mitchell (eds), *Combating Gender Violence in and around Schools* (pp. 207–16). Stoke-on-Trent: Trentham Books.

Leach, F. (2003) *Practising Gender Analysis in Education*, Oxford: Oxfam.

Leach, F. and Machakanja, P. (2000) *A Preliminary Investigation into the Abuse of Girls in Zimbabwean Junior Secondary Schools*. DFID Education Research Report No. 39. London: DFID.

Leach, F. and Mitchell, C. (eds) (2006) *Combating Gender Violence in and around Schools*. Stoke-on-Trent: Trentham Books.

Leach, F. and Sitaram, S. (2007) 'The sexual harassment and abuse of adolescent schoolgirls in South India', *Journal of Education, Citizenship and Social Justice*, 2 (3), 257–77.

Leach, F., Slade, E. and Dunne, M. (2012) *Desk Review for Concern: Promising Practice in School Related Gender Based Violence (SRGBV) Prevention and Response Programming Globally*. Dublin: Concern Worldwide.

Leach, F., Fiscian, V., Kadzamira, E., Lemani, E. and Machakanja, P. (2003) *An Investigative Study of the Abuse of Girls in African Schools*. Education Research Report No. 54. London: DFID.

Luke, N. and Kurz, K.M. (2002) *Cross-Generational and Transactional Sexual Relations in Sub-Saharan Africa*. Washington, DC: International Center for Research on Women.

Mac an Ghaill, M. (1994) *The Making of Men: Masculinities, Sexualities and Schooling*. Milton Keynes: Open University Press.

Mensch, B., Hewett, P.C. and Erulkar, A.S. (2003) 'The reporting of sensitive behaviour by adolescents: a methodological experiment in Kenya', *Demography*, 40 (2), 247–68.

Morrow, V. (2009) *The Ethics of Social Research with Children and Families in Young Lives*. Young Lives: an International Study of Childhood Poverty, Working Paper No. 53.

Nyanzi, S., Pool, R. and Kinsman, J. (2000) 'The negotiation of sexual relationships among school pupils in south-western Uganda', *AIDS CARE*, 13 (1), 83–98.

Oyěwùmí, O. (ed.) (2005) *African Gender Studies: A Reader*. New York: Palgrave Macmillan.

Parkes, J. and Heslop, J. (2011) *A Cross-Country Analysis of Baseline Research from Kenya, Ghana and Mozambique*. London: ActionAid. Available at: www.actionaid.org/publications/cross-country-analysis-baseline-research-kenya-ghana-and-mozambique.

Pattman, R. and Chege, F. (2003) *Finding Our Voices: Gendered and Sexual Identities and HIV/AIDS in Education*. Nairobi: UNICEF Eastern and Southern Africa.

Plan Togo (2006) 'Monitoring and evaluation with children'. Available at: http://plan-international.org/where-we-work/africa/publications/monitoring-and-evaluation-with-children.

Powell, M.A., Fitzgerald, R., Taylor, N. and Graham, A. (2012) *International Literature Review: Ethical Issues in Undertaking Research with Children and Young People*, for the Childwatch International Research Network, Southern Cross University, Centre for Children and Young People, Lismore NSW and University of Otago, Centre for Research on Children and Families, Dunedin, NZ.

Pryor, J. (1995) 'Hearing young children's voices in qualitative research: problems and possibilities', unpublished paper, University of Sussex, Brighton, UK.

Rivers, C.R. (2000) 'Shattered hopes: study of sexual abuse of girls', prepared for Metlhaetsile Women's Information Centre, funded by UNICEF Botswana.

Rossetti, S. (2001) *Children in School: A Safe Place?* Gabarone, Botswana: UNESCO.

Save the Children (2004) 'So you want to involve young children in research? A toolkit supporting children's meaningful and ethical participation in research relating to violence against children'.

Save the Children (2000) 'Children and participation: research, monitoring and evaluation with children and young people'.

Save the Children Sweden (2011) 'Violence against children in schools: a regional analysis of Lebanon, Morocco and Yemen', Manara Network, funded by SIDA.

Schenk, K. and Williamson, J. (2005) *Ethical Approaches to Gathering Information from Children and Adolescents in International Settings: Guidelines and Resources.* Washington, DC: Population Council.

Shariff, S. (2008) *Cyber-Bullying: Issues and Solutions for the School, the Classroom and the Home.* Abingdon and New York: Routledge.

Shumba, A. (2001) 'Who guards the guards in schools? A study of reported cases of child abuse by teachers in Zimbabwe secondary schools', *Sex Education*, 1 (1), 77–86.

Sikweyiya, Y. and Jewkes, R. (2011) 'Perceptions about safety and risks in gender-based violence research: implications for the ethics review process', *Culture, Health & Sexuality*, 13 (9), 1091–102.

Smith, P. (ed.) (2003) *Violence in Schools: The Response in Europe.* London and New York: RoutledgeFalmer.

Teni-Atinga, G. (2005) 'Beginning teachers' perceptions and experiences of sexual harassment in Ghanaian teacher training institutions'. Unpublished doctoral dissertation, McGill University, Canada.

Timmermann, G. (2003) 'Sexual harassment of adolescents perpetrated by teachers and by peers: an exploration of the dynamics of power, culture and gender in secondary schools', *Sex Roles*, 58, 5–6.

Tisdall, E.K., Davis, J. and Gallagher, M. (2009) *Researching with Children and Young People: Research Design, Methods and Analysis.* London: Sage Publications.

UNESCO (2012) *Education Sector Responses to Homophobic Bullying.* Paris: UNESCO.

UNICEF (2005) *Summary Report: Violence against Disabled Children.* Nairobi: UNICEF. Available at: www.unicef.org/videoaudio/PDFs/UNICEF_Violence_ Against_ Disabled_Children_Report_ Distributed_Version.pdf.

UNICEF, Plan International, Save the Children Sweden and ActionAid (2010) *Too Often in Silence: A Report on School-Based Violence in West and Central Africa.* Nairobi: UNICEF. Available at: www.e4conference.org/wp-content/ uploads/2010/04/14en.pdf.

UNICEF ROSA (2001) 'Corporal punishment in schools in South Asia', UNICEF Regional Office for South Asia.

UNICEF ROSA (2005) 'Regional consultation on violence against children in South Asia' (for the UN Study on Violence against Children), Islamabad, Pakistan, 19–21 May, Regional Office for South Asia (ROSA). Available at: www.unicef. org/rosa/VAC.pdf.

United Nations (2006) *Secretary-General's Study of Violence against Children.* New York: United Nations. Available at: www.unviolencestudy.org.

USAID (2003) *Unsafe Schools: A Literature Review of School-Related Gender-Based Violence in Developing Countries.* Washington, DC: USAID. Available at: www. usaid.gov/our_work/cross-cutting_programs/wid/pubs/unsafe_schools_literature_ review.pdf.

USAID/DevTech (2008) 'Safe Schools program: final report', DevTech Systems, Inc. for USAID.

Van Eerdewijk, A. (2004) 'The sexuality of girls in Dakar: seeking pleasure between discourses on danger'. Paper presented at the conference 'Pleasure and d anger revisited: sexualities in the 21st century', 30 June to 2 July, Cardiff University, UK.

WHO (2001) *Putting Women's Safety First: Ethical and Safety Recommendations for Research on Domestic Violence against Women.* Geneva: World Health Organisation.

Part II

Experiencing violence in the home and the school

4 Gender violence in the home and childhoods in Vietnam

*Kirrily Pells, Emma Wilson and
Nguyen Thi Thu Hang*

The majority of research on children and violence in the home has originated in the Global North, within a psychological framework which highlights the adverse consequences of violence for individual children's physical, cognitive and emotional development (Kitzmann *et al.* 2003). Few studies have explored children's own perspectives, experiences and responses, as actors within their own 'social worlds' (Overlien and Hyden 2009: 480). Not all children exposed to violence develop psychological difficulties, but rather generate their own meanings and responses to violence and so manage, or indeed succeed, in the face of adversity (Cairns and Dawes 1996; Boyden and Mann 2006).

This chapter draws on qualitative longitudinal research in Vietnam to explore children's responses to violence in the home. In Vietnam, domestic violence is recognised in law and policy as an infringement of human rights, a public health concern and an obstacle to economic growth and poverty alleviation. However, policies and programmes designed to address domestic violence rarely consider children (Hoang *et al.* 2013). Here, we examine how inequalities and hierarchies, both within and outside the home, shape how children learn about and experience multiple forms of violence in the home. We explore the varying tactics employed by boys and girls to negotiate violence, and the influence of violence on children's subjectivities, social relationships and schooling. We conclude by reflecting on appropriate policy responses to prevent and mitigate the effects of family violence.

Violence in the home and the everyday

Violence within the home is defined variously and interchangeably as domestic violence, intimate partner violence, interpersonal violence or family violence. Yet no common definition exists for any of these terms. In line with the 2007 Vietnamese Domestic Violence Control and Prevention Law, we use the broad term of violence in the home to encompass 'purposeful acts of certain family members that cause or may cause physical, psychological or economic injuries to other family members'. While acknowledging that violence in the home is a global phenomenon, the ways in which it is experienced and the exact forms it takes are shaped by specific contexts: 'the social and cultural dimensions of violence are what give violence its power and meaning' (Scheper-Hughes and Bourgois 2004: 1). Adopting the definition enshrined in Vietnamese law enables us to explore the disjuncture between national discourses and children's everyday lives as well as to engage with national and local policy environments.

Structural and interpersonal inequalities collide in violence in the home, in a dialectical relationship whereby structural violence, such as poverty, unequal gender relations and social exclusion, can be both a causal factor and an outcome of family violence (Terry 2004). This does not pathologise people living in poverty, but rather underscores the importance of situating family violence within a wider context (Merry 2009). Multiple forms of violence, whether physical, emotional or economic, 'can co-exist, nurture and sustain each other' (Morgan and Björkert 2006: 450). Within this chapter we explore a 'violence continuum' (Scheper-Hughes and Bourgois 2004: 19) whereby the 'violences of the everyday' (Kleinman 2000: 239), whether visible or hidden, in everyday relations are understood to be an extension of broader structural violence.

To understand how the 'violences of the everyday' operate we draw on Bourdieu's (2004) concepts of the habitus and symbolic violence. The concept of symbolic violence is intended to move beyond dichotomies of structure and agency by embedding the structures of the dominator within the body of the dominated, through 'the schemes of perception, appreciation and action', which Bourdieu (1977: 97) terms the habitus. Gender inequalities not only shape the habitus, but are also reproduced through the daily interactions and embodiment within the habitus (Reay 2004: 436). Rather than 'victims' adopting submission out of choice, symbolic violence reveals how the habitus of the dominated is 'the product of the objective structures, and also that these structures only derive their efficacy from the dispositions which they trigger and which help to reproduce them' (Bourdieu 2004: 341). This is not 'mechanical determinism' but rather 'invention within limits' whereby individuals have scope for creativity but shaped within the habitus' series of 'orientations and limits' (Bourdieu 2004: 95–6). Within this chapter we explore how children's habitus are shaped by violence in the home, and how children develop 'creative responses that are capable of transcending the social conditions in which it [the habitus] was produced' in particular through engagement with schooling and with social networks (Reay 2004: 434–5).

Methods and ethics

We draw on qualitative longitudinal data generated with children and their families living in contexts of poverty in Vietnam, as part of the Young Lives study.[1] These data consist of semi-structured interviews with children, young people and their caregivers, as well as focus group discussions with community members, which explored themes such as important changes and transitions in children's lives, health and well-being, relationships, schooling, work and experiences of public programmes and policies.

It is important to note that Young Lives is not a focused study of violence and researchers did not ask children and caregivers explicitly about violence. Rather, this theme was raised spontaneously in some accounts of family life, perceptions of well-being and so on. Fieldworkers are trained in the principles and standards set by Save the Children's 'Child Protection Policy' (Save the Children 2003). Serious cases of abuse and exploitation are referred to relevant authorities and service providers, or, where these do not exist, local teams may investigate informal support networks available to children and families (see Morrow 2009).

The qualitative longitudinal data used here is drawn from three sites, which were purposively selected from a possible 20 sites involved in the Young Lives household and child surveys in Vietnam (see Crivello *et al.* 2013). The selected sites – Van Lam, Van Tri and Nghia Tan (all pseudonyms) – were chosen to capture variation in location (rural and urban), ethnicity (Kinh and minority ethnic groups) and social and economic circumstances. Van Lam is a very poor mountainous community in the South-Central coast of Vietnam populated by many ethnic minority groups (mostly Cham H'roi); Van Tri is a prosperous rural area in the Red River Delta, with a high population density and good infrastructure; while Nghia Tan is an urban neighbourhood in Da Nang city, with average infrastructure where people are engaged mostly in manual labour.

We analysed data collected in 2007 and 2011 from 47 children, 23 girls and 24 boys, of whom half were 9–10 years (in 2011) and half 16–17 years, together with their caregivers (mostly mothers). The majority were Kinh and eight were of Cham H'roi ethnicity. From these 47, we selected six cases to analyse in greater depth (five girls and one boy), with these cases chosen purposively for the variety and depth in their narratives rather than attempting to seek out representative cases. Collecting data at two points in time enabled us to analyse how children's reflections on violence in the home changed over a four-year period.

We adopted a thematic analytical approach to identify patterns in responses to violence, and our case-based analysis then enabled close examination of how violence has shaped the individual biographies of the six selected cases over time. All data were cleaned, transcribed and translated in country, and all children and communities have been assigned pseudonyms to ensure anonymity. Below we situate the data in the changing context of gender hierarchies and violence in Vietnam.

Gender, family and violence in Vietnam

The phenomenon of family violence in Vietnam needs to be contextualised within a broader appreciation of the structural forces, both old and new, which influence the construction of gender hierarchies and the institution of the family. In a rapidly globalising world, family violence is both 'embedded in enduring patterns of kinship and marriage, but can be exacerbated by very contemporary political and economic tensions' (Merry 2009: 2). In Vietnam, processes of rapid socio-economic change combine with Confucian, Taoist and Socialist traditions to influence the construction of gender hierarchies (Rydstrom 2003; Schuler *et al.* 2006).

Confucian philosophy extols an idealised version of womanhood, based on the four feminine virtues of 'housework (cong), appearance (dung), speech (ngon) and conduct (hanh)' (Ngo 2004: 50). To achieve these virtues, women traditionally were primarily confined to the private sphere and to the service of the family. Moreover a woman was required to follow the moral code of the 'three obediences': 'at home she follows her father, married she follows her husband, widowed she follows her son' (Nguyen 1995 cited in Volkmann 2005: 26). Confucianism also places emphasis on male ancestral worship, and preference was traditionally given to sons as they embody both a 'symbolic and material' link with their 'patrilineage in the past, present, and future' (Rydstrom 2002: 363). Research on contemporary societal attitudes suggests that son preference is still evident in Vietnam, predominantly in rural areas and among lower-income groups (General Statistics Office 2008). This was illustrated by a woman from Van Tri in a focus group discussion who explained: 'I had two daughters, and my husband made me bear another child, a boy, that's the mentality of male supremacy.'

Vietnamese Socialist thought, like the Confucian virtues, promotes an idealised vision of femininity, albeit one that encompasses a wider array of productive and reproductive roles (Schuler *et al.* 2006). While the Socialist state has extended important legal protection to women and simultaneously encouraged women to play a more prominent role in public life, attention continues to be placed on their reproductive function (Drummond and Rydstrom 2004). This, in turn, has led to a convergence of state and private interests at the nexus of the family. Indeed, the state is active in ensuring that women foster the appropriate qualities for both the nation and the home. The 'brilliant worker, excellent housewife' (giỏi việc nước, đảm việc nhà) campaign, initiated by the Vietnam General Confederation of Labour in 1989, encouraged women to be diligent in their professional, social and familial duties and utilised a set of indicators (such as children's performance in school) to measure women's achievements. Commentators argue that such standards placed enormous pressures on women, who were not only expected to be economically astute and productive, but were also required to be self-sacrificing and prioritise familial harmony above all else (Schuler *et al.* 2006: 391). This was emphasized by participants in focus group discussions with community members, as explained by one woman who said:

> In order for a family to be happy, the woman has to suffer a lot . . . In order for the children to be happy and have a comfortable life, the mother has to tolerate a lot. The women suffer the most . . . For example, my husband doesn't earn lots of money, but I have to appease him whenever he raises his voice.
>
> (Female, age 50)

Not only do such discourses reinforce and legitimise power differentials between men and women, but in the context of domestic violence, seeking help from institutional sources (where these exist) may prove difficult for women, as in essence it represents a public admission of having failed to cultivate a 'cultured family'.[2]

Rydstrom (2004) in her research in rural Vietnam found that young people still strongly identify with Taoist constructs of 'cool' female ideals of gentleness and sweetness, and 'hot' male ideals of physical strength and hot temper, with these opposing but complementary forces generating a sense of 'harmony' between male and female bodies and interactions. Yet such conceptualisations may also serve to normalise men's violence, and in line with the Confucian philosophical tradition and contemporary Socialist ideals, they place an overwhelming responsibility on women to 'endure' in order to maintain the semblance of 'harmony' within the home (Rydstrom 2003).

Aside from these ideological influences, social relations and societal structures are undergoing huge transformations in Vietnam since the shift to a more market-oriented economy which began with the process of Doi Moi (renewal) in 1986. Favourable policies in education and health, combined with a growing urban labour market (for example the export-led garment industries), have provided new opportunities for women and are moulding young women's aspirations towards professional life (World Bank 2011).

Nevertheless, these transitions have been far from smooth and can jar sharply with traditional beliefs and gender norms. In Nghia Tan (an urban neighbourhood in Da Nang), views were divided in the community discussions over the extent to which economic growth has reduced or increased pressures within the home. On the one hand, poverty reduction was felt to reduce conflict:

> Ten years ago, family circumstances were difficult. The economy was bad while families had many children. Children asked for money to buy food and to pay for tuition fee. Husbands and wives didn't have any money, so they started arguing and fighting with each other . . . Now when the economy is better, lives are getting better too. When the economy gets better, that phenomenon also disappears.
>
> (Female, age 39, Nghia Tan)

On the other hand, some felt that improved economic opportunities for women threatened men's status and created new tensions within the home:

> Nowadays, women are likely to find a job more easily than men. The current trend is like that, for example, if the woman can do business while the man can't, the man has to stay home, and help out the woman. That is why the woman sometimes can dominate the man somehow.
>
> (Female, age 47, Nghia Tan)

None of the families who spoke of violence in the home had accessed formal support services, but depended instead on informal strategies. This finding echoes a national survey on domestic violence in Vietnam which found that 87 per cent of abused women did not seek any form of institutional support largely because they considered the violence to be nothing out of the ordinary and not serious enough (General Statistics Office 2010).

In the following section, we consider how the historical, cultural and gendered underpinnings of interpersonal violence in Vietnam permeate the individual narratives of violence of our six cases.

How children learn about and experience violence in the home

In children's accounts, violence was rarely present in one form, but manifested itself in myriad ways which were often concurrent and mutually reinforcing. Wider structural inequalities, including social and cultural norms, shaped both the occurrence of violence and children's understandings and daily interactions. Permeating many of the children's accounts was a view of violence as a private matter, which threatened to disrupt family harmony.

For example, No Ha was nine years old, of minority Cham H'roi ethnicity, and lived in Van Lam. She recounted a narrative of economic and emotional violence, punctuated by episodes of physical violence against her sisters and her by her father, who she feared: 'I am scared of his beating.' Since her mother left the family home when she was three years old No Ha resided with her father, his second wife and her two sisters. She described how she 'strongly wants' her mother to return and how 'we were much happier when living with my mother'.

No Ha's stepmother expressed concern that she is not able to care for the children as she would like, as she is required to work away from home in the fields, illustrating the competing demands of productive and reproductive roles assigned to women:

> If I didn't work, my husband would think that I was lazy, but if I did so, nobody at home to remind his children. Everybody talks about that . . . Of course if I stayed at home, it would be more convenient for them, as I could help take care of No Ha.

The importance of maintaining the facade of family harmony and ensuring violence within the home is kept as a private matter is implicit in many accounts.

Nga was the second oldest of six siblings and lived in urban Nghia Tan with her parents. In 2007, when Nga was 14, her father stressed the importance of parents giving children 'moral fibre' and commented that there were:

> a lot of cases that make a child's life become bad, for example parents do not live in harmony, the drunken father beats children, or the mother imitates her friends and doesn't do what father asks. The child witnesses these things, then feels discontented and leaves home, and his life will become bad as a result. Unhappiness is caused by the adults.

Nga described herself as an 'unhappy child' but did not elaborate on her home environment. However, when we interviewed her three years later she initially maintained this facade, agreeing with the statement that her family live in harmony. But later in the interview she explained that when the family were facing financial problems her father became violent, adding that he was frequently drunk:

> At night he goes to the bar, drinks to the point of nearly passing out, he's not like the others who drink and then go home and talk crap. My dad just drinks and then sleeps at the place, other people drink and then go home.

Both Nga and No Ha initially reproduced their caregivers' public positioning of harmonious family life, yet as they became older they became more critical and talked more readily about the violence in their homes.

Discussions of violence in the home often emerged gradually when children were asked about key events in their lives. Touching on the theme of family life, Lien, a 17-year-old girl from Van Tri, related how at age 12 her mother left home as a result of being physically beaten by her father and how as a young child she was privy to episodic violent physical acts between her parents:

> *. . . since 2005, has your father ever beaten your mother again?*
> He has sometimes.
> *In front of your very eyes?*
> No but I did hear them.

Children may experience violence directly (such as No Ha and Nga) or like Lien they may overhear their parents fighting. Dao, on the other hand (aged ten in 2011), learned about the violence from his brothers. He was the youngest of five sons and lived with his parents in Nghia Tan. His mother endured physical violence from her employers from a young age while working as a domestic servant. She married in order to escape this violent situation, despite her sister's advice: 'she knew then all his sisters and brothers were all very brutal . . . It was true; I was beaten since the first day I went there.' Not only has Dao's mother been beaten by her husband and his siblings, 'they didn't let me eat with them. I had to earn my living by myself'. She added that she was frequently ridiculed because of her lack of education and her husband would humiliate her by trying to get her to read aloud.

In recent years there has been partial reconciliation between Dao's parents and the family are living together again. Dao's mother was afraid of leaving her husband because it might bring dishonour to her father by contravening filial obedience, so she 'decided to endure in silence by myself'. She reported that 'I never expose my sad stories to any of my sons. But for example, the sad story that I told you today, if Dao is at home and he can hear, he will ask me a lot of questions and do some investigations to find out the truth'. She described how in the past her eldest son would tell his siblings: 'I remember our aunt beat my mother with a pole, when I was standing there and crying. I was a little boy, standing and crying. And I still remember up to now, I never forget it' and 'gradually, his brothers understand the situation'.

In contrast to Lien and No Ha, the violence experienced by ten-year-old An was predominantly symbolic. An lived with her maternal grandparents and her disabled mother in the Van Tri community. Her mother contracted encephalitis when she was an infant, which left her paralysed on one side and unable to speak. An's father never acknowledged her as his child. Her maternal grandfather's account suggested that had An been born a boy, this might not have been the case, or alternatively An would have had greater chance of being adopted by another family:

> . . . We decided to let the child be born. There was someone proposing to adopt the child. If the child were a boy, he would be adopted by others. In the end, the delivered child was a girl so no one wanted to foster her.
>
> *Did you and your wife make up your mind to care for the baby?*
>
> We had no choice at all.

Even prior to her birth, An was therefore subjected to symbolic violence because of the endurance of son preference in Vietnamese society (Zhang and Locke 2002). Ten years later the effects endured, increasing in potency as she has matured and become cognisant of the implications of her father's actions on her social positioning. Indeed, her grandfather described how she has been mocked by her peers and publicly ignored by her father:

> *Has she ever asked for permission that she wanted to go [see her father]?*
>
> No, she never said anything. In spite of being teased by others, she said nothing.
>
> *What about her father, did he want to see his daughter?*
>
> No, he also passed by our house and so did his wife and his father-in-law, but they all ignored us, particularly the child.

Although seemingly loved and nurtured by her mother and grandparents, An was acutely aware of the social and moral implications of her fractured family in a social context which places a high premium on family unity:

> . . . *what is your dream family?*
>
> A complete family
>
> . . . *what is 'complete'?*
>
> (silent)

The evidence presented here illustrates how children experience multiple forms of violence, indirectly and directly, with wider structural inequalities often shaping the occurrence and manifestation of violence in the home. In contrast, having a 'complete' or harmonious family featured at the top of ranked indicators of 'having a good life' for children in group discussions, across age, gender and location. The pervasiveness of the family harmony ideal influenced whether and how children disclosed violence. In the following sections we explore the role this plays in shaping children's responses to violence and their subjectivities.

Children's responses to violence

Children's responses to the violence they experience at home are complex and varied, influenced by age, gender, economic resources and social networks, as well as the nature of the violence experienced (Mullender *et al.* 2002). It is common for children to employ avoidance strategies (Overlien and Hyden 2009). In our study, for younger children these often involved distancing themselves from the violence physically, and for older children, emotionally. No Ha (aged nine), for example, described avoiding her father's beatings by removing herself from the family home and staying with her paternal grandfather, who consoled her, and intervened on her behalf: 'he shouted at my family.'

Similarly, Lam, age 11, told how she tried to hide when her father was violent. Lam lived with her parents and brother in Nghia Tan, and spoke of her parents' frequent arguments: 'there are only a few days when they don't [argue].' She described her father as 'very violent', hitting her mother and sometimes throwing her out onto the street. When this happened Lam hid in a corner because of distress and fear of her father throwing things: 'even if I cry they won't stop.' In contrast, Lam's brother, who was two years older, tried to intervene. Lam said her brother 'holds the big [bread] basket' and 'he says "stop, dad"'. However, her father continued fighting.

Older children often tried to distance themselves emotionally from episodes of physical violence, but they also spoke of intervening to alter the dynamics of violence, using different sets of strategies from when they were younger. As found in other studies, we found that older children tended to have more individual resources to navigate the situation and protect themselves physically and/ or emotionally, alongside more developed social networks outside the home (Mullender *et al.* 2002). Children rarely described directly intervening in episodes of physical violence, and where this did occur, it was older boys, such as Lam's brother, who adopted such strategies. Dao's mother recalled how her eldest son:

> called his brothers and asked them to take care of me, he told them 'You can fight against them' – my husband's brothers and sisters – 'if they insult our mother even verbally'. But I told my children not to insult them. I told my sons 'If you insult them by saying bad things behind them, they will hurt your mother'.

Older children also developed indirect strategies to try and protect their mothers (Katz 2013). The following examples of Nga and Lien illustrate how differential access to social and economic resources shaped their responses. When she was 15,

Nga did not pass the exam to progress onto higher secondary school and so she went to a continuing education centre, but because of fighting between students as well as not feeling that her studies were progressing, she decided to 'stay at home to help out my parents'. Since Nga left school, she stayed up late and went to the bar where her father had been drinking: 'I go wake him up and tell him to come home.' In this way she protected her mother by being the one to let her father back into the house when he was drunk. Nga also worked at her mother's café and gave her earnings to her mother.

In contrast Lien described having limited emotional and social support as she 'seldom confides' in her sister and is 'not so close' to her mother. She no longer had close contact with her childhood friends. In the absence of any other obvious recourse, the most attainable strategy was one of simultaneous acceptance and avoidance through emotionally distancing herself. When her mother was visibly upset, she encouraged her mother to accept 'her fate' and told her to 'let it be'. Her father also used fate to legitimise his violent actions: 'I still love my wife; however, it is our fate . . . I don't know why I turn out like this.'

We learn from the narrative of Lien's mother, however, that her own views were conflicted on whether to bring her private suffering into a public forum. Her desire to speak out was impeded not only by her loyalty to Lien but also by the social and cultural taboos associated with family disunity that were engrained within the local context:

> To be honest, there were times I really wanted to speak everything out loud but she [Lien] prevented me from doing so . . . I think many people know; however I don't want to tell them my story. Sometimes I tried to pretend there was no problem in our family so as to live a happy life. I don't talk much about it. It isn't something good to talk about.

Children can therefore co-construct symbolic violence, in which the other forms of violence (physical, emotional and economic) thrive. Bourdieu's conception of symbolic violence focuses on the ways in which the 'dominated, often unwittingly, sometimes unwillingly, contribute to their own domination by tacitly accepting the limits imposed' as a result of 'objective structures' shaping the subjective or habitus (2004: 341). In the cases of Lien and Lam we see how children are both subject to symbolic violence through the imposition of gender hierarchies within the home and society at large, as well as being mediators of symbolic violence. This helps shape their mothers' responses and reinforces dominant gender ideologies as both mother and daughter endure their 'fate' in order to maintain the appearance of familial harmony.

These narratives demonstrate the importance of understanding the multiple ways children respond to violence and how these are shaped by poverty, gender hierarchies and access to social and economic resources. Age is also a key factor. In our study, younger children appeared more confused and tried to remove themselves physically from the situation, whereas older children tended to have more developed strategies to help their mothers, whether through emotional protection, practical support and income generation, or encouraging acceptance of one's fate to avoid further repercussions or social ostracism. In turn these diverse strategies adopted by children inevitably influence their subjectivities and relationships in and out of school.

Influence of family violence on children's subjectivities, social relationships and schooling

Findings from group discussions with Vietnamese children conducted in 2011 illustrate how experiences of violence, both direct and indirect, influence children's perceptions and understanding of what constitutes a happy life for children. In an exercise on well-being, family violence emerged as an indicator of an unhappy life. For example, in Van Lam older girls included a 'father who beats after drinking' and 'parents who quarrel' as indicators of ill-being. But despite the overwhelmingly negative impact of violence in the home and the profound influence it has on children's subjectivities, what emerges from our findings is that children can still exhibit resilience in pursuing schooling and establishing social relationships (Katz 2013).

As Horton and Rydstrom (2011: 548) explain, male elders in Vietnamese society are entitled to command respect from and exert privilege over younger male relatives due to their closer links to their patrilineal ancestry. Older boys who challenged their father's violent behaviour verbally or physically (such as the brothers of Dao and Lam) would appear to be subverting these established masculine hierarchies. Yet such challenges to the established gender order can simultaneously be viewed as attempts by young men to assume the role of protector within the family (a responsibility waived and abused by their fathers), and to demonstrate recognised masculine traits of strength and control, thereby carving out masculine identities fitting with their stage in the life course.

Lien, however, described tensions with her mother. She reinforced, rather than challenged, dominant constructions of femininity by encouraging her mother to accept the violence as 'her fate', while her mother was keen to adopt a more defiant stance by speaking 'out loud'. Indeed we note how Lien's mother hoped for (but was repeatedly denied) a more unified and mutual positioning between daughter and mother – one that questioned established social norms. These contrasting accounts from Lien, Dao and Lam therefore highlight the way violence both shapes and permeates multiple and competing gendered subjectivities, which can co-exist within the same family context.

For Lien, Lam, Dao and An, the symbolic, physical and emotional violence which they witnessed or experienced did not seem to have affected their school achievements, with a focus on their studies possibly acting as a distraction from their difficult home environments. Lam and Dao both won awards for high performance in exams. Lien failed her high school entrance exam the first time round, but she has since passed and secured a place. In contrast, No Ha and her sisters were struggling on many fronts. No Ha was behind by two grades in school and, according to her stepmother, found reading difficult.

An actively tried to improve her social standing and respond to the constraints which had overshadowed her childhood. She was a good pupil at school and secured strong friendships. At the same time, she pursued positions of responsibility that could afford her social and moral recognition. As the class monitor, she enjoyed 'helping other pupils study good and be nice', and she described feeling honoured to have been selected for the Young Pioneer Union, entitling her to wear a red scarf as a visible symbol of recognition for her public position. This enabled her to challenge the gendered symbolic constraints in her life that had resulted from a lack of paternal recognition.

Whereas An, Dao and Lam had strong friendships at school, Lien felt different from other children because her 'family condition' meant she had to work. Nga explained that she had not had many school friends but instead socialised with 'a few good children who had to quit school because of their family situation'. This group of friends supported one another 'because their situation is just as difficult as mine', including giving money. This echoes other research on the inextricable links between poverty, stigma and shame profoundly felt by children (Walker *et al.* 2013). In the cases discussed here there appears to be an interconnection between poor material status and family violence and/or lack of family harmony which combine to create a sense of shame and being different for these children.

All the children in the study, with the exception of Dao, described difficult relationships with their fathers – the principal perpetrators of family violence in these selected cases. Lien found it very hard to talk about her father in the interview and to articulate her emotions. As described above, she employed a strategy of avoidance, preferring not to confront him or discuss the situation openly with other family members. Yet we were able to glean that she both loved him and understood that he was not a responsible man. Dao described loving both parents and identified his greatest wish for the future as 'I want my family to live together in harmony, and everybody to love each other'.

Our evidence supports findings from other studies which question the linear pathway that is often drawn between exposure to family violence and detrimental outcomes for children (Mullender *et al.* 2002; Overlien 2010). The effects on children's subjectivities in our study were complex and varying, yet all struggled to negotiate difficult home lives, often in isolation, and as found in other studies, there were indications at times that their outward resilience could be skilfully masking underlying difficulties (McGee 1997; Mullender *et al.* 2002).

Conclusions

Poverty and gender hierarchies shape children's habitus, specifically here through violence in the home. In contrast to psychological deterministic frameworks, in this chapter we have seen that children's responses are far from predictable. Children can both reproduce or resist violence, in highly inventive ways, with both positive and negative implications for their subjectivities, social networks and engagement with school. There is indicative evidence that children's age and sense of agency are important factors which mediate children's experiences and responses. Approaches to gender violence, particularly in the context of poverty, need to take better account of children as social actors, embedded in intergenerational relationships and situated in environments undergoing rapid social change.

The longitudinal design of our research enabled us to analyse changes in children's responses over time. At younger ages, children exhibited confusion and uncertainty about how to respond to violence. The home and the family therefore became domains to be actively avoided, both physically and emotionally. Older children however adopted multiple strategies to negotiate and challenge violence, often shielding their mothers from its effects, indirectly via their economic contributions, and also directly. Boys may become physically involved in attempting to stop violent episodes. Girls find alternative means to interrupt the pattern of violence, as in the case of Nga collecting her drunken father from the bar. Future research is needed to explore the longer term effects on young women and men's transitions to adulthood of growing up with family violence.

Children's habitus are also shaped by the social and economic resources at their disposal. The group discussions indicated that there was greater knowledge about violence in the home and more services available in Nghia Tan. In rural areas, such as Van Tri and especially more remote Van Lam, violence in the home is more normalised, by children as well as adults, perhaps exacerbated by a lack of alternatives for women. In urban areas, such as Nghia Tan, there are more wage earning opportunities for women and children as a result of economic growth, which are challenging the reproduction of gender hierarchies. However, the persistence of the ideal of family harmony in Vietnamese society and the continuing embodiment of family violence as a private matter means children and caregivers across all three sites are reluctant to seek support, even where services exist.

Children's responses are highly 'situational' (Overlien and Hyden 2009: 490), demonstrating varying degrees of agency and vulnerability at different time points (Katz 2013). Yet all responses, even those that could be perceived to be 'passive' – such as running away from violence as Lam and No Ha do – involve 'active choices' (Overlien and Hyden 2009: 492).

These findings offer a number of implications for policy. First, children affected by family violence can easily fall between the distinct policy domains that deal with child protection and domestic violence. As we have highlighted, 'everyday' violence in the home is often normalised and may not be as apparent to observers as an obvious child protection concern. At the same time, domestic violence interventions may not address the ways in which the needs of children can differ from those of their mothers. This is particularly important for cases such as No Ha where parental violence co-occurs with violence directed against children.

Second, given the high levels of school enrolment in Vietnam, particularly at primary level, schools provide an obvious entry point to reach children, not only to raise awareness on family violence and provide information and support, but also to foster norms around non-violent behaviours and relationships (Ellis 2008). In our study, a positive school experience could help bolster children's emotional resilience in the face of violence in the home. Finally any intervention designed to respond to violence in the home should be situated within a broader umbrella of public policies that work collectively to address the gendered structural constraints, such as poverty, that both enhance families' vulnerability to violence and shape their abilities to mediate the effects of such violence. Of critical importance will be to reconfigure policy messages to alleviate the burden on women to sustain happy and harmonious families in Vietnam and to utilise the 'transformative potential' of social protection (Devereux and Sabates-Wheeler 2004) to promote more equitable relations among households and communities.

Acknowledgements

We wish to thank the children and families participating in the Young Lives study for generously giving their time and sharing their experiences with us. We would also like to thank the team of researchers in Vietnam led by Vu Thi Thanh Huong. Helpful comments were received on an earlier draft from Paul Dornan, Nikki van der Gaag, Caroline Knowles, Virginia Morrow and Jenny Parkes.

Notes

1 Young Lives is an international study of childhood poverty which conducts large-scale household and child surveys with 12,000 children and their primary caregivers in four countries – Peru, Ethiopia, India (Andhra Pradesh) and Vietnam. The study is following two cohorts of children in each country over 15 years: 2,000 children who were born in 2001–2 and 1,000 children who were born in 1994–5. In addition, in-depth qualitative work is carried out with a sub-sample of 200 children and their caregivers. Young Lives is core-funded by UK aid from the Department of International Development (DFID) from 2001 to 2017, and co-funded by the Netherlands Ministry for Foreign Affairs from 2010 to 2014. For more details see: www.younglives.org.uk.
2 Article 29 of the 2003 Law for Emulation and Commendation states that the 'Cultured Family' title can be conferred on households which follow party policies and national laws, maintain 'harmonious, happy and progressive' families, and are economically productive.

References

Bourdieu, P. (1977) *Outline of a Theory of Practice*. Cambridge: Cambridge University Press.
Bourdieu, P. (2004) 'Gender and symbolic violence', in N. Scheper-Hughes and P. Bourgois (eds) *Violence in War and Peace: An Anthology* (pp. 339–42). Oxford: Blackwell.
Boyden, J. and Mann, G. (2006) 'Risk and resilience in children affected by armed conflict and forced migration', in M. Ungar (ed.) *Pathways to Resilience* (pp. 3–25). London: Sage Publications.
Cairns, E. and Dawes, A. (1996) 'Children: ethnic and political violence – a commentary', *Child Development*, 67 (1), 129–39.

Crivello, G., Morrow, V. and Wilson, E. (2013) *Young Lives Longitudinal Qualitative Research: A Guide for Researchers*, Technical Note 26. Oxford: Young Lives.

Devereux, S. and Sabates-Wheeler, R. (2004) *Transformative Social Protection*, Working Paper 232. Brighton: IDS.

Drummond, L. and Rydstrom, H. (2004) 'Introduction', in L. Drummond and H. Rydstrom (eds), *Gender Practices in Contemporary Vietnam* (pp. 1–25). Copenhagen: NIAS.

Ellis, J. (2008) 'Primary prevention of domestic abuse through education', in C. Humphreys, C. Houghton and J. Ellis, *Literature Review: Better Outcomes for Children and Young People Experiencing Domestic Abuse – Directions for Good Practice* (pp. 121–50). Edinburgh: The Scottish Government.

General Statistics Office (2008) *Result of the Nation-Wide Survey on the Family in Viet Nam 2006.* Hanoi: GSO.

General Statistics Office (2010) *'Keep Silent is Dying': Results from the National Study on Domestic Violence against Women in Viet Nam.* Hanoi: GSO.

Hoang, T.-A., Quach, T.T. and Tran, T.T. (2013) '"Because I am a man, I should be gentle to my wife and my children": positive masculinity to stop gender-based violence in a coastal district in Vietnam', *Gender and Development*, 21 (1), 81–96.

Horton, P. and Rydstrom, H. (2011) 'Heterosexual masculinity in contemporary Vietnam: privileges, pleasures and protests', *Men and Masculinities*, 14 (5), 542–64.

Katz, E. (2013) 'Domestic violence, children's agency and mother-child relationships: towards a more advanced model', *Children and Society* early online version, doi: 10.1111/chso.12023.

Kitzmann, K.M., Gaylord, N.K., Holt, A.R. and Kenny, E.D. (2003) 'Child witnesses to domestic violence: a meta-analytic review', *Journal of Consulting and Clinical Psychology*, 71 (2), 339–52.

Kleinman, A. (2000) 'The violences of everyday life: the multiple forms and dynamics of social violence', in V. Das, A. Kleinman, P. Ramphele and P. Reynolds (eds), *Violence and Subjectivity* (pp. 226–41). Berkeley: University of California Press.

McGee, C. (1997) 'Children's experiences of domestic violence', *Child and Family Social Work*, 2 (1), 13–23.

Merry, S.E. (2009) *Gender Violence: A Cultural Perspective.* Chichester: Wiley-Blackwell.

Morgan, K. and Björkert, S.T. (2006) '"I'd rather you'd lay me on the floor and start kicking me": understanding symbolic violence in everyday life', *Women's Studies International Forum*, 29 (5), 441–52.

Morrow, V. (2009) *The Ethics of Social Research with Children and Families in Young Lives: Practical Experiences*, Working Paper 53. Oxford: Young Lives.

Mullender, A., Hague, G., Imam, U., Kelly, L., Malos, E. and Regan, L. (2002) *Children's Perspectives on Domestic Violence.* London: Sage.

Ngo, T. (2004) 'The Confucian four feminine virtues (tu duc): the old versus the new – ke thua versus phat huy', in L. Drummond and H. Rydstrom (eds), *Gender Practices in Contemporary Vietnam* (pp. 47–73). Copenhagen: NIAS.

Overlien, C. (2010) 'Children exposed to domestic violence: conclusions from the literature and challenges ahead', *Journal of Social Work*, 10 (1), 80–97.

Overlien, C. and Hyden, M. (2009) 'Children's actions when experiencing domestic violence', *Childhood*, 16 (4), 479–96.

Reay, D. (2004) '"It's all becoming a habitus": beyond the habitual use of habitus in educational research', *British Journal of Sociology of Education*, 25 (4), 431–44.

Rydstrom, H. (2002) 'Sexed bodies, gendered bodies: children and the body in Vietnam', *Women's Studies International Forum*, 25 (3), 359–72.

Rydstrom, H. (2003) 'Encountering "hot" anger: domestic violence in contemporary Vietnam', *Violence Against Women*, 9 (6), 676–97.

Rydstrom, H. (2004) 'Female and male "characters": images of identification and self-identification for rural Vietnamese children and adolescents', in L. Drummond and H. Rydstrom (eds), *Gender Practices in Contemporary Vietnam* (pp. 74–95). Copenhagen: NIAS.

Save the Children (2003) *Child Protection Policy*. London: Save the Children Alliance.

Scheper-Hughes, N., and Bourgois, P. (eds) (2004) *Violence in War and Peace: An Anthology*. Oxford: Blackwell.

Schuler, S., Hoang, T., Vu, S., Tran, H., Bui, T. and Pham, V. (2006) 'Constructions of gender in Vietnam: in pursuit of the "three criteria"', *Culture, Health and Sexuality*, 8 (5), 383–94.

Terry, G. (2004) 'Poverty reduction and violence against women: exploring links, assessing impact', *Development in Practice*, 14 (4), 469–80.

Volkmann, C.S. (2005) '30 years after the war: children, families, and rights in Vietnam', *International Journal of Law, Policy and the Family*, 19 (1), 23–46.

Walker, R., Kyomuhendo, G., Chase, E., Choudry, S., Gubrium, E., Nicola, J., Lødemel, I., Leemamol, M., Mwiine, A., Pellissery, S. and Ming, Y. (2013) 'Poverty in global perspective: is shame a common denominator?', *Journal of Social Policy*, 42 (2), 215–33.

World Bank (2011) *Vietnam Country Gender Assessment*. Washington, DC: The World Bank.

Zhang, H.X. and Locke, C. (2002) 'Contextualising reproductive rights challenges: the Vietnam situation', *Women's Studies International Forum*, 25 (4), 443–53.

5 Children's perceptions of punishment in schools in Andhra Pradesh, India

Virginia Morrow and Renu Singh

Introduction

One of the success stories of the Millennium Development Goals[1] has been the increase in enrolment of children in primary schools. However, little attention has been paid to the daily experiences of children in school, from their viewpoints, and the extent to which corporal punishment[2] is used to control boys and girls in overcrowded classes with lack of teaching material, and teachers with limited classroom management skills. Even less attention has been paid to parents' views about their children's experiences at school. Corporal punishment is widely used in schools globally (UN 2006), despite international concern about the effects on children and the implications for their capacity to benefit from school. Severe and sometimes fatal injuries to children are reported from across India (Covell and Becker 2011). This raises questions as to why the practice is so persistent. Norms and social values relating to what makes a 'good' schoolgirl or schoolboy shape how children are expected to behave, and how adults behave towards to children. The implicit links between childhood poverty and the gendered nature of corporal punishment are rarely explored. In India, violence against girls is now high on the political agenda, after the horrific fatal gang-rape of a female student in Delhi in 2012 led to widespread demonstrations demanding an end to sexual violence against girls and women. However, more normalised forms of violence may go unnoticed or unquestioned, and limited academic attention has focused on children, and how patriarchy leads to gendered differences in the way boys and girls are treated at home, school and society at large. Social divisions based on caste, class and socio-economic status remain predominant, and violence against the powerless by those in power is common. This extends to schools where teachers 'control' the students through corporal punishment. Yet as Jeffrey (2012) has noted, 'the extent and nature of corporal punishment and bullying in schools . . . in the global South is a topic that urgently requires research' (p. 792).

This chapter, like the previous chapter, presents research evidence from Young Lives[3] about the prevalence of school corporal punishment among a sample of children in Andhra Pradesh, India. The chapter is structured as follows. First, we review existing literature, then we describe the methods and our approach to research ethics. The following section presents survey findings, before turning to analysis of qualitative data exploring corporal punishment from the points of view of children (aged 7–15) and their parents. Our findings indicate that violence in the form of corporal punishment of children in schools is endemic. Through analysis of children's and parents' perspectives, we consider the ways in which corporal punishment practices are shaped by norms and practices in families, schools and communities, and the links to gender and poverty. The chapter concludes with a discussion of the implications for policy and further research.

Corporal punishment in the international research literature

Up to the 2000s, research on corporal punishment tended to be dominated by US studies of child abuse, from a developmental psychology perspective, focused on parental use of corporal punishment, and on outcomes for children in adolescence and adulthood (Ember and Ember 2005). Though they may disaggregate by SES, gender and ethnicity, these studies tend not to theorise power imbalances on the basis of gender, generation or poverty. Further, as Ripoll-Núñez and Rohner (2006) note: 'research is limited by the fact that the targets of punishment – children themselves – are only rarely asked to be the source of information. Thus little is known about children's perceptions of their own experiences with corporal punishment' (pp. 231–2).

Recent research with children on physical and emotional punishment for Save the Children Sweden in the Southeast Asia and Pacific region from a human rights perspective found high levels of children reporting a range of forms of punishment, including corporal punishment (Ennew and Pierre Plateau 2004; Beazley *et al.* 2006). Some research on physical punishment in schools incorporates children's accounts (for example, Payet and Franchi 2008; Parkes and Heslop 2011; Twum-Danso 2013). However, few studies have explored the gendered dimensions of corporal punishment in schools (see Morrell 2001; Dunne *et al.* 2006; Parkes and Heslop 2011; Rojas 2011; and Chapter 6 in this volume, for exceptions). Dunne *et al.* (2006) distinguish between *implicit* gender violence related to everyday institutional structures and practices, and *explicit* gender violence, which relates to overtly sexualised encounters. Corporal punishment, they suggest, is a form of implicit gender violence since even though it may not be visibly or directly gendered it may reinforce gender differentiation through the ways in which it is practised by male and female teachers, or the messages it conveys about how girls or boys should behave, or indeed that the strong have control over the weak within genders. Morrell (2001) links corporal punishment and constructions of masculinity in South Africa. He notes that:

> In African schools, corporal punishment was used on boys and girls alike. It both symbolized and secured hierarchical dominance (of adult over child, learned over learner, male over female). In gender terms, bluntly put, it taught boys to be tough and uncomplaining, and it taught girls 'their place' – to be submissive and unquestioning.
>
> (p. 142)

Dunne *et al.* (2006) note that the 'gender regimes' of school are a crucial aspect of the hidden curriculum and that, while corporal punishment is often highly visible, 'it is implicitly gendered and in many developing world countries it is part of normal institutional life' (p. 82).

Understanding corporal punishment in context: legislation, school practices and childhood in India

Theoretically, from a Foucauldian perspective, school corporal punishment is a form of discipline that involves teachers controlling children's bodies in order to control their minds, and thus maintaining the social order. In *Discipline and Punish*, Foucault noted that discipline includes methods that:

> made possible the meticulous control of the operations of the body, which assured the constant subjection of its forces and imposed on them a relation of docility-utility . . . Many disciplinary methods have long been in existence – in monasteries, armies, workshops. But, in the course of the 17th and 18th centuries, the disciplines became general formulas of domination.
>
> (Foucault 1977: 137)

Foucault argued that 'discipline produces subjected and practised bodies, "docile" bodies' (Foucault 1977: 138). Thus, regulation and surveillance become internalised though Panopticon disciplinary controls. One of the aims of primary education was to 'train docile children . . . to "fortify", to "develop the body", and to prepare children for a future in some mechanical work' (Foucault 1977: 210–11). As Rojas notes in her analysis of children's experience of discipline in schools in Peru, 'discipline, and in particular school discipline, is linked to strategies of control applied to maintain order' (Rojas 2011: 5). The use of corporal punishment in schools involves adults (teachers) wielding power over children.

In order to understand punishment practices in India today, it is important to reflect on the social history of education systems and the use of corporal punishment. There is no specific historical study of corporal punishment in Indian schools (as far as we are aware – though see Sen (2004) on punishment of juvenile offenders in colonial India), but legal frameworks imposed during the colonial era appear to have been based on the traditional common law defence of 'reasonable chastisement' (Vohito 2011). Harber (2004), when describing the origins of mass schooling in France, Germany, the UK and the US, notes that authoritarian forms of schooling dominated, with 'the perceived right of teachers to punish inherent in the need to maintain control and order in the traditional schools setting' (Harber 2004: 73). Vohito suggests that in British colonies, 'corporal punishment using canes and whips was institutionalised in schools and in penal systems; and much missionary teaching promoted its use among parents' (Vohito 2011: 67). Colonial schooling systems displaced less authoritarian methods of education in India, when only elite castes and boys were educated (systems which, of course, perpetuated inequalities). Girls from upper-caste families received education within their homes. Students lived with their *guru* ('dispeller of ignorance', Sanskrit) who was held in great esteem. The *gurukul* system gave way to mass schooling under British rule, and the development of stark power disparities between teachers and pupils. Military schools set up by the colonisers in India further institutionalised corporal punishment (Ellis 2011).

In the post-colonial period, there have been considerable efforts to end corporal punishment in schools. India ratified the UN Convention on the Rights of the Child in 1992, and has copious policies that ban corporal punishment in schools, including the Right of Children to Free and Compulsory Education (2009) which guarantees school for children between the ages of six and 14. Elementary schooling has expanded, including phenomenal growth in low-fee private schooling (Singh and Sarkar 2013; Woodhead *et al.* 2013). However, this rapid expansion has not been matched by comparable increases in the teaching workforce. There is a shortage of teachers in government schools, and class sizes are very large, putting pressure on teachers to control high numbers of children, in both the private and the government sector (Singh and Sarkar 2013). The use of corporal punishment in schools also needs to be understood in the context of teaching practices. Balagopalan and Subrahmanian (2003) note that teachers in India tend not to make learning interesting. Learning by rote and reading out loud are common classroom practices and are difficult for children who speak a local dialect. Further structural constraints mean that resources are not available and entrenched hierarchies (such as caste) affect everyday practices. Kumar (2010) notes the low social status of primary school teachers and the poor quality training that they receive, and a lack of political will to address the use of corporal punishment in schools.

Use of violence in India is widespread, and news media frequently report violence (by the army, police, in homes and workplaces). However, there is very little research about how violence is linked to cultures of masculinity and femininity in India, the forms that masculinity and femininity take, and how these intersect with caste/ethnicity/class/age (though see Kakar 1978; Manjrekar 2011). For children in Andhra Pradesh, norms relating to femininity mean that girls are required to be docile and submissive, and not to be 'caught' being 'naughty', though they may be punished in differing ways. Constructions of masculinity may mean that boys are supposed to be able to accept physical punishment and to withstand pain.

No official statistics on corporal punishment in schools are kept, but research on child abuse suggests that about two-thirds of children experience corporal punishment in school, slightly more boys than girls. The Government of India commissioned research that included a sub-study with 3,163 children aged 5–18 in 13 states, who were asked about physical abuse by teachers. In all age groups, 65 per cent reported being beaten at school. Of those reporting corporal punishment, 54 per cent were boys and 46 per cent were girls (Kacker *et al.* 2007: 52). But most children do not report or confide in anyone (see Bartholdson 2001; Chakraborty 2003). Being hit on the palms with a cane by a teacher is common practice, but teachers use a range of other punishments, including forcing children to kneel in uncomfortable positions, slapping or spanking and beating on the knuckles (National Commission for Protection of Child Rights 2010). Child abuse and corporal punishment are viewed as distinct from each other in many contexts, and where corporal punishment is accepted, a distinction is made on the basis of the extent of harm and motivation. This slippery slope is probably one of the strongest arguments against corporal punishment – outlawing it prevents excesses. The next section describes the methods and approach to research ethics, before moving to a presentation of the results.

Methods and ethics

In order to explore children's experiences of corporal punishment in Andhra Pradesh we draw on data from Young Lives. Young Lives samples are not representative, but pro-poor.[4] A survey is carried out every three years (2002, 2006, 2009) with 3,000 children and their caregivers, and is complemented by qualitative research (2007, 2008, 2010) in four communities with a nested sample of 25 children from each cohort (the older cohort were born in 1994, the younger cohort in 2001/2), roughly equal numbers of boys and girls, from a range of caste and language backgrounds, their caregivers (mostly mothers, but occasionally both parents), and other key figures in the community. Young Lives surveys are not dedicated child protection prevalence surveys, but rather general surveys of children's well-being, experiences of poverty, and progress. While the survey asked a question about being beaten by teachers, the qualitative research is more loosely framed, and research teams are encouraged to follow what children are willing to talk about, within a broad set of topics, including well-being, transitions (moving school), and time-use and daily experiences. Local research teams conducted interviews in homes, fields or in community premises, and schools. Like most studies of violence, we rely on self-reports and various factors such as research context, cultural considerations and children's agency in research may affect disclosures of violence.

A range of qualitative methods are used, including one-to-one interviews, group discussions and creative activities (such as drawings of a child 'doing well'/'doing badly' and body-mapping[5]). Corporal punishment emerged as a concern on numerous occasions, including group discussions about what constitutes a child 'doing well', children's descriptions of what they like and dislike about school, and so on. Qualitative interviews are voice-recorded, transcribed and translated.

We present descriptive statistics from the child survey conducted in 2009 (Round 3) with 1,900 younger cohort children (aged 7–8 years) and 753 older cohort children (aged 14–15 years), together with some findings from the qualitative element of the Young Lives School Study.[6] Significance tests were carried out using Pearson's chi-squared tests and unpaired two-sample t-tests as appropriate. Qualitative data were coded by themes, using Atlas.ti qualitative data analysis software. For this chapter, a thematic approach has been used, by extracting all mentions of corporal punishment by children and caregivers across all three rounds of data collection, then further sorting these by topics (see Crivello *et al.* 2013).

Asking children about their experiences of corporal punishment at school raises profound questions about research ethics and the responsibilities of researchers to report instances of violence, as also discussed in depth in Chapter 3. Arguably, 'it is unnecessary to collect data about such experiences in order to promote what is a fundamental human right' (EPOCH 2012: 19). The dilemma lies in the fact that children not only risk harm, but are reporting an illegal activity. Questions are likely to be raised in the readers' minds about why action was not taken by researchers to challenge the use of corporal punishment, and why children were not removed from situations where they risk harm. On balance, we feel it is helpful to raise awareness about the use of corporal punishment and the effects on children at the broader, social policy level. Here, a balance was struck between intervening in children's lives, and raising awareness (see also Powell 2012). As EPOCH (End Physical Punishment of Children) (2012: 19) suggests, research findings can be used 'to raise awareness about the reality of children's experiences of corporal punishment, to counter myths, and to add weight to arguments' that might be used in campaigns to improve practice, especially where legislation may have been passed, but is not effective.

Survey findings: prevalence of corporal punishment

Overall, our findings indicate clearly that physical punishment in schools is highly prevalent, as shown in Figure 5.1.

The 7–8-year-old cohort were significantly more likely to have witnessed and experienced corporal punishment than the 14–15-year-old cohort, with over two-thirds of the younger children having been physically punished at school in the past week, compared with one-third of the older children.

Among children aged 14–15 years of age, we note differences by sex with boys reporting punishment more frequently than girls (see Figure 5.2). Children from urban locations (compared to rural) and children from the poorest quintile (compared to the least poor) also reported higher levels of punishment.

There were also significant differences in the younger group (see Figure 5.3). As with the older children, more boys experienced violence than girls, though for both girls and boys it was commonplace. Poorer children were more likely than less poor children to report punishment. However, in contrast to the older cohort, punishment was higher in rural settings. Thus it appears that there was a less sharp distinction in the use of corporal punishment between boys and girls in the younger cohort. This may be because corporal punishment is part of the socialisation of younger children, but when they are older it is no longer seen as an appropriate way to discipline young women, while 'toughening up' young men is still normative. This is to an extent reflected in our analysis of qualitative data, which we turn to now.

Girls' and boys' views on punishment in school

Corporal punishment was observed by fieldworkers to be a sensitive topic but one that was widely mentioned during qualitative data gathering. Many punishments

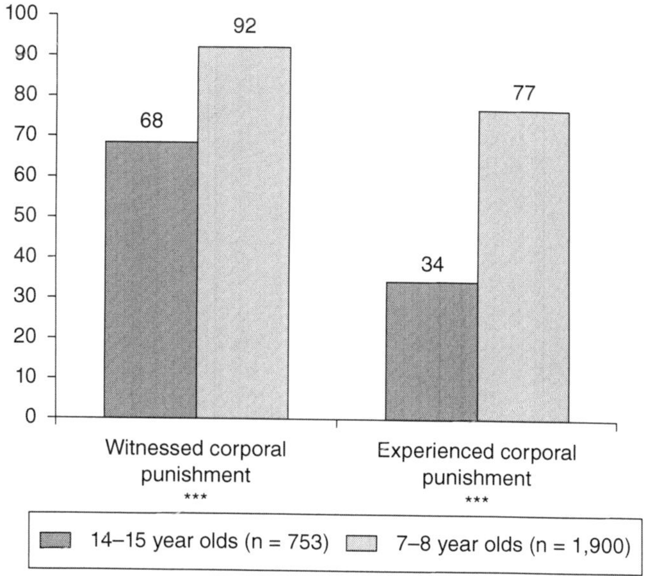

Figure 5.1 Children's experiences of physical punishment in last typical week by cohort

Notes: * p<0.05, ** p<0.01, ***p<0.001.

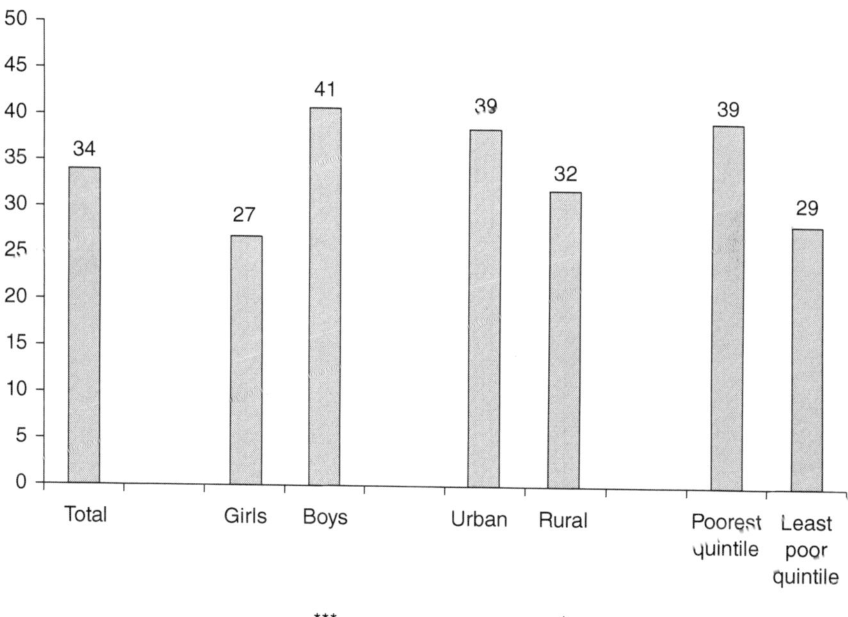

Figure 5.2 Children experiencing physical punishment in last typical week of school, aged 14–15 years

Notes: * p<0.05, ** p<0.01, ***p<0.001.

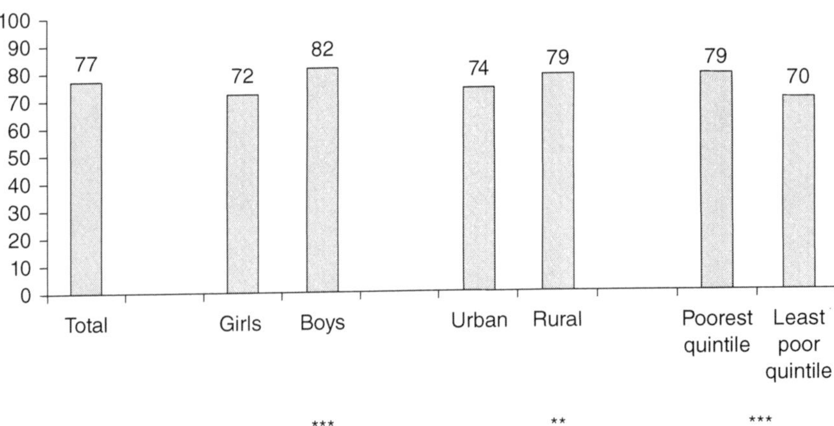

Figure 5.3 Children experiencing physical punishment in last typical week of school, aged 7–8 years

Notes: * p<0.05, ** p<0.01, ***p<0.001.

were linked to the poor conditions for teaching and learning in schools. Fieldwork teams noted that children were being taught in very overcrowded classrooms, with a minimum of 40 students per class, sometimes as many as 125:

> Children sitting in the back rows of the class were often engaged in other activities during lessons. Large class sizes were also noted by younger children as a reason for children to be beaten. Children explained that their teacher was very frequently absent, and they were taught by other teachers trying to compensate by managing more than a class at a time. As the number becomes unmanageable, teachers use a stick to control the children, hitting them if they can't say the words. That is why all the children were scared of them.

Other forms of punishment were also described in group discussions. One 8-year-old girl explained that her teacher had asked her to do a *goda kurchi* (sitting on the edge of the wall by balancing on the legs, a form of punishment widely used in India) and her leg was swollen. Another child explained that in the 1st standard, the teacher used to beat very little, but in 2nd standard, they are beaten hard: 'they beat so that we learn and we are becoming big, but it hurts'.

A range of punishments were used with both boys and girls, with children expressing discontent about both physical and verbal forms. *Goda kurchi* and verbal abuse was described by one of the 9–10-year-old boys in a group discussion at a government school:

The teachers beat with sticks and rulers and make us sit on our haunches –
our legs swell up. They also abuse us, and use foul language, 'you look like
bullocks and donkeys – the herdsman is better than you' – this makes us very
sad.

Girls and boys spoke of a range of reasons for punishment. Some referred to
corporal punishment as a way of controlling unruly behaviour or behaviour that
flouted school rules, as the following extract from a report of a group discussion
with 7–8-year-old girls and boys (2008) shows:

> Teachers beat the students if they make noise, fight each other, making noise
> by knocking the bench, grabbing pens or money from each other; if they are
> not neat, and if they make the classroom untidy. They all claimed at first that
> they were never beaten by the teachers, and it is others who were beaten.
> When explored further, however, Rahul was beaten by the teachers more –
> 10 times. All were beaten for making a noise, for knocking the plates when
> taking midday meal, for not writing properly, for not working on maths
> properly . . . the teacher beat them with a stick . . . brought by the students
> from the nearby bushes. Teachers use only thin sticks which are not dry.
> The dry ones will break easily, and if they are wet will not break and will be
> sharper. Hence teachers always keep only the wet, thin stick with them.

Other reasons included being absent from school for work, illness, or attending
family celebrations, missing classes, not doing their homework, not reading well,
making mistakes, getting poor marks in exams, not wearing uniform, not having
the right equipment, not paying the teacher for extra lessons – one girl said, 'my
teacher beats me if I don't go to the private class' Another girl mentioned that
children were punished for making a noise, especially if the teacher is getting
phone calls or writing his accounts. Shanmuka Priya (aged ten) explained:

> If we don't study, they beat us. If we ask other children for help, they beat
> [us]. I went to drink water without asking sir, so he beat me that time.
> They said all children should come back to class by the time they count ten
> after the interval. But I went home [to use the toilet]. After coming back to
> school, he beat me. Once he beat me when I did not study.

This girl's mother described how her daughter is frightened of going to school.
Boys and girls mentioned going home at lunchtime to use the toilet, as toilets in
schools are often inadequate and unsanitary.

Linking corporal punishment to poverty

As well as poor conditions in school, poverty in homes clearly influenced school
discipline practices. Living in poverty meant that children were sometimes not

in a position to follow the rules and expectations of formal schooling. Children described being punished for not having uniform or the right equipment, or money to pay fees. Anwar (aged ten) said: 'If we don't get notebooks, then teachers will beat us.' Yaswanth (aged 15) described how he sometimes missed school: 'if uniform is not there [ready], I don't go because the PT master will beat me.' At high schools, responsibility for administering corporal punishment to children was often assigned to a particular male teacher.

One mother mentioned that the only thing her seven-year-old daughter says about school is that teachers beat her:

> She studies well, she goes regularly and returns, but when there is no dress [uniform] and when we delay the fee payment then she will not go, she refuses to go . . . she says she will not go and she hides behind that wall . . . and says that 'sir will beat me, they will beat me'.

From Young Lives data, it appears that economic constraints and family circumstances mean that boys and girls in rural areas engaged in seasonal agricultural work on family land, and missed school for days, weeks or months at a time. Tasks are gendered, and boys described having to get up in the middle of the night to switch on irrigation pumps when the electricity supply is available, which made them tired at school the next day. Girls typically undertook domestic chores before and after school. Girls and boys engaged in cotton pollination work. When they did return to school, they faced punishment. Ramya (aged 12) said: 'I feel very bad when teacher scolds me. I like to be regular to school, do home work, but I cannot do it all. It is difficult, but I have no choice but to do it.' Ranadeep (aged 13), also involved in cotton pollination work, described missing school to work, and when he returned to school: 'They [school management] beat us . . . They hit us because I didn't go to school for one month, and they have taught the lessons and I missed [them].'

Though older boys rarely spoke directly about their fears of punishment, their mothers spoke of their sons' emotions. Ranadeep's mother explained:

> My boy scolds me for this. He liked going to school, but we stop him, he makes a lot of argument. Otherwise, we cannot run the family, we don't get labourers in time and there is no other way for us, so we had to do it like that. When he is absent without intimation to teachers, they shout at him and he is terrified . . . His father goes there and informs them . . . they scold us, they say, how will he get on if he is absent for such a long time? . . . we try to pacify them by telling them about our problems at home.

Girls and younger boys, however, talked more openly about their fears and sadness. Ramesh (aged ten) described how he felt about changing school:

> I was very afraid [of changing schools] as the school was bigger, and my earlier one was small. We have PT Sir [physical training teacher], they said he beats the children a lot. I was very frightened.

Vinay, a Scheduled Tribe boy aged 15, complained about the unfairness meted out on boys, who he perceived as being more likely to be punished than girls:

> They [teachers] will give a preference to teachers' children, but for other children they won't motivate, but discourage them . . . If we ask why they are doing . . . that, they will give a severe punishment for a small mistake . . . and beat us . . . He [a teacher] beat one student very badly because he did not get good marks in [an] exam . . . other girls also got less marks but left them without any punishment, but this boy got punishment. This boy got 33 out of 100 but another girl got 8 marks but she did not get any punishment.

Vinay's account lends some support to the gendered nature of corporal punishment in this context, helping to 'toughen' boys in preparation for manhood.

Some children mentioned that they and their parents do not question the use of corporal punishment for fear that the child may not receive 'care' and attention from teachers in the future. When Santhi, age 15, was asked whether such incidents were reported to the headmaster, she replied, 'we do not tell, if we tell, this sir will not care for us. He will not teach well'. Her friend added, 'he will not take care of us, he will avoid us'. In this case 'care' seems to imply attention from the teacher.

Fear of further punishment meant that children did not tell their parents about physical punishment they experience at school. For example, in a group discussion, a nine-year-old boy said: 'I do not like my school, since the teachers beat me badly. They beat with a stick on my back, even if we are sitting and talking.' When the researcher asked: 'Do you not complain to your parents?' he replied: 'No, because they only beat because we must study well. My mother will thrash me very hard, if she knows I am not answering in class.' This seems to support a discourse of learning through strictness, which seemed to be a widespread view in schools and in homes. Corporal punishment was excused, taken for granted and even supported by some, since 'they beat so we learn'. At the same time, children often criticised the practice when deemed inequitable or unjust.

'It is for their own good': parents' views

Parents, like their children, were ambivalent about corporal punishment. Sometimes parents expected and demanded it of teachers, as the mother of a nine-year-old boy explained: 'Nowadays, the teachers don't beat the students . . . but it should be necessary sometimes to keep them in control. So we ourselves ask them to be strict with the students.'

Some parents colluded with the practice perhaps because they felt helpless to influence change, as in the case of Sahiti's mother, who said: 'If Sir beats [the children], we do not say anything. We tell the child that it is for your own good.'

Some parents, however, did feel able to question the practice, as discussed by the mother of a seven-year-old boy:

> In the sense that children are afraid of the sir [teacher], if children complain against the teacher, they don't care, because they are determined to educate the children. A few days ago, sir has called for a parents' meeting, explained one of the children had taken the parents to the school, as the child was beaten as a punishment. Parents also questioned the teacher for beating the child, he must have thought somebody else would come . . . hence he decided to call a meeting with all the parents to discuss this, and said that 'everybody knows about me, whatever I do is for your children's education, if children don't care [about] me here in school and you at home, then how are they controlled, how can I teach if they are not controlled?' And [he] also requested not to misunderstand. [He said] 'Children are banged [hit] once or twice to control and teach them, and you should not make it an issue, madam'. He explained this to all, as one of the parents questioned him, because that is done for the benefit of the children, he said he punished only troublemaking children and not all children, he doesn't wish to punish good children.

This example suggests that this teacher felt he could discuss corporal punishment openly with parents. It is also clear that parents had differing views. The teacher appeared to think he could reach consensus by explaining the reason (to control and teach) and the extent (only one or two bangs). So he was setting his own boundaries, and expecting parents to agree, despite flouting the law. As noted in other studies, punishment that is not excessive but sufficient to induce fear is viewed as signifying care (Morrell 2001; Parkes and Heslop 2011).

On the other hand, some parents had removed children from school because of corporal punishment. The mother of a ten-year-old boy described how her child no longer wanted to continue at school following a beating:

> My son discontinued going to a private school, when he fell sick after being beaten by the teacher. He does not wish to continue schooling any more. I am not allowed to enter the school to even meet the headmaster and am too scared to complain against the teacher. After spending so much money, my son is not studying. I tried to explain that teacher beats you for your betterment – they are not your enemies, but he does not wish to continue his studies.

This parent was fearful of confronting the institutional practices of the school. Another mother explained how 'my daughter was small, she was frightened, and said she will not go to school. She was crying, so I went and told . . . [the teacher] not to hit'. So it seems that the parents, as well as the children, have rules for the kinds of corporal punishment that are acceptable – bounded by how severe, the reason, and so on. Caste status and educational background are likely to influence parents' confidence to challenge teachers directly.

While corporal punishment is widely used, not all teachers use it. In one horrific case, a mother told us how corporal punishment had stopped at a local school after a boy was killed: 'one student was beaten severely for not attending . . . he went to [get] a samosa . . . The boy was dead on the spot. Since then, they put in a system of not beating the students.' In this case, the practice changed despite the wishes of the parents: 'we ourselves ask them to beat on their backs or on the hands, otherwise the students will become stubborn, without any fear.'

In other cases, though we did not systematically research whether there were any schools using 'positive discipline' and/or rights-based approaches, parents talked about positive relationships between children and teachers. Schools were places of learning and creativity, as well as discipline and control. The mother of Santhi, an older cohort girl, said about her child's school:

> It is good. They [teachers] mingle closely with the students . . . they try to remove the fear from the students by constantly talking to them, moving freely and helping them to read. Teaching them how to behave . . . But when they are not able to do well it is definite that they get a scolding.

When asked 'do they beat the children of this age [14–15-year-olds] too?' the mother replied:

> Not exactly beating. They say some harsh words. These children will not wait till they get beatings. Usually they don't beat girls. She never complained that she was beaten in school . . . they are all grown-up children. They will not tolerate scoldings, leave alone thrashings. If there is any bigger problem the parents are summoned. However, it has never taken place. Most of the parents are job holders, and they have self-esteem and ego.

In previous rounds of qualitative data, Santhi had complained about teachers beating her, but her mother indicates that older children will not tolerate corporal punishment. However, Santhi is an exception, because her family is 'middle class', and had moved to a town to access what they perceived to be high-quality schooling. These examples suggest that use of corporal punishment is classed, gendered and age-related.

Conclusion

In India, as in many countries, laws banning corporal punishment in line with the UN Convention on the Rights of the Child may be out of kilter with everyday realities. Changing social policies send clear messages about practices that are not acceptable, but the eradication of corporal punishment in schools globally is proving difficult, and India is no exception. We have found that girls and boys alike experience routine violence, with boys experiencing particularly high levels. This needs to be understood in contexts of social norms related to how children should be raised, and what schooling should be like. The use of corporal punishment is condoned by parents and, to an extent, children, within bounds. However, blaming specific groups (teachers and/or parents) will not enable progress to be made, and risks alienating teachers already under pressure because of overcrowded classrooms, poor infrastructure and poverty situations. We also need to be cautious about problematising situations in developing countries at the risk of constructing 'truths' 'about social realities in specific contexts' (Dunne *et al.* 2006: 76). Approaches need to develop not only from the top down, but from communities, families and teachers upwards, to find ways of working together to change practices (Morrow and Pells 2012). There is some indication of shifting attitudes because, although corporal punishment is experienced by all social groups, some older children and parents[7] in better-off communities mentioned challenging corporal punishment by teachers. Learning from the ways in which parents and children challenge teachers' practices could usefully be channelled into community-led strategies to influence attitudes about corporal punishment.

In global policy debates, much emphasis has been placed on the role of education as the solution not only to reducing cycles of poverty in developing countries, but also to addressing gender violence. However, the evidence presented here suggests that we must question this. Violence as an integral part of schooling may have consequences for boys' and girls' development that go beyond the here-and-now of childhood to social and economic consequences in adulthood, as children experience fear and risks of injury while at school. In India, this needs to be understood in the context of high expectations that parents and children have of schools, despite the very low levels of learning that children achieve (ASER 2013). Some children dislike school for many reasons, but if they discontinue school because of their experience of corporal punishment, and if they learn that the use of violence is the solution to behaviour that is out of line, then formal schooling may inadvertently be reinforcing both cycles of poverty and the use of violence. Children want to study, but practices within schools may inhibit their learning. As we have seen, there are links in parents' and children's minds about the use of corporal punishment at home, and this may legitimate its use in schools and vice versa (cf. Morrell 2001). Corporal punishment is also serving to reinforce norms about gender, childhood, and about caste/class status, in the differential ways in which it is administered. Thus the regulation of bodies to regulate minds in schools that Foucault described is likely to reproduce pernicious inequalities in unforeseen ways.

Finally, it is increasingly recognised that understandings of child protection need to encompass broader definitions of violence, and more holistic responses (Bourdillon and Myers 2012). Ongoing debates are setting new goals for the post-2015 development agenda. The UN High-Level Panel have proposed Goal 2 on girls' (and women's) empowerment to 'Prevent and eliminate all forms of violence against girls and women'. Goal 3 sets minimum learning standards, emphasises the importance of 'quality education', and recognises that globally, 'there is an education, learning and skills crisis', because 'vast numbers of children cannot read or do basic maths after multiple years of schooling' (UN 2013: 36). However, Goal 3 makes no mention of corporal punishment in schools. This means that a substantial dimension of violence in girls' as well as boys' lives is overlooked, reinforcing gender stereotypes of girls (and women) as the inevitable victims of male aggression and violence. This is a missed opportunity. As Pinheiro notes: 'Schools are uniquely placed to break the patterns of violence by giving children, their parents and communities the knowledge and skills to communicate, negotiate and resolve conflicts in more constructive ways' (UN 2006: 112).

Acknowledgements

The authors thank the children, families and other community members who participate in Young Lives research, Professor Uma Vennam and team in Tirupati, Emma Wilson for expert research assistance, Zoe James, Jenny Parkes, Kirrily Pells and Caine Rolleston for helpful comments.

Young Lives is core-funded from 2001 to 2017 by UK Department for International Development (DFID) and co-funded by the Netherlands Ministry of Foreign Affairs from 2010 to 2014 for the School Study. The views expressed are those of the authors. They are not necessarily those of, or endorsed by, Young Lives, the University of Oxford, DFID or other funders.

Notes

1 The Millennium Development Goals were agreed in 2000 and set targets relating to (*inter alia*) child survival and enrolment in primary schools.
2 The UN Committee on the Rights of the Child General Comment No. 8 (2006) defines 'corporal' or 'physical' punishment as: 'any punishment in which physical force is used and intended to cause some degree of pain or discomfort, however light. Most involves hitting ("smacking", "slapping", "spanking") children, with the hand or with an implement – a whip, stick, belt, show, wooden spoon, etc. But it can also involve . . . kicking, shaking or throwing children, scratching, pinching, biting, pulling hair, or boxing ears, forcing children to stay in uncomfortable positions, burning, scalding or forced ingestion . . . corporal punishment is invariably degrading. In addition, there are other non-physical forms of punishment that are also cruel and degrading, and thus incompatible with the Convention . . . These include, for example, punishment which belittles, humiliates, denigrates, scapegoats, scares or ridicules the child' (UN Committee on the Rights of the Child 2006: 4). Art. 19 of UN Convention on the Rights of the Child requires states to protect children from 'all forms of physical or mental violence' while in the care of parents or others.
3 Young Lives is an ongoing longitudinal study investigating the changing nature of childhood poverty in four developing countries, Ethiopia, India (Andhra Pradesh), Peru and Vietnam, over a 15-year period, 2002–17 (www.younglives.org.uk).
4 Using sentinel site sampling, 20 sites per country were selected with oversampling of sites in poor areas. The sites include urban and rural areas, representing a range of regions and contexts that reflect ethnic, geographic and political diversity. Within each sentinel site, 100 households with a child aged between six and 18 months (younger cohort) and 50 households with a child between seven and eight years (older cohort) were randomly selected. The sample is divided into quintiles (groups of equal size) according to a wealth index, where the lowest quintile (bottom 20 per cent) of families are considered to be the 'poorest' and those in the highest quintile (top 20 per cent) the 'least poor'.

5 Body-mapping is a visual method to elicit people's experiences of health and harm. It involves using a large sheet of paper with an outline of a body that enables children to identify parts of the body affected (Cornwall 1992).
6 An additional School Study was initiated in 2010 to gain a better understanding of children's school experiences, and included qualitative interviews with children (aged 9–10) and caregivers in three sites with 30 children and families (see Singh and Sarkar 2013; Woodhead *et al.* 2013, for further details).
7 In June 2013, a Public Interest Litigation was filed in Hyderabad by a parent to challenge the inaction of the State of Andhra Pradesh in preventing corporal punishment (www.deccanchronicle.com/130616/news-current-affairs/article/petition-filed-high-court-against-corporal-punishments).

References

ASER (2013) *Annual Status of Education Report (Rural) 2012.* New Delhi: Pratham.

Balagopalan, S. and Subrahmanian, R. (2003) '*Dalit* and *Adivasi* children in schools: some preliminary research themes and findings'. *IDS Bulletin,* 34 (1), 43–54.

Bartholdson, O. (2001) *Corporal Punishment of Children and Change of Attitudes: A Cross Cultural Study.* Stockholm: Save the Children.

Beazley, H., Bessell, S., Ennew, J. and Waterson, R. (2006) *What Children Say? Results of Comparative Research on the Physical and Emotional Punishment of Children in South East Asia and the Pacific.* Save the Children Sweden.

Bourdillon, M. and Myers, W. (2012) 'Development, children and protection'. *Development in Practice,* 22 (4), 437–47.

Chakraborty, K. (2003) *A Comparative Study on Violence in Three Slum Communities in Kolkata.* Save the Children UK, West Bengal Office, India.

Cornwall, A. (1992) 'Body mapping in health RRA/PRA'. *RRA Notes,* 16, 69–76.

Covell, K. and Becker, J. (2011) *Five Years On: A Global Update on Violence against Children.* NGO Advisory Council Report for follow-up to the UN Secretary-General's Study on Violence against Children.

Crivello, G., Morrow, V. and Wilson, E. (2013) 'Young Lives longitudinal qualitative research: a guide for researchers'. *Technical Note 26.* Oxford: Young Lives.

Dunne, M., Humphreys, S. and Leach, F, (2006) 'Gender violence in schools in the developing world'. *Gender and Education,* 18 (1), 75–98.

Ellis, C. (2011) '"Snapshots" of the classroom: autobiographies and the experiences of elementary education in the Madras presidency, 1882–1947'. *Childhood,* 18 (3), 384–401.

Ember, C. and Ember, M. (2005) 'Explaining corporal punishment of children: a cross-cultural study'. *American Anthropologist,* 107 (4), 609–19.

Ennew, J. and Pierre Plateau, D. (2004) *How to Research the Physical and Emotional Punishment of Children.* Save the Children, Bangkok, Thailand.

EPOCH (Global Initiative to End All Corporal Punishment of Children) (2012) *Ending Legalised Violence against Children. Global Report 2012.* Available at: www.endcorproalpunishment.org.

Foucault, M. (1977) *Discipline and Punish.* Harmondsworth: Penguin.

Harber, C. (2004) *Schooling as Violence.* London: RoutledgeFalmer.

Jeffrey, C. (2012) 'Commentary: youth and development'. *European Journal of Development Research,* 23 (5), 792–6.

Kacker, L., Varadan, S., Kumar, P., Mohsin, N. and Dixit, A. (2007) *Study on Child Abuse: India 2007*. New Delhi: Ministry of Women and Child Development.

Kakar, S. (1978) *The Inner World: A Psychoanalytic Study of Childhood and Society in India*. New Delhi: Oxford University Press.

Kumar, K. (2010) 'Banning is just the beginning: corporal punishment in schools will prove tenacious'. In NCPCR *Eliminating Corporal Punishment in Schools: A Study*. New Delhi: NCPCR (National Commission for Protection of Child Rights).

Manjrekar, H. (2011) 'Ideals of Hindu girlhood: reading Vidya Bharati's *Balika Shikshan*'. *Childhood*, 18 (3), 350–66.

Morrell, R. (2001) 'Corporal punishment and masculinity in South African schools'. *Men and Masculinities*, 4 (2), 140–57.

Morrow, V. and Pells, K. (2012) 'Integrating children's human rights and child poverty debates: examples from *Young Lives* in Ethiopia and India'. *Sociology*, 45 (5), 906–20.

National Commission for Protection of Child Rights (NCPCR) (2010) *Eliminating Corporal Punishment in Schools: A Study*. New Delhi: NCPCR.

Parkes, J. and Heslop, J. (2011) *Stop Violence against Girls in School: A Cross-Country Analysis of Baseline Research from Ghana, Kenya and Mozambique*. London: Action Aid/Institute of Education.

Payet, J. and Franchi, V. (2008) 'The rights of the child and "the good of the learners": a comparative ethnographical survey on the abolition of corporal punishment in South African schools'. *Childhood*, 15 (2), 157–76.

Powell, M. (2012) *Ethical Principles, Dilemmas and Risks in Collecting Data on Violence against Children. A Review of the Available Literature*. Child Protection Monitoring and Evaluation Reference Group, UNICEF and others.

Ripoll-Núñez, K. and Rohner, R.P. (2006) 'Corporal punishment in cross-cultural perspective: directions for a research agenda'. *Cross-Cultural Research*, 40, 220–49.

Rojas, V. (2011) '"I'd rather be hit with a stick . . . grades are sacred": students' perceptions of discipline and authority in a Public High School in Peru'. *Working Paper 70*. Oxford: Young Lives.

Sen, S. (2004) 'A separate punishment: juvenile offenders in colonial India'. *Journal of Asian Studies*, 63 (1), 81–104.

Singh, R. and Sarkar, S. (2013) 'Teaching quality counts: how student outcomes relate to quality of teaching in private and public schools in India'. *Working Paper 91*. Oxford: Young Lives.

Twum-Danso, A. (2013) 'Children's perceptions of physical punishment in Ghana and the implications for children's rights'. *Childhood*, 20 (4), 472–86.

UN (2006) *UN Secretary-General's World Report on Violence against Children*.

UN (2013) *A New Global Partnership: Eradicate Poverty and Transform Economies through Sustainable Development. The Report of the High-Level Panel of Eminent Persons on the Post-2015 Development Agenda*. New York: United Nations.

UN Committee on the Rights of the Child (2006) *General Comment No. 8*.

Vohito, S (2011) 'Africa: growing momentum towards the prohibition of corporal punishment'. In J. Durrant and A. Smith (eds) *Global Pathways to Abolishing Physical Punishment* (pp. 67–82). London: Routledge.

Woodhead, M., Frost, M. and James, Z. (2013) 'Does growth in private schooling contribute to Education for All?' *International Journal of Educational Research*, 33 (1), 65–73.

6 Corporal punishment, capabilities and well-being

Tanzanian primary school teachers' perspectives

Sharon Tao

A burgeoning literature elucidates the detrimental effects of corporal punishment on children, including physical, psychological and emotional harm (Newell 1989; Gershoff 2002); reduced moral and social development (as children do not learn the 'wrongfulness' of behaviours, but learn to avoid punishments instead) (Hoffman 1983; De Veer and Janssens 1994); and increases in aggression, antisocial behaviour and lack of self-control (Straus 1990; Lazerele 2000). Investigations of corporal punishment within educational settings have demonstrated similar physical, mental and emotional effects, particularly in developing country contexts (Youssef *et al.* 1998; Leach and Machakanja 2000; Morrell 2001; Dunne *et al.* 2006).[1] Within Tanzanian schools in particular, a survey of 500 primary and secondary students demonstrated that children feared teachers 'who shout, use bad language and caning' (Mkukuta Secretariat, Poverty Eradication Division 2007: 15). Another study found that excessive corporal punishment was linked to truancy and dropout (Kuleana Children's Rights Centre 1999). A third study also documented secondary students stating that '[corporal punishment] doesn't help me change', and 'it makes me lose focus on my studies' (Feinstein and Mwahombela 2010: 406). These research findings come despite the Tanzanian government's ratification of the United Nations Convention on the Rights of the Child (CRC) in 1991 which states that children should be protected against physical as well as psychological violence (United Nations 1989). Although the CRC was ratified, corporal punishment is still legal in Tanzanian schools, though limited to four strokes only to be administered by head teachers (Ministry of Education and Vocational Training 2008). The research evidence, however, suggests that regular teachers continue to practise corporal punishment (McAlpine 2008; Frankenberg *et al.* 2010); which speaks to the difficulty of changing teachers' attitudes and behaviours even though legislation is in place. This points to the need to understand further the complex interconnections between social norms, reasoning and lived experience that prompt teachers to use corporal punishment.

This chapter will explore possible explanations for teachers' ongoing use of corporal punishment, particularly with regard to the varying practices of male and female teachers, as well as how they inflict different types of corporal punishment based on the sex of their students. These explanations will be framed through the lens of the Capability Approach, and I will argue that repeated acts of violence could be viewed as a product of teachers negotiating capability constraint. Empirical data collected at three Tanzanian primary schools will be used to demonstrate how constraints on teachers' occupational and personal well-being are frequently caused by environmental conditions linked to impoverished educational contexts, social conditions mediated by gender relations, as well as capability conflict with students; and that corporal punishment is often the product of teachers attempting to exercise agency within constraint. By reframing corporal punishment in this manner, I hope to generate a more nuanced understanding of corporal punishment that challenges over-simplified victim–perpetrator dichotomies, avoids blaming teachers, and instead helps enhance educational strategies to reduce physical punishments in schools.

Understanding why adults come to use corporal punishment

Although there is a large literature on the negative effects of corporal punishment on children, research attempting to explain corporal punishment from the *adult's* perspective is far less common. Xu *et al.* (2000) posit that an adult's level of cultural, human and social capital determines their propensity to use corporal punishment at home. Owen and Wagner (2006) discuss how in American Evangelical Protestant schools, religious ideology shapes teachers' values and their subsequent use of corporal punishment. Morrell (2001) argues that there are strong connections between home and school modes of discipline in South Africa, and that corporal punishment persists because parents use it in the home and support its use in school. Humphreys (2008) argues that accepted gender regimes in Botswana value masculine authority, thereby perpetuating the use of corporal punishment by male teachers (to maintain power) and female teachers (to assert authority in relation to their subordinated feminine identities). One study of note attempts to broaden the set of reasons for adults' use of corporal punishment by organising a variety of interconnected 'societal causes' into *distal, mezzo* and *proximal* levels (Straus 2010: 9). In this framing, factors at broader distal levels increase the occurrence of those at subsequent levels, and the more these factors are present at the individual or proximal level, the greater the likelihood corporal punishment will occur. For example, Straus (2010) delineates several distal level factors related to corporal punishment, such as low levels of education, the presence of war, the presence of punitive deities, inequality in society and cultural norms that tolerate violence in general. Out of these broad demographic and institutional patterns, shared cultural norms tolerating violence suggest the most *direct* relationship to corporal punishment, as they imply that approval of violence in one sphere of society may enhance approval in other spheres (Straus 2010). With regard to Tanzania, corporal punishment has long been an institutionalised form of reprimand as 'corporal sanctions were part of colonial attempts to open hegemonic dialogue . . . by enforcing legitimate violence across various segments of the colonial society' (Bernault 2007: 77). Years after its introduction, corporal punishment is still used as a judicial sanction for adults today, which most likely influences the acceptability of corporal punishment as a reprimand in other areas of Tanzanian life.

Straus' (2010) mezzo factors related to corporal punishment include legal permission, cultural beliefs that it is harmless, normative expectations that it should be used and the experience of corporal punishment as a child. These mezzo factors bridge broader institutional structures with people's actual conduct via specific policies, norms and belief systems. For example, corporal punishment as a judicial reprimand is replicated in schools via the law that allows head teachers to use it at their discretion. An implicit belief system is also replicated at the school level through claims that it instils respect, makes children change their behaviour, improves performance and is not a form of physical abuse (Durrant 2005). Unfortunately, if head teachers (who are legally allowed to use corporal punishment) have a strong allegiance with this belief system, they may use corporal punishment quite extensively themselves, as well as 'overlook' its use by teachers.

Finally, Straus' (2010) proximal level is comprised of factors that are highly correlated with individuals who use corporal punishment, such as high levels of stress, receiving advice to use it, experiencing domestic violence, having authoritarian parenting practices and having a large household. In analysing these proximal factors, the only one that is directly derived from broader distal and mezzo levels is receiving advice to use corporal punishment (although authoritarian parenting practices may be tangentially related to this). The other factors however, reflect constraints on an adult's sense of well-being, which in turn could affect her interpretation of a child's 'negative' behaviour as well as exacerbate any tension stemming from that interpretation. For example, a Tanzanian teacher may already be predisposed to use corporal punishment by the distal and mezzo norms that justify its use, however, if her personal well-being is also affected by proximal factors (such as experiencing domestic violence and being responsible for many children), her overall stress level may be elevated, shortening her patience and triggering an unreasoned judgement of a child's 'negative' actions. At such a point, the teacher's predisposition to use corporal punishment may come into play and her heightened stress level may also exacerbate the intensity of force with which she administers corporal punishment.

This example speaks to the need to unpack the black box that obscures the interplay between social structures, adults' personal states and children's 'provoking' behaviour. There is also a silence in Straus' work with regard to how gender affects the use of corporal punishment. Although issues of gender are implicit in proximal factors such as domestic violence, an explicit unpacking is needed to provide more nuanced and detailed understandings. In an effort to build on and expand Straus' delineation of such social factors, I decided therefore to investigate teachers' personal experiences through the lens of the Capability Approach. This approach arguably can provide a very precise conceptualisation of well-being, as well as tools to analyse how environmental factors (particularly within poverty contexts), personal factors (such as skill sets and training – or lack thereof) and social factors (such as gender dynamics, gender norms and gender identities) may enhance or constrain it. Below I explain the elements of the perspective that help us interpret the use of violence by teachers.

The Capability Approach conception of well-being

The Capability Approach (CA), developed by Amartya Sen, emerged as an intellectual response to various approaches traditionally used for the evaluation and measurement of well-being, as it critiqued the 'information bases' on which they were predicated (Sen 1999). For example, welfare economics utilised income as the information base for evaluation and although Sen (1992) acknowledged that income was an important resource for well-being, he argued that there were components of well-being that were not directly acquirable with income (such as being healthy, or being able to make choices). He argued that current spaces for evaluation did not account for the fact that different people attained different levels of well-being when given the same income or bundle of goods. He suggested that instead of focusing on the *means* that might facilitate a good life, we should instead focus on the *actual living* that people manage to achieve; and more importantly, the *freedom* that people have to achieve the types of lives they want to lead (Sen 1999). This alternative view bore the information base of *functionings*, which are the 'beings and doings' that people have reason to value; and *capabilities*, which are the opportunities or substantive freedoms that people have for realising these functionings.

Capabilities can be both expanded or constrained by *conversion factors*, which can be delineated into *personal conversion factors* (such as intelligence, physical ability and skill sets); *environmental conversion factors* (such as geographical location, infrastructure and logistics); and *social conversion factors* (such as social norms and gender relations, roles and identities) (Robeyns 2005). If the conversion factors that block capability freedom can be reconciled, a person would then be judged to have an expanded capability, and her well-being would be evaluated either based on the capabilities she has available to her, or on the functionings that she chooses to realise (Sen 1999). Sen's preferred view of well-being – as a product of the enhanced or constrained opportunities surrounding the beings and doings that people value – has provided a new way in which to understand well-being and, as I will argue later, teachers' use of corporal punishment. Constrained capabilities in a teacher's personal life (such as not being free from domestic violence) may contribute to an overall low level of well-being, thereby elevating stress levels that can trigger the use of corporal punishment; and constrained capabilities in a teacher's occupational life (such as not being able to control numerous children) may also contribute to a more immediate sense of poor well-being. This latter view of reduced classroom well-being also implies that students' actions are what often constrains teachers' valued beings and doings.

This conflict between students' and teachers' capabilities relates to Sen's (1999: 192) discussion of 'co-operative conflict' in which different parties have congruent and conflicting interests within a group. Decision-making takes the form of pursuing co-operation (with the necessary suppression of some interests), however the power dynamics and patterns of behaviour that produce co-operation may not, in some contexts, be particularly egalitarian. In the case of Tanzanian classrooms, co-operation seems to be very much gained in favour of the teachers' interests through the use of corporal punishment. However, with a better understanding of what these interests are and how they might be constrained, alternative methods to gain co-operation might be elicited, which do not require the complete suppression of students' interests nor involve the threat of violence. Using empirical data from Tanzania I demonstrate how female and male teachers' valued beings and doings were indeed constrained by such capability conflicts with students, as well as through impoverished environmental factors and gendered social relations inside and outside of schools.

Investigating teachers' well-being in Tanzania

The findings discussed in this chapter are drawn from a larger project, which sought to understand the values, beliefs and lived experiences of Tanzanian teachers (Tao 2013). I collected data from the Arusha region in Tanzania between June and November 2010 at three government primary schools: a rural school with 1,253 students and 25 staff; an urban school with 1,448 students and 39 staff; and a peri-urban school with 1,867 students and 31 staff. Despite their differing environments, all three schools had similar levels of material deprivation (general lack of textbooks, classrooms and desks, amongst others), a lack of in-service training for teachers (particularly surrounding issues of gender, classroom management and children's rights) and student populations from generally low socio-economic backgrounds. The ratio of female to male teachers varied at each school (rural: 68 per cent women; urban: 95 per cent women; peri-urban: 81 per cent women). There were also variations in teachers' age, levels of experience and ethnic backgrounds, but greater homogeneity was apparent in characteristics such as religious affiliation (Christian), socio-economic level (low) and qualification (completion of lower secondary and teacher training college).

Since the central focus of my research was to provide nuanced explanations for a variety of teachers' practices, I utilised ethnographic case studies. My methods included focus groups, semi-structured and informal interviews, questionnaires and participant observation with teachers, as well as with head teachers, school management committees, and District Education Officers. I did not intend specifically to investigate corporal punishment; however, at the first of my three case study schools, I became extremely troubled by the amount of corporal punishment being used and subsequently decided to investigate the topic further by adding questions to my research instruments. Since I had previously been a volunteer teacher at this school and was reasonably fluent in Kiswahili, I was able to engage in many informal conversations with teachers, managers and students about this sensitive topic. My participant observation role as a full-time member of staff (which entailed teaching Standard 3–6 English in classes of 65–120 students) facilitated close relationships with teachers and students, and provided insights into the daily conditions, pressures and politics that teachers face. It also provided ample opportunities to observe corporal punishment at each school.

In my discussions with teachers, many explicitly voiced their disdain for caning. Neema[2] from the rural school, for example, stated: 'I don't like caning because the aim is not to cane them. The aim is to educate them and make them understand. But also I don't like them to make noise and to disturb the class.' Similarly Elias from the peri-urban school noted, 'When I'm here at school, things that frustrate me and worry me is when I cane a child and it hurts them. If you punish a pupil and you hurt them very badly, it makes me anxious'. However, when asked to clarify why they still used corporal punishment, teachers stated that they felt 'forced' to use it because of their working environments. As Aisha from the peri-urban school explained:

> The government does not want us to cane, but still we cane even though it is not allowed. We are completely prohibited to cane. If you are caught caning, you get a serious letter or you can get transferred. You are taken to another place where it is worse to teach. But without caning, the kids do not listen.

This demonstrates the dilemmas that teachers at all three schools had to constantly negotiate – knowing that corporal punishment is prohibited and punishable (and should not be condoned from a normative perspective), yet feeling the need to use it from a practical or instrumental perspective. Interestingly though, the three head teachers in this study had differing interpretations of the law that prohibits caning, and their resultant policies towards corporal punishment varied greatly.

It was clear, for example, that corporal punishment at the peri-urban school was condoned and freely used by the head teacher. In an informal conversation, a male teacher admitted that the head teacher 'expected' all the men to use the cane. This expectation could be related to contextual associations between strength and violence with masculinity, which also serve to maintain power within both gendered and generational social relations (Demetriou 2001). Such accepted gendered social relations require male teachers to use corporal punishment to maintain 'a masculine authoritarian disciplinary system', and require female teachers to use corporal punishment to assert their authority within this system (Humphreys 2008: 537). This was indeed the case at this peri-urban school, however at schools with female head teachers, the masculine authoritarian disciplinary system – which is broadly endemic to Tanzania as a whole – was enacted in different ways. For example, at the urban school, the female head teacher did not herself cane, nor pressurise her teachers to use corporal punishment. Instead, caning was the responsibility of the 'deputy head teacher of discipline', which meant that although corporal punishment still occurred, it was formalised, assigned to one person, and administered in private spaces. However, like the peri-urban head teacher, the urban head teacher did not explicitly disallow corporal punishment either, and would 'overlook' its informal use by her staff. Conversely, at the rural school, the female head teacher's interpretation of the law was quite literal in that she did explicitly tell teachers they were not allowed to cane. In following the legislation, she was the only one allowed to cane for 'severe' wrongdoings (such as stealing or fighting); and the school's protocol entailed documenting the child's name, reason for punishment, the use of four strokes, and the child's signature. However, this did not preclude teachers using corporal punishments that were 'hidden' from the head teacher.

Therefore, although the two female head teachers accepted the use of corporal punishment to differing degrees, this difference demonstrates that caning was not used as explicitly to maintain a masculine authoritarian disciplinary system, as was demonstrated by the male head teacher. Instead, the female head teachers' interpretations of the law were fluid with regard to which behaviours warranted punishment, and what they implicitly and explicitly expected from their teachers. Moreover, set against these interpretations and expectations were teachers' own anxieties about what was occurring in their classrooms and how this often constrained their well-being. Below I will attempt to unpack these tensions from a teacher's perspective, and demonstrate how corporal punishment happens as a result of teachers' attempting to exercise agency in the face of constraint.

Constraint on teacher capabilities in the classroom

In interviews and questionnaires that sought to identify broad functionings that teachers valued, both female and male teachers prioritised their valuing of 'being able to help students learn' and 'being able to control class' in order to facilitate this end. However, as Amani from the peri-urban school described, there were many types of student behaviours that constrained his ability to control and teach his class:

> I try to let [my students] know that, 'please, when I am teaching here in class, I don't like a pupil who is talking, I don't like a pupil who is walking here and there . . . maybe I'm teaching maths and you are studying Kiswahili. I don't like it. You have to listen because at the end of the period I will give you questions. When I give you questions, because you were not listening, you will not answer properly'. And that is something that I hate so much. So sometimes I have to beat them – to cane them.

This quote illustrates how corporal punishment happens when students constrain a teacher's capability to teach by doing things such as talking, moving about the classroom, or doing homework for another subject. This points to a capability conflict between students valuing 'being able to move about class' or 'being able to finish homework for a different subject', and Amani's valuing of 'being able to help students learn'. When these sets of valued capabilities conflicted, co-operation was gained with the suppression of the students' interests; and although reconciliation of capability conflict can be gained in a variety of ways, as Amani admitted, he often chose a more violent method.

Another primary constraint on 'being able to help students learn' was overcrowded classrooms, not only because the sheer numbers of pupils spread time and resources thin, but overcrowding also bred environments where talking and noise-making were inevitable. As Aisha from the peri-urban school stated, 'When you teach they make noise, they laugh, I think it is because there are so many in class'. Teachers seemed resigned to the fact that large classes and a lack of resources were systemic problems that they could not change, but they felt they could contend with noisy children who were constraining their capability 'to be in control' in order 'to help students learn', as Elias from the same school explained:

> If you punish a pupil and you hurt them very badly, it makes me upset. But that is caused because of the high concentration of pupils in the class. It's very hard to control them in the class, so sometimes I have to use a stick. It causes me frustration and anxiety . . . But sometimes the environment forces me to use the stick.

This view – that caning is a 'forced' option – demonstrates that teachers do not often have alternative non-violent classroom management techniques at hand; so even if a teacher does not like to cane, she often feels that is the only way to contend with the constraint of a noisy class.

Another instance of being 'forced' to cane was discussed by Aisha from the peri-urban school who stated, 'I don't like caning, but it is necessary. If you don't cane, the students will just keep talking and not learn. You tell them one time, two times, three times, and they do not listen. It makes me angry'. This quote suggests how corporal punishment is used first because students constrain a teacher's capability to teach, but then this constraint is exacerbated as the repeated ignoring of a teacher's requests constrains two other valued capabilities – 'being respected' and 'being free from shame' (or rather, 'not losing face'). Darwall (1977) delineates two forms of respect that can be related to what teachers valued in this study: *recognition respect*, which consists of giving appropriate recognition or consideration to an individual by virtue of their role or position; and *appraisal respect*, which is predicated on a judgment of an individual's behaviour or achievements. In Aisha's case, recognition respect seemed to be an entitlement to be gleaned by her position as a teacher, and students ignoring her requests constituted constraint on this capability. With regard to appraisal respect, this was contingent upon Aisha meeting various expectations set by broader discourses and codes of conduct (such as having an obedient class); thus, when students repeatedly ignored Aisha, not only was her recognition respect constrained, so was her appraisal respect, as having control of her class was a common expectation she was assumed to meet. In addition to this, issues of respect and shame often carry gendered significations, and as discussed previously, in a masculine authoritarian disciplinary system (in which Aisha's peri-urban school very explicitly engaged), female teachers often have to negotiate 'contradictory positions of masculine authority and subordinated femininity' (Humphreys 2008: 529), and corporal punishment is used as a tool to assert their authority, particularly with male students who ignore them. Thus, constraint by students on Aisha's recognition and appraisal respect produced corporal punishment that took many forms – as an expression of frustration, as a form of retaliation after being shamed, and as a method to re-establish respect where gendered identities can take precedence over age and authority relations. Thus, the single lash of a stick could constitute a teacher contending with multiple forms of constraint (although often unbeknownst to them). It is difficult to know which constraint was dominant in any one instance of corporal punishment; however by reframing it in this way we can start to see how individual acts of corporal punishment often represent complex networks of interrelated meanings, subject positions and intents.

Constraint on teachers' capability to follow protocol

In focus groups and interviews, many teachers articulated their fear of being seen as doing a poor job. In fact, teachers at all three schools were very anxious about the surveillance activities of the education administration and the power they wielded in being able to transfer or fire a teacher. In discussing the school inspectors, Shabani from the rural school commented:

> I've counted [inspector] visits and so many times they've threatened. So many times they visit and they threaten more than help . . . to show that we are not doing our work well, we are not teaching as well as they want, things like that. I get worried and anxious every time they come.

This fear foregrounds the implicit valued functioning of 'following teacher protocol', which teachers valued not because it was intrinsic to the type of working lives they wanted to lead, but because their livelihoods were threatened (via transfer or firing) if they *didn't* value such a functioning. Given this somewhat obligatory valued functioning, we can start to see how corporal punishment can occur as a result. Teachers learn from treatment by inspectors and their managers that the only way to get people to do what is expected of them is through threat of punishment. They then transfer this thinking to the students who determine their success at following teacher protocol, as in the case of duty teacher tasks. As Amani from the peri-urban school stated:

> When I'm on duty, there is no other way [than to use corporal punishment] because there are a lot of kids. And there is pressure from the school leader. If you are on duty and the head comes and sees that the school is dirty, he will yell, 'You, teacher on duty! Why is the school dirty?'.

In a poverty context such as Tanzania, a lack of educational funding means that all janitorial duties are the responsibility of the students and the duty teachers; thus in Amani's school, only two teachers are in charge of making sure 1,800 students complete chores within a 30-minute period before and after school. These chores are often based on and reinforce broader gendered divisions of labour, such that girls sweep and mop classrooms and boys water plants and pick up rubbish. In addition to this problem, when children stray from these chores, a teacher's capability to follow protocol is constrained, and I observed teachers using corporal punishment that resembled the quick pokes and prods used by local animal herders to keep order and guide the pack. Like herding, this use of the cane was not necessarily anger driven; however, if constraint by students started to impede on the secondary valued functioning of 'being free from shame' (which is contingent on successfully following teacher protocol), then corporal punishment as an expression of anger and retaliation was very quickly produced.

Constraint on teachers' duty-bound capabilities

During focus groups and interviews, many teachers articulated that they valued 'teaching "good" behaviour' which entailed life skills and codes of societal conduct. For example, Salima from the urban school explained:

> We teach them how to live a self-reliant life. We teach them how to dress their bed, to wash their clothes; we teach them that they must be clean. Sometimes in the assembly we check them, if they are dirty, we punish them so that they learn how to be clean. This teaches them that when they go home they must wash their clothes and their body, so that they come to school clean. This will help them when they grow up, so that they will be accepted by society.

One could posit that the capability to be successful in teaching good behaviour is constrained when students constantly demonstrate 'bad' behaviour such as coming to school 'dirty'. Other infringements on 'good behaviour' were also related to issues of gender and poverty, such as girls coming to school late because of their morning chores at home, or children coming to class without proper notebooks, pens or uniforms. When faced with these particular capability constraints, teachers did not feel any personal affront and were thus less likely to have anger influence action. Instead, teachers' actions lay in the belief that it was their duty to cane students so that they would 'learn good behaviour' and thus 'be accepted by society'. This duty-bound form of corporal punishment seemed to be underpinned by the reasoning 'spare the rod, spoil the child' as it primarily acted as a consequence for students' wrongdoings, and secondarily acted as a tactic to prevent more wrongdoings in the future. Headteachers also reinforced this belief system which thus turned caning into the protocol for 'bad behaviour' infringements, which entailed quick lashes of a stick, systematically administered to groups of pupils.

In the rural school where caning was prohibited, teachers used what they perceived to be 'non-violent' punishments, such as making children squat with their hands in the air, or do frog jumps and push ups. Although these activities could be argued to be violations of students' physiological and psychological integrity, they did not violate the 'no caning' rule and were thus allowed; and were most likely used due to the predominant belief that behaviour could only change through punishment. Although these punishments were systematically administered to both boys and girls, the way they were received could have significant gendered effects. Humphreys (2008) argues that girls' fear of being beaten and punished (combined with fear of humiliation by both teachers and male students) often prevents them from participating orally in class; and Connell (1987) states that this lack of participation is frequently ascribed to girls' 'natural' shyness or docility, thus reinforcing dominant notions of femininity. In addition, Humphreys (2008) argues that the systematic corporal punishment of low-achieving male students often leads to further classroom rebellion (which leads to further beatings) or truancy/dropping out (in order to avoid more beatings).

In addition, punishments were used for more 'severe' wrongdoings, however, in these instances, the duty-bound forms of caning seemed to be subsumed by the need to dole out a more judicial form of corporal punishment. As Amani from the peri-urban school discussed:

> Ahh, let me be a little bit honest. That [caning] you mentioned, I do practise it. You see? I practise it in class, on duty, and when someone comes with the habit of stealing money. Having a sexual affair with an older man. And students leaving school when they are supposed to be here. I play all those roles. But for me, I try to hold back my anger.

Here, Amani discusses how he does not administer corporal punishment as an expression of anger but rather as a 'duty' that is required by his role as a judge, jury and purveyor of punishments for severe moral wrongdoings. Unfortunately in these instances, students are rarely given a voice or allowed to defend themselves, and clearly, teachers can make many questionable assumptions when they play the role of judge. For example, we can see that Amani's judgement about sexual relationships assumes that it is only girls that have affairs, and that these affairs are usually with older men. Clearly, he deems girls having sexual relationships as morally wrong, and his acknowledgement of older men speaks to an underlying assumption that these are exchange relationships of sex for money/goods. Similar instances of this type of relationship have been reported in Mozambique, Ghana and Kenya (Parkes and Heslop 2011; Chapter 9, this volume), in which girls are seen by adults as both strategically seeking out these situations (in the face of extreme poverty), or more likely being coerced into them, given the large age and status inequalities of the men involved. Amani's view denotes an instant vilification of girls having affairs, irrespective of the circumstances that may have led to them, raising questions about the fairness and suitability of teachers being judges, juries and purveyors of punishments. Parents too expected and insisted that teachers take these roles – as I observed on two occasions when parents asked *all* teachers at the peri-urban school to supplement and legitimise the punishments that they gave at home. In these instances, the teachers felt pressured to use corporal punishment and, since the severity of wrongdoings also incited moral outrage, many felt justified in administering punishments that included harsh verbal abuse, slapping, kicking and sustained lashing with sticks. Moreover, different forms of abuse seemed to be performed along gendered lines; with female teachers administering interrogations and verbal abuse within the private sphere of the teachers' office, and male teachers administering physical punishments in the public sphere of the school grounds. This not only reinforced the expectation of a male perfor-mance of violence, but also made the child an example to others, which furthered the likeness of these punishments to representations of a form of justice.

Finding spaces to transform violence

I have attempted to reframe corporal punishment as a product of capability con-straint and conflict within school contexts. Such an analysis has provided detailed understandings of the different meanings, subject positions and intents behind corporal punishment; and by further unpacking the points at which social norms and teacher agency intersect with constraint, we can start to see ways in which transformative strategies to reduce corporal punishment could be seeded. For example, Tanzanian teachers often valued 'being able to control class' (in order to help students learn). However, as a result of constraints such as having classes of 80–120 students, a lack of training in classroom management, and capability conflict with children, teachers were not able to have control and successfully teach their lessons, resulting in frustration, loss of face, and further pressure from the head to gain control. However, when teachers tried to exercise agency within these constraints, corporal punishment was often used to reconcile capability con-flict with students and gain a constrained form of control. It is during this process that we can see how social structural elements condition teachers to use corporal punishment. Alternatively if a teacher possesses a strong ability to resist social structures via reflexive deliberation, she might decide to use a different classroom management tool with which to exercise agency (if, of course, she is aware of others). However, if her temper is heightened due to her constrained capabil-ity, her ability to reflexively deliberate may be hampered and her use of corporal punishment may reflect an unconscious reflex that has been set by her previous social conditioning.

Given this understanding, it seems that possibilities for intervention could entail the acknowledgement of these processes and the encouragement of reflex-ive deliberation through the careful challenging of the social norms that justify the use of corporal punishment. Of course, encouraging reflexive deliberation during the heat of frustration and anger may be a difficult proposition. Ongoing discus-sions with teachers prompting them to question the value of corporal punishment might prove fruitful, at least in reducing the intentional, more controlled forms of corporal punishment. For example, Chege (2006) discusses how prompting teachers to reflect on their own experiences of violence and gendered norms from their childhood allowed Kenyan teachers to be more empathetic and reduce the amount of violence in their teaching practice.

With regard to the other capabilities such as 'being able to follow protocol' and 'teaching good behaviour', there are two areas which interventions could address: first, the types of protocols and duty-bound activities that teachers have; and second, beliefs about changing student behaviour. In the case of the former, head teachers are the locus of control for teacher protocols such as duty teacher tasks. If a head teacher can find creative ways to reduce the pressure surrounding these tasks, then teachers' capability to follow successfully duty teacher protocols would be enhanced. Amani at the peri-urban school suggested that duty teacher tasks be shared by *all* teachers at all times, as opposed to just two teachers on rotation. If head teachers could also create working environments where reprimand or loss of face is not imminent if protocols are not achieved, and where men are not expected to perform their masculinity through violence, this might alleviate some of the major triggers for corporal punishment.

In addition, head teachers also set the explicit and implicit codes for student behaviour (for anything from cleanliness to theft), including teacher protocols for how to deal with lapses. Student codes of conduct could be reviewed, particularly those which students understandably have problems meeting (such as living far away and thus arriving late). Teacher mandates to use corporal punishment to deal with 'poor behaviour' could also be challenged: for example, the head teacher's explicit prohibition at the rural school of using corporal punishment did reduce severe and frequent caning.

This leads to another area in which intervention could occur – one where teachers are exposed to and convinced of alternative ways to change student behaviour. As discussed previously, teachers often glean from authoritarian treatment by their managers that the only way to get people to do things is through punishment; they then transfer this thinking to their students by using corporal punishment as the most effective and easiest way to improve behaviour. Unfortunately, caning does often provide an easy and immediate way to gain short-term compliance from children. But if alternative non-corporal techniques to change student behaviour (such as positive reinforcement) were framed as an even easier and more effective way for teachers to successfully follow protocol and change behaviour in the long-term, they might have more purchase. Although corporal punishment provides an immediate anger release for teachers, many are aware that caning can be physically and emotionally exhausting; thus positive reinforcement and praise for students could also be presented as techniques that are much easier to implement.

Finally, all of the above-mentioned strategies should also be located within a broader discussion of female and male teacher and student identities, in order for teachers to be conscious of the tacit gender regimes that function (and that they are complicit in) at their schools. As Humphreys (2008: 538) states, teachers need to become aware of how their gendered identities

> relate to practices of corporal punishment, to the broader gendered disciplinary system within which corporal punishment is located, and to the gendered structures of wider society. Only then will it be possible to start reconceptualising school gender relations as less adversarial, authoritarian and punitive in nature.

These discussions could take place during pre- and in-service training both for teachers and head teachers. Training seminars could be designed to provide spaces for teachers and heads to reflect on their gendered identities and how these relate to their belief systems, protocols, students and use of corporal punishment. These seminars could also allow teachers to share non-violent classroom management techniques that are grounded in context and experience, and not imposed by a cultural outsider. This is quite significant as Makuru, the chairman of the peri-urban school management committee, noted:

> this organisation from Mwanza, they are called Kuleana. They came there with their rules. Children's rules. Children will not do work in the house. Children shouldn't be hit. Where do those rules come from? Are these coming from outsiders? From our culture here? When they introduced these rules, did they come in touch with the culture and see if the culture agrees?

Clearly, there is a mistrust of interventions and international conventions promoted by non-Tanzanians, as they are deemed to be an imposition of another worldview and to harbour an implicit judgement of and lack of sensitivity towards Tanzanian culture. These points were discussed at length with a Tanzanian 'critical friend' who stated that before any outsider (such as myself) could even think of suggesting non-corporal classroom management techniques, I would first have to prove that they worked in my class of 120. If I could not demonstrate that I could gain control and respect in my own classroom, then Tanzanian teachers would not be inclined to listen to me. I believe this to be a fair condition, which shows that any alternative techniques for classroom management or changing child behaviour must be situated in context and show proof of success before teachers will entertain trying them; otherwise, corporal punishment will continue to be viewed as the best way for teachers to achieve their valued functionings. In successfully using some classroom management techniques suggested by my critical friend, I was able to open up discussions with fellow teachers at my school. Given the interest teachers had in these discussions, and the disdain that many teachers expressed about caning, it would seem that providing in-service seminars that provide a space for teachers to share their home grown alternatives could prove to be fruitful.

That said, it is hoped that the analysis in this chapter has been able to provide explicit connections between broader social structures, teachers' values, their contexts, conflicting capabilities with students, and the processes through which these combine to produce corporal punishment. The benefit of reframing corporal punishment in this way is that it not only fosters detailed explanations of why it occurs, but that it can engender punishment reduction through more nuanced and creative strategies.

Notes

1 This body of literature uses a gender lens to unpack the negative effects of corporal punishment in schools in developing country contexts. For example, Youssef *et al.* (1998) discuss how boys experience more frequent and harsher forms of corporal punishment from teachers than girls in Egypt; Leach and Machakanja (2000) discuss

how sexual aggression from boys and some male teachers is largely tolerated and 'normalised' in junior secondary schools in Zimbabwe, Morrell (2001) discusses how domestic patterns of discipline promote the continued use of corporal punishment at schools in South Africa, and Dunne *et al.* (2006) review research and interventions regarding the effects of gender violence in schools in a variety of Asian and African contexts.

2 All names have been changed to protect participants' privacy and confidentiality.

References

Bernault, F. (2007), 'The shadow of rule: colonial power and modern punishment in Africa'. In F. Dikötter and I. Brown (eds), *Cultures of Confinement: A History of the Prison in Africa, Asia and Latin America* (pp. 55–94). Ithaca, NY: Cornell University Press.

Chege, F. (2006), *Teacher Identities and Empowerment of Girls against Sexual Violence.* Florence: UNICEF Innocenti Research Centre.

Connell, R. (1987), *Gender and Power: Society, the Person and Sexual Politics.* Stanford: Stanford University Press.

Darwall, S. (1977), 'Two kinds of respect'. *Ethics*, 88 (1), 36–49.

De Veer, A. and Janssens, J. (1994), 'Victim oriented discipline, interpersonal understanding and guilt'. *Journal of Moral Education*, 23 (1), 165–82.

Demetriou, D. (2001), 'Connell's concept of hegemonic masculinity: a critique'. *Theory and Society*, 30 (3), 337–61.

Dunne, M., Humphreys, L. and Leach, F. (2006), 'Gender violence in schools in the developing world'. *Gender and Education*, 18 (1), 75–98.

Durrant, J. (2005), 'Corporal punishment: prevalence, predictors and implications for child behaviour and development'. In S. Hart, J. Durrant, P. Newell and F. Power (eds), *Eliminating Corporal Punishment: The Way Forward to Constructive Child Discipline* (pp. 90–146). Paris: United Nations Educational, Scientific and Cultural Organisation (UNESCO).

Feinstein, S. and Mwahombela, L. (2010), 'Corporal punishment in Tanzania's schools'. *International Review of Education*, 56 (1), 399–410.

Frankenberg, S., Homqvist, R. and Rubenson, B. (2010), 'The care of corporal punishment: conceptions of early childhood discipline strategies among parents and grandparents in a poor and urban area in Tanzania'. *Childhood*, 17 (4), 455–69.

Gershoff, E. (2002), 'Corporal punishment by parents and associated child behaviours and experiences: a meta-analytic and theoretical review'. *Psychological Bulletin*, 128 (1), 539–79.

Hoffman, M. (1983), 'Affective and cognitive processes in moral internalisation'. In E. Higgins, D. Ruble and W. Hartup (eds), *Social Cognition and Social Development: A Sociocultural Perspective* (pp. 236–274). New York: Cambridge University Press.

Humphreys, S. (2008), 'Gendering corporal punishment: beyond the discourse of human rights'. *Gender and Education*, 20 (5), 527–40.

Kuleana Children's Rights Centre (1999), *Does Corporal Punishment bring about Discipline?* Dar es Salaam: Kuleana Children's Rights Center.

Lazerele, R. (2000), 'Child outcomes of non-abusive and customary physical punishment by parents: an updated literature review'. *Clinical Child and Family Psychology Review*, 3 (4), 199–221.

Leach, F. and Machakanja, P. (2000), 'Preliminary investigation into the abuse of girls in Zimbabwean junior secondary schools'. *Gender and Education*, 9 (1), 69–87.

McAlpine, K. (2008), *The State of Child Protection in Tanzania*. Dar es Salaam: TEN/MET.

Ministry of Education and Vocational Training (2008), *Education Sector Development Programme*. Dar es Salaam: The Government Printer.

Mkukuta Secretariat, Poverty Eradication Division (2007), *Tanzanian Children's Perceptions of Education and their Role in Society*. Dar es Salaam: Research on Poverty Alleviation (REPOA).

Morrell, R. (2001), 'Corporal punishment in South African schools: a neglected explanation for its persistence'. *South African Journal of Education*, 21 (4), 292–300.

Newell, P. (1989), *Children are People too: The Case against Physical Punishment*. London: Bedford Square Press.

Owen, S. and Wagner, K. (2006), 'Explaining school corporal punishment: evangelical Protestantism and social capital in a path model'. *Social Justice Research*, 19 (4), 471–99.

Parkes, J. and Heslop, J. (2011), *Stop Violence Against Girls in School: A Cross-Country Analysis of Baseline Research from Ghana, Kenya and Mozambique*. London: ActionAid.

Robeyns, I. (2005), 'The Capability Approach: a theoretical survey'. *Journal of Human Development*, 6 (1), 93–114.

Sen, A. (1992), *Inequality Re-examined*. Cambridge, MA: Harvard University Press.

Sen, A. (1999), *Development as Freedom*. Oxford: Oxford University Press.

Straus, M. (1990), 'Ordinary violence, child abuse and wife beating: what do they have in common?'. In M. Straus and R. Gelles (eds), *Physical Violence in American Families: Risk Factors and Adaptations to Violence in 8,145 Families* (pp. 403–24). New Brunswick: Transaction.

Straus, M. (2010), 'Prevalence, societal causes and trends in corporal punishment by parents in world perspective'. *Law and Contemporary Problems*, 73 (1), 1–30.

Tao, S. (2013), *Rethinking Teacher Quality: Using the Capability Approach and Critical Realism to Provide Causal Explanations for Teacher Practice in Tanzania* (unpublished PhD thesis). London: Institute of Education, University of London.

United Nations (1989), *Convention on the Rights of the Child*. New York: Office of the United Nations High Commissioner for Human Rights.

Xu, X., Tung, Y. and Dunaway, R. (2000), 'Cultural, human, and social capital as determinants of corporal punishment: toward an integrated theoretical model'. *Journal of Interpersonal Violence*, 15 (1), 603–30.

Youssef, R., Attia, M. and Kamel, M. (1998), 'Children experiencing violence II: prevalence and determinants of corporal punishment in schools'. *Child Abuse & Neglect*, 22 (1), 975–85.

Part III

Negotiating gender violence

7 'You don't want to die. You want to reach your goals'

Alternative voices among young Black men in urban South Africa

Ariane De Lannoy and Sharlene Swartz

In South Africa, popular media and academic readings alike have long portrayed young Black men as offenders, immoral, disconnected from the older generations and involved in violent crime, including gender based violence (Wood and Jewkes 2001; Sangar and Hadland 2008; Clowes *et al.* 2010; Lefko-Everett 2012; Ward *et al.* 2012a). News of the many brutal acts of violence continue to feed what Posel (2005) has termed the 'scandal of manhood', the problematising of (especially Black) men in post-apartheid South Africa. Much of the violence literature sees young men as subscribing to, or performing, a violent hegemonic masculinity that arises out of struggle and is aimed at dominating other, more vulnerable members of society: children, women, or other less powerful men (Morrell 1998). Such analyses seldom include the experiences of those young men who choose not to join the ranks of 'troubled' men around them, nor do they address the dilemmas and complexities faced by those who do at some point in time engage with violence. Drawing on a longitudinal, in-depth study, in this chapter we argue for the need to hear and understand 'alternative masculinities' in post-apartheid South Africa, and to bear in mind that even hyper-masculine, violent identities are fluid, and dependent on context. It is in that fluidity that (additional) opportunities for change may lie.

Deprivations, aspirations and masculine identities in post-apartheid South Africa

Hegemonic masculinities are dominant cultural images of what it means to be 'a real man', and include being successful, respected, in control, tough and providers for their family (Morrell 2001: 7; Morrell *et al.* 2012). These ideals are created in men's immediate local environments and through more globally connected institutions such as mass media and corporate world advertisements, influencing the ways in which men construct a desired male identity for themselves (Connell 1995; Salo 2003). In a context of severe levels of inequality and deprivation, the position of 'a real man' and the respect that comes with it are not easily gained through traditional pathways such as education, high income jobs or middle-class lifestyles that boast beautiful houses and fancy cars. Hegemonic masculinities may also be earned and defended through violent behaviour, acted out towards the more vulnerable in society.

South Africa's discriminatory apartheid past led to the social, political and economic exclusion of millions of those deemed 'non-white'. Spatial segregation by race meant that vast numbers of people classified as 'Coloured' or 'Black' were forcibly removed from inner cities and suburbs that were proclaimed 'Whites only', to be left in under-serviced townships on the cities' peripheries. Racist rules and regulations restricted free movement of people of colour, their access to education and the labour market. The situation left Black lower-class men grappling to create different ways of asserting themselves (Xaba 2001). Morrell (2001) indicates how, throughout South Africa's history, hegemonic masculinities have therefore become related to violence, which is aimed at creating fear and demanding an instant recognition of status and respect.

The post-1994, democratically elected ANC government installed regulations and policies aimed at undoing the inequalities of the past. The education system is now officially unified, presented as a cornerstone of the democracy and a means to create a more equal society. Labour market restrictions have been lifted and an extended social welfare system of grants and pensions now helps to alleviate the worst kinds of poverty. The country's dominant discourse emphasises potential upward mobility for those previously discriminated against, supported by state-led interventions such Affirmative Action and Black Economic Empowerment. Nevertheless, high levels of poverty and inequality remain. Young people are especially vulnerable, with high levels of school dropout and unemployment (Census 2001; Cloete 2009; National Youth Development Agency 2011). Violence and homicide are commonplace in young lives, and leading causes of death among young men in the country (Burton 2008), with young Black men most affected (Swartz *et al.* 2012). With surroundings and institutions that do not offer the necessary kinds of support, strategies and possibilities for upward mobility, it is often assumed that 'many young Black males must . . . look at their futures . . . with a sense of desperate manhood' (Ratele 2001: 249). Repeatedly, work on the position of young men in contemporary South Africa has linked barriers to upward mobility and the development of oppositional and violent forms of masculinity (Wood and Jewkes 2001; Xaba 2001; Noonan 2012; Panday *et al.* 2012).

We too in previous work have noted that continued inequality and deprivation leave Black youth with little social and economic autonomy, whilst having high aspirations for a better, successful and respectable life. These ideals tap into the post-apartheid discourse of 'equal opportunities for all' (Swartz *et al.* 2012; Soudien 2003, 2007).

We have argued that the continued disempowerment of the majority of youth, alongside the ambitious aspirations, can easily lead to a sense of alienation and exclusion from the larger democratic experiment. This alienation lies at the basis of young men's and women's engagement with what Swartz[1] (2010) has termed *Ikasi style*, which 'comprises violence, sex, alcohol and substance abuse, as well as music, recreation, fashion and other diversions' (Swartz *et al.* 2012: 28) and is an expression of young adults' attempts to create a sphere of belonging at least within the township environment. We have argued that Black township youth engage with alternative ways of 'becoming', and alternative networks of belonging to the broader South African collective while in fact they remain excluded. Ikasi style then, is a reaction against and perpetuation of the 'woundedness' of the South African state (Swartz *et al.* 2012) that makes especially young men link the use of violence to issues of 'respect' (see also Oduro *et al.* 2012: 283). This argument brings us close to the literature that describes the formation of a violent hegemonic masculinity in a context of deprivation, and that views gang affiliation and violent crime as young men's attempts to create a sense of belonging and status (Bility 1999; Ward *et al.* 2012b).

In this chapter, however, we examine the experiences of young men who, despite seeing their 'dreams deferred', despite the pressures and attractions of Ikasi style, engage in a precarious process of trying to define themselves in ways that are not, no longer, or not only related to anti-social behaviour. We argue that the strong emphasis on violent hegemonic masculinities underlying much of the work on young men and gang affiliation 'fails to capture masculine diversity' (Morrell 2001: 3; see also Walsh and Mitchell 2006). It may therefore overlook the identity creation processes of young men who try to find a way of belonging also within the broader South African context (Kinnes 2000; Pinnock 1982; Samara 2005).

This chapter begins to address this gap. It illustrates a number of ways in which young men negotiate conflicting masculine identities in a context of poverty, blocked opportunities and the temptations of 'Ikasi'. We use Bourdieu's and Giddens' theories of identity creation as theoretical tools to engage with the narratives of four young men. Before presenting the data, we introduce the empirical study itself and consider the theoretical frame used in this chapter.

Researching young men in South Africa's townships

The data we draw on are from a longitudinal study on young men and women in low-income townships on the peripheries of Cape Town (De Lannoy 2008), which used both quantitative and qualitative methods to explore the ways in which Black township youth make decisions about their education and construct their identities in post-apartheid South Africa. Here we report on a subsection of the work, and draw on interview and observational material collected over a two-year period (2005 and 2006) with 20 young people aged between 14 and 22, who were selected on the basis of having made significant decisions regarding their schooling the year before the study started. A period of collaboration with the non-governmental organisation Southern African Environmental Program (SAEP), which supports youth who wish to rewrite their final matric examinations, led to one young woman being invited to participate in the study. Other participants were selected using snowballing. They all shared comparable socio-economic backgrounds, school circumstances and peer and family pressures.

De Lannoy conducted interviews in English, with occasional help with translation from a fieldwork assistant when language proved a problem. Being a foreign (Belgian), White woman conducting research in African areas may have affected the research, potentially having 'enabled some things to happen and perhaps closed down other things' in the course of the project (Parker 2005: 30). To help mitigate this, care was taken to use a variety of fieldwork methods over an extended period of time, including individual and group interviews, alongside observational work. Informed by the young adults' frequent complaints that there was 'nothing to do' in the townships, participants were regularly invited to accompany the researcher to local activities including hip hop jam sessions, theatre and beach outings.

The conceptual framework for analysing the qualitative data bridges sociological and psychological perspectives on youth identity and school engagement (see De Lannoy 2011). Drawing on Bourdieu's theoretical work on class reproduction, the analysis looked at different forms of 'capital' or resources available to young people. Bourdieu (1977) argued that cultural, social and symbolic capital, alongside economic capital, influence one's life chances and social outcomes. Children from lower-class backgrounds, he argued, lack the necessary kinds of 'capital' to enable upward social mobility. They lack the requisite knowledge and information ('cultural capital') of the educational and labour market to make informed choices. They lack the financial means ('economic capital'), the status or prestige ('symbolic capital') and the networks ('social capital') that would provide them with more leverage to be allowed into the better educational institutes or jobs. Bourdieu argued that young people born into a lower-class environment are aware of the barriers surrounding them; they therefore adjust their aspirations downwards and change their behaviour accordingly. However, Giddens (1991) asserts that the process of identity creation is 'a trajectory of development from the past to an anticipated future', consisting of 'a complex diversity of choices to be made (with) . . . little help as to which options should be selected' (1991: 80). He argues that even in situations of deprivation, individuals retain the ability to explore options for different life paths. However, when making such choices, especially in the absence of clear guidelines, individuals are confronted with 'radical doubt' (1991: 86): Giddens claims it is impossible to escape the thought that the strategy or lifestyle chosen is but one of the possible options available, creating always a level of anxiety.

Bourdieu's and Giddens' theories are useful for understanding the endless processes of trial and tribulations, doubt and 'rudderlessness' that have been described in earlier work on the lives of Cape Town's poorest township youth (Henderson 1999;[2] Ramphele 2002[3]). For example, in her study of township youth at the time of the transition, Henderson (1999) found young adults trying out various life paths in their search for identity. Some, who consciously attempted to find better schools outside the townships, were accused by others of being a 'sell out', no longer committed to the struggle for freedom for all. Henderson discussed the range of responses:

A social situation characterised by fragile social relationships demands of children that they be dexterous, resourceful, adaptable, that they take responsibility. Such dexterity can however lead to a lack of focus, a mercurial adaptation to circumstance and a lack of future orientation.

(1999: 32)

Our narratives similarly reveal the 'endlessness' in the process of trial and error as young men juggle, alternate or 'try out' different types of manhood. The following sections present the cases of four young men, Thando, Nezile, Lungile and Lutho, all living in the sprawling, low-income townships of Khayelitsha and Nyanga. Both areas rank high on the country's crime statistics. Unemployment rates are 51 per cent and 56 per cent respectively, and fewer than 25 per cent of youth in the areas have completed their high school examinations (Statistics South Africa 2012). The four cases have been chosen from the larger sample as powerful illustrations of the complex realities South African youth face. They illustrate the strong attraction of violent crime and gang affiliation, but also demonstrate how individual young men attempt to resist these temptations.

Juggling identities in a context of deprivation and violence

You don't want to die, you want to reach your goals

Thando was 19 years old at the time of our first interview. He was living in Nyanga, approximately 26 km out of the city centre. He was born and spent his childhood in the rural Eastern Cape with his grandparents, but had moved to Cape Town at the age of 12 'to get a better education', and came to live with his mother, half brother, aunt and his aunt's children. A year later his mother and both grandparents died. His aunt took on the care for both himself and his younger brother Lungile, but the family was barely managing to keep heads above water. The little income there was consisted of the rent charged to a befriended family for using a backyard room. The main house looked in desperate need of care, with visible holes in the ceiling and doors hanging without hinges. Conversations with a neighbouring home-based care organisation indicated that Thando and his brother regularly went without food.

Thando described how stressed and lost he felt after the loss of his close family members, and he visibly trembled when he spoke about his mother:

> Sometimes you lose loved ones, you feel left alone; you don't feel good anymore . . . Because I have no mother and all my friends have mothers . . . My mama was always on my side you know, always had good impressions [of] me.

He talked about how losing her had made his life much more uncertain and how it had increased his responsibilities to levels that were clearly too high for him to carry alone. The impoverished situation of his aunt's house made him realise that he not only had to look after himself – 'buying yourself clothes and food' – but that he might also have to take on the care of the others in the household:

> Sometimes when I look at this home, I think of how many years it will take me to build this home? . . . will I finish this home? Will I build this home? Will I be responsible for my brother and my cousin? After that . . . myself.

The wish to escape his perceived responsibilities, to be independent and not remain stuck in a situation of structural poverty emerged in Thando's story, when he said: 'sometimes I wish I had my things, don't bother no one, just do my thing'. This wish to 'have his own things' led him to reflect on the temptation to commit crime:

> It's very hard sometimes because there are a lot of things that are happening. The things that other youngsters do; robbing, sometimes you wanna do robbing [so that you would also have some money] but you think . . . you don't want to die; you want to reach your goals.

During the two years of the study, however, Thando resisted the attraction of gang affiliation and crime. He maintained a focus on his goals for a better future life. He fostered friendships with young men who had similar ideals in life, concentrated on going to the gym in his spare time, and made conscious choices to stay away from certain friends, as he perceived them as people who might try to 'corrupt' him: 'I talk to them, but they don't listen to me. Some of them, I don't walk with them . . . anymore because they gonna corrupt me too'. He maintained a steady focus on his education. He was a learner at one of the local high schools and at the end of his time there, Thando passed the national grade 12 examination. He wished to study further and, through that path, be independent and in a position to take care of others in future. He repeatedly said he wanted to take on his responsibility 'as a man' and caregiver in the house, look for a job and help put his brother through school before taking up tertiary education himself.

Thando was very much aware of the restrictions and responsibilities poverty was placing on him. He was aware, also, of the choices he could make – engaging with violent crime, or not, for example. In the absence of any clear guidance from adults in his life, he decided against violent crime and in favour of the long-term oriented life path based on education. His choices were not made without doubt. Thando believed that educational success would offer a route to the masculine requirement to succeed, provide and control, but frequently wondered whether he would ever reach that aspired adult life.

If someone always calls you stupid, why would you still make an effort?

One young man in particular had chosen exactly the path Thando spoke of avoiding, embodying aspects of Ikasi style and engaging in crime and violence. At the start of the study, Nezile was 19 years old and shared a house with his mother, stepfather, stepbrother and the latter's girlfriend in the sprawling township of Khayelitsha. All adults in the house earned an income and his house was in a considerably better state than that of the other young men in the study, more spacious, well maintained, with working sanitation and electricity. However, Nezile described his home situation as problematic and abusive, with low levels of understanding between him and the adults in the household.

When asked to tell us a little bit more about himself, Nezile almost immediately referred to the place of violence, crime, drugs and weapons in his life. He admired the toughness of older men in the community who 'had done bad things', and at the age of 13, he had started smoking drugs and stealing money. At 14, he was 'introduced to weapons', and decided he wanted to have his 'own gang', the main aim of which was 'to get known'. He had wanted to gain a position of power, 'to be someone' who was known and feared in the area:

> The thing is that we wanted to get known . . . like when we enter in a place where they [another gang] are known, everyone would just fear, they are scared. We wanted it to be like that with my gang . . . We wanted to be the most feared, like . . . It's saying we want to rule every gang there is, be the only gang that is feared even if the other gang comes.

Nezile's words express an idealised hyper-masculine identity in which power over others is gained through instilling fear. His comments reflected the impact of peer pressure, a violent society and the inability to connect to either his home or school environment. Although he never rejected the potential value of education for upward mobility, he described his own schooling as boring, with frequently absent teachers, or 'an irritating teacher, and a very slow teacher, or a teacher that is always upset'. He complained that there had been too much theoretical teaching and too little practical work. To make things worse, his mother and stepfather would regularly call him 'dumb' or 'stupid', conveying that he was not living up to their expectations: 'And then, if someone always calls you stupid, why would you still make an effort?'

Nezile's account shows how his attraction to gang life was influenced by his inability to perform well in school, the demoralising language in his home environment, the influence of peers, the seemingly easy access to guns and drugs, and the lack of chances to combine work with studies.

Even then, he told us that he had been trying to quit 'the life' lately. Someone had been shot because of him, and he felt guilty. He now also realised the threat to his own life, fearing he might get killed himself. Gang life no longer awarded its promised position of power and success, but increased the anxiety, insecurity and confusion around his life and future possibilities. He said that he was constantly worried that 'maybe one day, something is going to happen'. He never knew 'what tomorrow is going to bring'. Yet, while he said that he was now aware of the wrongfulness of crime, he still enjoyed and exerted his position of power among younger friends whom he could introduce to crime:

> they gonna do it and I'm not gonna stop them. I like it when they do it also . . . let's say you are walking down the street, I come and rob you. My friends are still here: they don't know about robbing, they don't know that stuff. I rob you. I'm gonna tell them to do it and force them to do it, seeing at the same time that it is wrong, but I want them to do it.

Nezile did take a job later, first as a (badly paid) waiter, and then as a DJ, looking for 'gigs outside of the location [township]'. The physical distance from the troubled area in Khayelitsha seemed to make it easier for him to shift his attention to another desired way of achieving manhood. Moreover, he had revived old ties with an ex-girlfriend who, he said, was 'ambitious, studying and all that. She wants to get something out of life'. He was now considering going to night school to pass his matriculation exam and wondered if, in that way, he would 'one day be the man I want to be. I see myself running a business, me, sitting in my own office'. He made concerted efforts to keep a distance from the friends he used to hang out with: "cause I told myself that I don't wanna go with the friends that are my age or older than me, you see. 'Cause they are gonna make me do bad things again'.

During the entire period of the study, Nezile experimented with various versions of manhood he could imagine for himself, sometimes inspired by the images presented in the media. Yet he remained uncertain about how his life would eventually work out. Having realised the dead-end road of gang-related power and status, he sought alternative ways to reach the kind of future masculinity to which he aspired. He remained uncertain of whether or not he would succeed by means of education, and how soon that education would pay off:

> You see people on the TV, and I saw this advert yesterday, this guy who has a briefcase and a suit and he was driving. So I'm like, if I finished my standards and everything, would I have been that person immediately or would I have to struggle to be that person? . . . so I thought maybe next year I will try again, try to be that person on TV.

While Nezile's shifts in search of one kind of masculinity or another seemed to unfold sequentially in trial and error mode, some young men juggled and shifted between the apparently contrasting identities simultaneously, while others attempted to maintain a more coherent identity, as in the following case of Lutho.

I am a learner here at school

Lutho was 15 years old at the time of our first interview. He was born in the rural Eastern Cape and spent a large part of his childhood with his father's family, but when he came on holiday to Cape Town in 2002, he decided to stay. He lived in Khayelitsha with his mother and two younger twin brothers and described their relationship as 'open' and supportive, motivating him to do well at school. The family lived in a small, informal house and survived on the mother's part-time income and food parcels she received from a local NGO. Lutho recounted how one day a young man in his school had protected the learners from an attack by a gang in which he was at the same time a member:

> [A] group of gangsters called Izinyoka [came] to the school, there was a fight and one gangster at the school protected us and tried to stop them. They started shooting at the office and he stopped them.

The young man had stopped the others by saying 'No, I am a learner here at school and I want to protect the school. If you want to kill me, you can kill me, I don't care'.

Lutho's account illustrates how identities are multiple and related to place and space (Rosenberg and Gara 1985). The young man Lutho referred to, juggled his identities as a gangster outside of school, with belonging to a group of non-gang related pupils during school hours. This is a clear example of how gang affiliation does not necessarily imply adherence to an anti-school culture. It also indicates that youth who are considered gangsters can be viewed as friends by their peers. This might especially be the case when they are away from their context of gangsterism, or when their gangster status may bring benefits, like protection. Lutho says that he considers this young man who protected him at school as his friend, and clarifies that 'maybe there is someone who wants to do something bad to me . . . then I just tell him'.

Walking these thin lines of friendship, Lutho displayed a very strong belief in self-control, being careful not to get too involved with peers who might demand the return of a favour. He explained: 'I don't feel comfortable, because I don't trust, he would kill, maybe he is doing that because there is something he wants from me.' He clarified that he would spend only short periods of time with this friend: 'I will leave on time, I won't stay the whole evening . . . maybe about 30 minutes later I go.' He continued to make it clear that he was not intending to join a gang or become involved in gang-related acts of violence. He hoped to complete high school and continue studying 'something with electricity' so that he could help the people in the communities around him who were living without electricity. For him, education was clearly a path to a better future: 'I think school is important because as you can see nowadays, in order for you to get a good job, you need to get well educated.'

Lutho's ability to 'remain focused' was supported by his social network: friends, church, a supportive home, a cousin who was a doctor and to Lutho a clear example of the kind of positive impact education could have on his life. Lutho described how he and his friends supported each other by talking about school and homework; they spent hours together in the library or church:

> We are doing lots of things together like going to the library and going to the church together. And we just sit and talk together, we don't do those bad things or get involved in crime. We support each other and if one of us is having a problem, we help each other.

The support he finds at his church, and his religion, further strengthened his belief in self-efficacy (Bandura 1995), his inner conviction that he could walk his own path. When others tried to convince him to join in criminal activities, he said he 'just ignore(d) them'.

I just let them

Lungile, Thando's 17-year-old half brother, did consider young men who commit serious crimes truly as his friends, and unlike Lutho, he did not ignore them, nor did he choose to 'leave on time'. His support system was weaker than Lutho's and the temptations to hang out with those who engaged in violent crime, stronger. He described how the loss of his mother and grandparents made him sad and lonely, and how the desire to join a gang emerges from loss and a sense of alienation:

> You see . . . most of the gangsters don't have parents so some other day it makes me wanna be in a gang and sometimes, I just . . . [think I want] to be hijacking [cars], to smoke tik tik [a local drug] because . . . they're the same as me. They don't have parents.

Even though Lungile identified with those who 'don't have parents' and referred to friends in gangs, he claimed that he did not join in their activities, because he 'see(s) it is wrong. Killing a person is not good'.

He did, however, take care not to distance himself from them openly. His quiet acceptance of their acts of violence and their apparent acceptance of his non-involvement offered him the chance to feel he belonged:

> Most of my friends are hijacking . . . and I'm still with them, but I don't do hijacking . . . I can't just discriminate them or . . . I just leave them, I let them do what they do you see, because if I stop them, like I say 'guys, what you're doing is wrong', that . . . it's like I'm a better person to them. It's like I'm making myself a better person to them. So I just let them.

Lungile's positioning towards his friends testifies to the pressure not to stand out and risk evoking feelings of jealousy and envy (cf. Bray *et al.* 2010). If he distinguished himself from the young people with whom he would otherwise identify, Lungile might pay too high a price of social exclusion.

Unlike his older brother Thando, Lungile desired to 'live a fancy life'. Brand name clothes and a nice car were elements through which he wished to express himself yet financial deprivation made that impossible. Between the pull of a 'popular culture' and the wish to remain 'on track' with his education, Lungile looked for ways to balance the two. While his brother chose to stay away from gangsterism, to endure his current situation, to consider – and, where possible, consciously plan – the next steps to be taken in his life, Lungile found it more difficult to reconcile his present situation with his wish to be part of Ikasi style, or what he called 'the trend'. He attempted to accommodate the seemingly competing goals: he chose to 'walk with his friends', but not to get involved with their crimes. He tried to look for a school which he felt would suit him better than the school he attended, one with more facilities – computer rooms, a library, 'proper sports fields' – that might make his time spent on education more enjoyable and 'less boring'.

Conclusion

The narratives of the young men discussed in this chapter indicate that deciding what kind of man to be in post-apartheid South Africa 'does not come easily' (see also Walker 2005: 235). In some respects, our findings are similar to Walker's (2005), who described the existence of 'alternative (that is, non-violent) masculinities' among young working-class men in Soweto. She sees them as new 'embryonic forms of male selfhood' (2005: 236), shaped in a post-struggle era and clearly tapping into the discourse of possibility in post-apartheid South Africa. Our own and Walker's observations invite us to move beyond viewing young Black men as perpetrators, gangsters, and lacking a vision for the future. All four young men described in this chapter aspired to hegemonic masculine identities of being a successful, respected man, able also to provide for their families and sometimes for their broader communities. In a context of violence, crime and enduring deprivation, however, they faced multiple constraints, and they tried various pathways in order to achieve their aspired manhood. Some, like Nezile, chose to try to gain respect and status through exerting violence and power onto others. Others, like Thando and Lutho, consciously chose to stay away from that path. Nezile's story illustrates, however, that even though the use of violence and crime may be chosen in an attempt to gain a position of respect at one particular time in life, such choices are not static. Decisions around which path to follow are dependent on time and place.

While all four young men lacked the economic capital to enable easy upward mobility, we saw no downward adjustment of aspirations that might be predicted by Bourdieu's theory of class reproduction. While they were well aware of the deprivations in their lives, their aspirations were influenced by a belief in the dominant achievement ideology that regards individual effort and education as the way to success. However, in line with Giddens' theory on identity creation (1991), their choices entailed doubt or anxiety. For some, like Lutho, bolstered by his support network within the family and church, the decision to pursue an education seemed easier than for the others. Others, however, moved between different identities, or created 'in-between' versions that would leave room for adaptation when necessary. Their choices and pathways seemed more precarious and 'fragile', much as Henderson (1999) pointed out about the youth she worked with at the time of the country's transition to democracy. Some, like Thando, feared that choosing a path of education would exclude them from their peer group and communities, and others, like Nezile, doubted whether education would deliver on its promise. This may explain why some took the risky position of 'walking with gangsters' in the present, whilst imagining a future life away from gangs.

For these young men there was a trial and error process of juggling identities, and decisions about which path to follow were made in the absence of clear guidance, amid family breakdown, high levels of unemployment and institutions that do not manage to offer effective support. We do need to acknowledge that we presented findings from a small, unrepresentative sample of youth in Cape Town. Further research would need to explore how applicable these findings are to broader youth cohorts in South Africa, looking very specifically at the ways in which young men construct their aspired male identities and following them for a prolonged period of time along the pathways they try out.

Nevertheless, listening to these young men's aspirations and anxieties has enabled us to start to think about the ways in which various institutions could intervene at several levels in young people's lives. Preliminary suggestions for interventions that can help reduce violence among young men might be to look at the possibilities for strengthening the care structure surrounding them (social and cultural capital), attempting to mitigate the levels of anxiety that come with having to make choices on their own. Within the educational system, clearer guidance around educational and career choices (cultural capital) is needed to help young men think through their future life paths and possibilities within and beyond their 'bounded' contexts. Policies and interventions might bear in mind the fact that young men find it easier to choose against a path of violence and crime if the economic means are available for them to create their aspired male identities. This can inform the thinking around interventions such as the Youth Wage Subsidy or an educational system that would combine apprenticeships with study. Finally, interventions aimed at 'changing men' might be informed by the fact that young men might not need much 'changing', as the possibility for change lies within their own understanding that violence is not or need not be part of their aspired identity.

Notes

1 Swartz (2010) conducted a qualitative study in Cape Town with 37 township youth aged 14 to 20, over a period of 16 months. Her work focused primarily on the moral influences in the lives of young people in Ikasi.

2 Henderson (1999) described the lives of 16 young people growing up in the deprived township of New Crossroads, Cape Town. She described youths' social context as characterised by 'fragility' (the low economic standing of their households, their experiences of mobility and caregiving, the violence surrounding them, power dynamics in relationships, and 'senses of self that are continuously being worked upon' (1999: 25–6)). Yet within such contexts of fragility, Henderson stresses the ability of youth to maintain a sense of agency.

3 Ramphele (2002) also documented the lives of 16 young adults, boys and girls, growing up in New Crossroads. She describes in detail the stories of two 'successes': young people who managed to 'make something of themselves' and who managed to get into the stream of upward mobility, despite growing up in a context of extreme poverty, and in a society where institutions such as family and school are often blatantly failing to offer support.

References

Bandura, A. (1995). *Self-Efficacy in Changing Societies.* Cambridge: Cambridge University Press.

Bility, K. (1999). 'School violence and adolescent mental health in South Africa: implications for school health programs'. *Sociological Practice: A Journal of Clinical and Applied Research,* 1 (4), 285–303.

Bourdieu, P. (1977). *Outline of a Theory of Practice.* Cambridge: Cambridge University Press.

Bray, R., Gooskens, I., Kahn, L., Moses, S. and Seekings, J. (2010). *Growing up in the New South Africa: Childhood and Adolescence in Post-Apartheid Cape Town.* Cape Town: HSRC Press.

Burton, P. (2008). *Snapshot Results of the CJCP National School Violence Study.* Centre for Justice and Crime Prevention, Research Bulletin, no. 2, Cape Town, April 2008.

Cloete, N. (2009). *Responding to the Educational Needs of Post-School Youth. Determining the Scope of the Problem and Developing a Capacity-Building Model.* The Centre for Higher Education and Transformation. Available at: www.chet. org.za/books/responding-educational-needs-post-school-youth (accessed June 2014).

Clowes, L., Lazarus, S. and Ratele, K. (2010). 'Risk and protective factors to male interpersonal violence: views of some male university students'. *African Safety Promotion Journal,* 8 (1), 1–18.

Connell, W. (1995). *Masculinities.* Berkeley: University of California Press.

De Lannoy, A. (2008). 'Educational decision-making in an era of AIDS'. Unpublished PhD thesis, University of Cape Town.

De Lannoy, A. (2011). 'The stuff that dreams are made of: narratives on educational decision-making among young adults in Cape Town'. *Journal of Education,* 51, 53–72.

Giddens, A. (1991). *Modernity and Self-Identity.* Cambridge: Polity Press.

Henderson, P.C. (1999). 'Living with fragility: children in New Crossroads'. Unpublished PhD thesis, University of Cape Town.

Kinnes, I. (2000). 'Gang warfare in the Western Cape: background'. Monograph No. 48, From urban street gangs to criminal empires: The changing face of gangs in the Western Cape, June 2000. Available at: www.savi.uct.ac.za/wp-content/ uploads/2012/12/Mono48.pdf (accessed June 2014)

Lefko-Everett, K. (2012). *SA Reconciliation Barometer 2012. Ticking Time Bomb or Demographic Dividend? Youth and Reconciliation in South Africa.* Cape Town: The Institute for Justice and Reconciliation.

Morrell, R. (1998). 'Of boys and men: masculinity and gender in Southern African studies'. *Journal of Southern African Studies,* 24 (4), 605–30.

Morrell, R. (ed.) (2001). *Changing Men in Southern Africa.* Pietermaritzburg: University of Natal Press.

Morrell, R., Jewkes, R. and Lindegger, G. (2012). 'Hegemonic masculinity/ masculinities in South Africa: culture, power, and gender politics'. *Men and Masculinities,* 15 (1), 11–30.

National Youth Development Agency (2011). *Our Youth. Our Future. The Integrated Youth Development Strategy of South Africa, 2012–2016.* Johannesburg: National Youth Development Agency.

Noonan, M. (2012). *Violence and Gang Youth in South Africa: More Complex than 'Black Menace'*. Consultancy Africa Intelligence, Discussion Paper. Available at: www.consultancyafrica.com (accessed June 2014).

Oduro, G., Swartz, S. and Arnot, M. (2012). 'Gender-based violence: young women's experiences in the slums and streets of three sub-Saharan African cities'. *Theory and Research in Education*, 10 (3), 275–94.

Panday, S., Ranchod, S., Ngcaweni, B. and Seedat, S. (2012). 'The situation of the youth in South Africa'. In C. Ward, A. Dawes and A. Van Der Merwe (eds), *Youth Violence: Sources and Solutions in South Africa* (pp. 95–140). Cape Town: UCT Press.

Parker, I. (2005). *Qualitative Psychology: Introducing Radical Research*. Berkshire: Open University Press.

Pinnock, D. (1982). *The Brotherhoods: Street Gangs and State Control in Cape Town*. Cape Town: David Phillip.

Posel, D. (2005). 'The scandal of manhood: "baby rape" and the politicization of sexual violence in post-apartheid South Africa'. *Culture, Health and Sexuality: An International Journal for Research, Intervention and Care*, 7 (3), 239–52.

Ramphele, M. (2002). *Steering by the Stars: Being Young in South Africa*. Cape Town: Tafelberg Publishers.

Ratele, K. (2001). 'Between "ouens": everyday makings of black masculinities'. In R. Morrell (ed.), *Changing Men in Southern Africa* (pp. 239–53). Pietermaritzburg: University of Natal Press; London: Zed Press.

Rosenberg, S. and Gara, M.A. (1985). 'The multiplicity of personal identity'. In P. Shaver (ed.), *Self, Situations and Social Behavior: Review of Personality and Social Psychology* (pp. 87–113). London: Sage Publications.

Salo, E. (2003). 'Negotiating gender and personhood in the new South Africa'. *European Journal of Cultural Studies*, 6 (3), 345–65.

Samara, T. (2005). 'Youth, crime and urban renewal in the Western Cape'. *Journal of Southern African Studies*, 31 (1), 209–27.

Sangar, N. and Hadland, A. (2008). 'Challenging patriarchal scripts? A gender analysis of South Africa's community print media'. *Agenda: Empowering Women for Gender Equity*, 22 (77), 4–17.

Soudien, C. (2003). 'Routes to adulthood: becoming a young adult in the new South Africa'. *IDS Bulletin*, 34 (1).

Soudien, C. (2007). *Youth Identity in Contemporary South Africa: Race, Culture and Schooling*. Cape Town: New Africa Books.

Statistics South Africa (2012). *Census 2011: Municipal Report, Western Cape*. Pretoria: Statistics South Africa.

Swartz, S. (2010). *Ikasi: The Moral Ecology of South Africa's Township Youth*. Johannesburg: Wits University Press.

Swartz, S., Hamilton Harding, J. and De Lannoy, A. (2012). '*Ikasi style* and the quiet violence of dreams: a critique of youth belonging in post-apartheid South Africa'. *Comparative Education*, 48 (1), 27–40.

Walker, L. (2005). 'Men behaving differently: South African Men since 1994'. *Culture, Health and Sexuality*, 7 (3), 225–38.

Walsh, S. and Mitchell, C. (2006). '"I'm too young to die": HIV, masculinity, danger and desire in urban South Africa'. *Gender & Development*, 14 (1), 57–68.

Ward, C., Dawes, A. and Van Der Merwe, A. (eds) (2012a). *Youth Violence: Sources and Solutions in South Africa*. Cape Town: UCT Press.

Ward, C.L., Artz, L., Berg, J., Boonzaler, F., Crawford-Browne, S., Dawes, A., Foster, D., Matzopoulos, R., Nicol, A., Seekings, J., van As, A.B. and van der Spuy, E. (2012b). 'Violence, violence prevention, and safety: a research agenda for South Africa'. *South African Medical Journal*, 102 (4), 215–18.

Wood, K.M. and Jewkes, R.K. (2001). '"Dangerous" love: reflections on violence among Xhosa township youth'. In R. Morrell (ed.), *Changing Men in South Africa* (pp. 317–36). Pietermaritzburg: University of Natal Press; London: Zed Press.

Xaba, T. (2001). 'Masculinities in a transnational society'. In R. Morrell (ed.), *Changing Men in Southern Africa* (pp. 105–24). Pietermaritzburg: University of Natal Press; London: Zed Press.

8 Young men and structural, symbolic and everyday violence in Lima, Peru

Ana Maria Buller

Introduction

According to the WHO World Report on Violence and Health being a young man is 'a strong demographic risk factor' for violence (Krug *et al.* 2002: 25), especially if this young man lives in a country with an emerging economy. Latin America, for instance, shows higher rates of violence among young people when compared with other regions in the world (Mercy *et al.* 2002). Furthermore, violence seems to be exacerbated by large urban contexts, with cities such as Rio de Janeiro, São Paulo, Mexico City, Lima and Caracas accounting for more than half the total of the national homicide rates (Briceno-Leon and Zubillaga 2002). However, these statistics refer to a small percentage of the population of young men living in these conditions, reflecting a set of marginal behaviours and not necessarily a generalised set of attitudes in poor communities (Mullins 2006). Traditional public health approaches to the study of young people and risk behaviours – including interpersonal violence – tend to consider individual characteristics, such as social status, age and ethnicity, as risk factors, which can inadvertently generate a blaming discourse in which young people with certain characteristics are widely stigmatised as 'youth-at-risk' (Kelly 2000; Sharland 2006). In trying to understand young men's interpersonal violent behaviour, we need to go beyond the individual and explore structural and contextual factors, but in doing so we need to be careful not to assume that individuals are passive recipients of structural forces.

Drawing on findings from the ethnographic study I conducted, in this chapter I discuss the experience and negotiation of structural, symbolic and everyday violence amongst young men in the socially excluded neighbourhood El Agustino in Lima, Peru. According to Farmer (2004) structural violence is the result of forces of oppression and discrimination, which occurs in a systematic manner and usually entails a historical dimension (Alcalde 2006). This holds true for El Agustino, where violence – as we will see in this chapter – has become normalised and operates at different levels. In the medical anthropology and sociological traditions, structural violence is defined as macro forces that result in particular patterns of social suffering (Farmer *et al.* 2004). According to Kleinman (2000), the local is central in understanding the influence of macro processes. Hence, it is in the everyday practices and interactions, in the so-called *everyday life violence* (Scheper-Hughes 1992), where structural violence finds its main manifestation. The concepts of *symbolic violence* and *misrecognition* (Bourdieu and Wacquant 2004) describe the way structural violence operates upon individuals. According to Bourdieu the main idea underlying the concept of symbolic violence is that individuals are immersed in and therefore unable to recognise the systems or conditions that generate the structural violence or the stigmatisation; individuals assume, for example, that the poor conditions are justified and that they are a result of their own actions. This is what Bourdieu calls misrecognition, referring to the violence that can be committed with the compliance of the oppressed.

In line with Bourdieu's Theory of Practice (Bourdieu and Nice 1977), if we consider El Agustino with its normalised violence to be the *field* where the interviewees have been socialised, it can be inferred that this pervasive violence has contributed to form their *dispositions* and consequently their *habitus*[1] (Bourdieu 1990), which in turn regulate their social practices. I argue that a structurally violent and stigmatising[2] context, such as El Agustino, generates 'negative' dispositions, such as feelings of unworthiness leading to self-denigration, envy, resentment, suspicion, lack of respect for the law and aggressiveness. But also 'positive' dispositions such as striving to survive, competitiveness, a sense of community, solidarity with fellow sufferers, creativity and resourcefulness. These dispositions are differentiated by gender, with young men internalising the image of the provider and income-generator as a central component of their gendered habitus, whilst women internalise a nurturing role.

Bearing these concepts in mind, the main aims of this chapter are to trace the connections between structural, symbolic and everyday violence – along the idea of a *continuum of violence* (Scheper-Hughes and Bourgois 2004), considering how violence becomes normalised and the consequences of this for masculine subjectivities. In doing so I aim to resist too linear explanations of the genesis of violence, such as the idea of the intergenerational cycle of violence (Widom 1989), a model widely adopted (Violence and Injury Prevention Programme WHO Regional Office for Europe 2007) but strongly criticised due to the lack of methodologically strong supporting evidence (Ertem *et al.* 2000; Newcomb and Locke 2001; Dixon *et al.* 2009) and conflicting results (Thornberry *et al.* 2012). Moreover, this model implies a linear directionality which does not take into account the role played by structural or symbolic violence and other contextual factors, such as the social environment and cultural norms (Wright and Fagan 2013). I hope that the discussion of the ways in which young men experience and negotiate violence in this setting contributes to enriching the understanding of interpersonal violence among young men from deprived contexts. By framing the discussion in terms of choice, I aim to distance myself from discourses which can reinforce the already disenfranchised status of underprivileged young men, and instead highlight their capacity to challenge and contest their own milieu despite the adverse conditions.

The chapter is structured as follows. After a brief description of the setting and study, I outline the most salient characteristics of structural violence found in El Agustino, and then draw on extracts of my interviewees' life narratives to illustrate how this structural violence percolates into interpersonal violence across social interactions and settings. I discuss how young men generate different negotiation strategies to adapt to pervasive violence and conclude by reflecting on the multi-purpose role that violence has on young men's lives in economically deprived and troubled communities, and the implications of the results for policy-making and the design of tailored interventions.

The setting

Peru is a middle-income country, which despite its steady economic growth in the last decade is still characterised by one of the most unequal distributions of income in the world (Iguíñiz Echevarría and León Castillo 2011). Of its 30 million inhabitants, 27.8 per cent of the population live in poverty, with 6.3 per cent of these living in extreme poverty (Instituto Nacional de Estadistica e Informatica 2007). Despite a decentralisation policy, Peru's governance is highly centralised with most of the decision-making and administrative power exerted by the central government based in the capital, Lima. The country suffered ten years of internal war against terrorism in the 1980s, when an estimated 69,280 people were killed or went missing (Comisión de la Verdad y Reconciliación 2003). Given the brutality of the attacks and their location primarily in the rural areas of the highlands many people were forced to leave their towns and migrate to the coastal cities, particularly to Lima. Once in the capital they soon became part of the socially excluded population, living on the periphery of the city. Today one-third of the total population lives in Lima. This migration resulted in an accelerated and unplanned growth of the city. The capital is divided into 43 districts. One of them, El Agustino, is the site of this study.

Situated towards the east of Lima and characterised by high levels of poverty, El Agustino is one of the most deprived districts in the capital with 22 per cent of the total population (Inter-American Development Bank 2010) of 190,474 living in poverty. I chose El Agustino as my study site above other districts with similar demographic characteristics because of the presence of strong grassroots organisations and NGOs working with young people, which could facilitate my entry into the community to conduct my research.

The study

Following previous studies aiming to explore young people's everyday practices (Burton 1997; Lightfoot 1997; Farrer 2002), I chose an ethnographic approach using in-depth narrative interviews with young men and women, semi-structured interviews with stakeholders and participant observation as data collection tools. During the 12 months of my fieldwork in 2008 I went to El Agustino on a daily basis, with a total immersion period of six weeks when I moved to live there. In choosing the participants for the study I considered their age, working/ studying status and area of residence within El Agustino – within these criteria

I tried to diversify the sample as much as possible. My final sample was comprised of 45 young men (16 to 26 years), 15 women (16 to 76 years old) and 19 stakeholders (mainly members of local religious and secular third sector organisations working with young men, health sector staff and local authorities such as the local government and police force representatives). Ethical approval was granted by the Universidad Peruana Cayetano Heredia in Lima and the London School of Hygiene and Tropical Medicine. Pseudonyms have been used to ensure anonymity.

Structural violence

The violence of poverty

While conducting my fieldwork, I was invited to take part in domiciliary visits alongside the social workers of a juvenile justice project. This gave me the opportunity to observe directly the living conditions of the inhabitants of El Agustino. Most houses were unfinished, made out of a mixture of concrete and adobe, with cardboard and corrugated iron panels as roofs, often without basic services such as sewerage and electricity. Electricity connections were mostly unlicensed, made by extending cables from the street lighting to the house, with exposed cables hanging from the walls. It was common to find three or four generations living in the same space, with many adults and children sleeping in the same room and sharing beds.

Extreme poverty in El Agustino went beyond infrastructure and services. Experiences of growing up in a household where there was not enough money to secure a meal everyday were not uncommon. Economic hardship meant that parents had to work extra hours, limiting their time with their children and having to rely on family members such as grandparents or uncles for their care. Many interviewees described how they felt a 'burden' for their families, having the urge to start working early on in life and failing to recognise their human right to be nurtured and protected by their primary carers. Given the usual lack of father figure and the traditional expectations of men as providers and protectors, young men felt it was their responsibility to contribute to the household income and to protect their mothers even as young children. Alejandro, for example, told me that he had started working when he was eight years old:

> I sold bread too, because I didn't like my mum to be out on the street alone. I was afraid that something might happen to her and I'd be at home . . . I didn't like that.
>
> (Alejandro, male, 16 years old)

Many of the young people stopped attending school once they started working. This jeopardised their possibilities to find a stable job later on in life, as not finishing secondary education meant that they were not qualified to enrol in further education. Thus, poverty and its consequences became a violent and vicious circle from which it was difficult to break as an individual.

Political and institutional violence

More than 15 years after the Shining Path's[3] main leader and principal collaborators were caught, the terrorist legacy still shaped the social organisation and the lives of people in El Agustino. Many of the interviewees knew someone whose relative had been murdered as a result of terrorism or in some cases had lost someone in their own family. During that time, civil liberties had been restricted and repressive actions taken by the government and enacted through the military forces. This meant that people were trapped between two forces and left vulnerable and scared. Terrorist acts also had a 'prospective impact', affecting the future lives of young men and women who did not experience it directly:

> The terrorists destroyed all my documents, and I've been all this time, during 22 years, studying and being part of Peru without really being part of it . . . I don't have a national identity card . . . That is something that prevents me from working and developing as a person, right?
>
> (Juan, male, 22 years old)

At the institutional level, local government employees – and politicians in general – were perceived as inefficient and untrustworthy. Despite acknowledging that the incumbent mayor had improved the district in terms of security and infrastructure, the generalised perception was that local government employees achieved their positions by connections, caring mostly about their own political agenda. Similarly the police force and more generally the justice system were perceived as unreliable and corrupt, often colluding with criminals, instead of protecting the – law-abiding – population. Interviewees considered it pointless to report anything to the police, unless they were prepared to offer them some money. Many reported being detained and beaten up before charges against them were proved. Taking bribes from parents of minors caught in some illegal activity was also usual. Police officers threatened parents with sending their underage children to a detention centre if they did not give them money. Accounts of abusive behaviour, such as insults and beatings, directed even towards minor detainees were frequent:

> Yes, they hit you, on the sole of your feet they hit you with that police stick . . . they hit you with all their strength on the sole of your feet or wherever it lands, and you just have to cope with it, that's your pay back for what you did on the street.
>
> (Lucas, male, 23 years old)

The police were not seen as a force of protection but as a source of oppression (Winton 2004; Fine and Kuriloff 2006), which led to feelings of neglect, mistrust and the need for the community to take justice into their own hands.

Violence was also evident in schools. There was a physical dimension, with teachers hitting students or even promoting fights in the classrooms. But there were other manifestations, such as corruption of teachers, who would charge money to those students in danger of failing a year. This practice was so institutionalised that some teachers offered the 'service' of coordinating with all the other teachers and calculated a total price which the student had to pay to pass the academic year:

Cesar (male, 21 years old):	I had to bribe the teachers in third, fourth and fifth years of secondary school to not fail, because if I didn't I would have failed . . .
AM:	Oh really?
Cesar:	Of course they make deals, they are the worst, they like money!
AM:	How much do they charge?
Cesar:	Each teacher, each subject course is like 50, 30 soles, or sometimes there were some that were nicer and would ask you to bring them highlighters, pens, anything, or there was another teacher that was known in the 'business', yeah? You'd give him all the money and he'd make a bill and he'd talk with each teacher.

Violence was also evident in the way the education system dealt with the so-called 'problematic students'. Young men were deemed problematic if they had learning difficulties or they were not able to concentrate in class, or they were violent or missed classes. The most common way of dealing with these students was to send them to a school with other 'problem students'. When young men were expelled or left school, they spent their spare time on the streets, which made their participation in gangs and violent football fan groups, or *barras bravas*, more likely. Thus, it was a system that did not offer a solution to the young men, but instead deepened and complicated their problems, as Gustavo's experience suggests:

Gustavo (male, 24 years old):	I mean, when I was . . . 13, they expelled me. So then I had like two years without studying. [. . .]
AM:	And when you stopped studying did you start participating even more [referring to street gangs]?
Gustavo:	Of course! Participating more in the gang.

Football clubs and the dynamics they generated among their football followers were particularly violent. Football seemed to provide an escape from the day-to-day hardships of life in El Agustino and these football clubs profited from the fanaticism reigning among these young men, as described by Beto in a discussion about what football meant to him: 'Passion, how should I explain this to you . . . If I go to the stadium I chant, chant, chant the whole 90 minutes' (Beto, male, 27 years old).

The clubs had a system, in which they organised districts by areas, and selected a leader for each area. These leaders were given a set number of tickets for each match, which they sold at a low price or gave for free to 'loyal' followers. Loyalty was assessed by match attendance but most of all by participation in confrontations with followers of the opposite team. The system generated fierce violence not only against other team followers but also among the followers of the same team. Factions fought over becoming the area and district leaders in order to have control over the tickets and the followers in their sector.

The violence of everyday life

People living in El Agustino have to learn to deal with everyday/direct violence from very early on in their lives. I witnessed situations in which very young children were shouted at and addressed with abusive language. Corporal punishment as a way to educate children was one of the most common forms of violence reported in the family setting. The following excerpts show the scope of the aggressive acts towards children:

AM:	And did you hit your kids when they misbehaved?
Blanca (female, 43 years old):	Not with a whip . . . but with my hand, sometimes a slap, or a punch or a kick, now I realise it wasn't the right thing to do.

> She [my mum] would wet my body and put electricity on me, ouch!
>
> (Andres, male, 19 years old)

> My mum, when she got mad, she would throw knives at me. I remember one day she threw a knife at me and I ended up with a cut.
>
> (Miguel, male, 25 years old)

Despite acknowledging the negative impact of parents' violence in their lives and expressing related feelings of anger and sadness, most interviewees justified their parents' violence and thought they deserved it. Many spoke of their parents' hard lives, and the aggression and traumatic events they had experienced in their own upbringing. During the interviews, stories about domestic violence between parents also emerged, usually triggered by the father coming home drunk or intoxicated, household financial issues or suspicions of – or actual – infidelity. On many occasions, children (especially sons) tried to protect their mother or siblings by physically confronting their father. Intra-familial violence was a complex phenomenon taking place between different members of the family and mediated by their relation to each other, their age and gender.

Outside the domestic sphere, street violence was reported as constant and dangerous. In contrast to violence in the household, I did not find any attempt to justify this kind of violence. Interviewees seemed to consider street violence as unfair, having detrimental consequences for innocent people who happened to be in the vicinity when violent events took place. Most of the violence on the street occurred between antagonistic football gangs or rival school groups, and in the form of crimes such as assaults, armed robberies and sexual violence, mostly against women. As shown in the following extracts, the violence between opposing football gang members could reach serious levels, including the use of rudimentary weapons such as forks, knives, machetes and broken glass bottles and in a few cases it could also include guns.

> We stuck a fork in his back or shoulder. Or we would cut his hair, we would cut it to bother him, we would cut his hair leaving a patch without hair.
>
> (Martin, male, 16 years old)

> I stabbed him twice, once in the lung and the other one on his foot, I did it, because he had done it to me too, that is why I stabbed him twice.
>
> (Enrique, male, 22 years old)

Interpersonal violence could also be found in the school setting. As well as the violence by teachers discussed earlier, violence happened among students and between groups from rival schools. The so-called 'wars' between different schools' students usually happened in the areas surrounding the schools and entailed throwing stones and attacking buses containing members from the rival school. Violence at school was particularly directed against individuals considered different for some reason, such as the 'geeky' ones, the introverts or the ones from different neighbourhoods. Many young men struggled whilst at school, and learned that they needed to fight back and be aggressive themselves in order to survive in a highly violent environment. As in the context of the street, interviewees reported that in the school context it was important to build a reputation for yourself. As Pablo (male, 27 years old) put it, 'it was like the law of the jungle, where the strongest wins'. Pupils were potentially in danger inside the classroom, during the break, in the bathrooms and outside the school:

AM: So there were fights every day?
Juan (male, 21 years old): Potentially yeah, the typical 'I'll see you after school', or you'd go to the bathroom, people from the older year could get you, hold your neck, push you against the wall, or something like that, there was a period when they did that to me.

Again gender played an important role in school violence, with the most extreme experiences of violence taking place at single-sex boys' schools. Many young men acknowledged that attending a boys' school was quite frightening because of the bullying and the fights. Some interviewees said they preferred mixed-sex schools because the presence of women made violence milder.

As described in the previous section, manifestations of violence in El Agustino could be found in different contexts and across social relations, used by different actors at different times. This led to a 'normalisation of violence', in which for many young men aggression seemed to be the assumed, preferred and the most effective course of action, to solve problems and react to conflict. Violence was expected and became the default way of solving problems. Another characteristic which became apparent from the interviewees' narratives was that violent events were usually interconnected. Hence, in the narratives, it was often possible to identify episodes of violence preceding, and leading to, other episodes of violence. Most of the time, the roles of victim and aggressor were combined or alternated over time, and over contexts. Many of the interviewees associated their violent reactions to having witnessed or been victims of their fathers' displays of violence at home. The psychologist of the chaplaincy confirmed the interconnectedness of violence. She told me that while most of the time young people would come to see her about problems they had 'on the street' and with other young people, when asked about the situation at home, they also reported problems in the household, which often included violence. This, in turn, generated feelings of resentment and anger:

AM:	What are the main causes of violence? Is it just the money . . . ?
Vera (psychologist):	No, no, no. There is a lot of resentment towards parents, a lot of revenge . . . When they come to therapy, there's a moment when they commit to the work and they are able express how bad they felt when they were beaten up, when they [their parents] tried to drown them in a water bucket because they misbehaved, when they were whipped, when they were kicked out of the house so one of the parents could have sex with someone else without them seeing it, and left them wandering the streets, that leaves a mark on them. So then, when they grow up, they are like you did something to me I will get back at you.

The psychologist also discussed how shifts in the positioning of the subject regarding violence were set in motion by feelings of anger and revenge. Revenge, in particular, seemed to be a strong motivating factor for shifting from the position of a victim of violence to an agent of violence in a 'tit-for-tat' logic that seemed to underpin many of the violent manifestations in El Agustino:

Yes, I turned more aggressive, I mean, my dad would hit me at home, but on the street, when I went to play football, well I wanted to hit everybody, I yelled at everybody, I mean, I realised that that made me more aggressive.

(Sebastian, male, 24 years old)

Negotiating violence

As shown in the previous sections, in El Agustino structural and institutional violence were ubiquitous and interwoven with everyday forms of direct violence. Rather than fortifying the social order, institutions seemed to add to the violence and to the experience of ill treatment and chaos. But not all the interviewees reacted in the same way, and individuals reacted differently to violence on different occasions. Here I delineate the three main strategies for negotiating violence I found in the interviewees' accounts: engaging in violence themselves (directed to others or to themselves), avoiding it or sublimating it.

Engaging in violence

A common way of dealing with violence was to get involved in it, becoming an agent of violence and retaliating when necessary. Reasons for getting involved in violence varied from person to person, according to the circumstances, and sometimes in contradictory ways. For instance, some interviewees, who expressed their decision to stay away from stealing and street fights in the neighbourhood, resorted to undertaking 'eviction jobs' for the construction sector, in order to make some money. These jobs entailed forcing squatters out of a house, through the use of violent force and guns. It could also entail violently 'discouraging' a construction contractor from bidding for a particular job. When finishing the fieldwork, I learned that one of my informants had been charged and incarcerated for shooting the son of a contractor, who had interfered whilst my informant was beating the father up. The original plan had been only to 'warn' the contractor, but his son's interference changed the situation and my informant ended up charged with homicide. This informant had been adamant about his decision to stay away from gangs and football fans' activities, but he gave up resisting violence when he was offered a significant sum of money for this job. Similarly, Esteban told me about his and his friends' decision to no longer participate in theft and football fans' fights. Paradoxically, he explained to me that in order to persuade members of his group to comply with the agreement to avoid violence, they threatened to beat them up:

Esteban (male, 17 years old):	Yeah we've all stopped, now we say we will hit whoever wants to go.
AM:	Whoever, what?
Esteban:	Whoever wants to go, we beat up, so nobody goes, nobody wants to go, because that is what we have agreed, we only go to the stadium.

I found a further example of this contradiction within the accounts of violence against children. Some parents used violence in order to teach their children *not* to be violent, *not* to fight between siblings, for instance. In the following extract, we can see that this father beat his kids because they had been fighting with each other. The father complains that they are family and they should not be fighting, however, he hits them quite brutally himself, according to Ruben's account:

> He turned the radio on really loud, and he locked up the room, he shut his room and left the radio in the kitchen, high volume, so you couldn't hear, and I was there for quite a while, I went upstairs and I heard boom!, boom!, as if they were hitting a horse, when they whip him, I heard that, boom!, 'ouch!, stop it dad', boom!, 'ouch!, ouch!', and I heard my dad saying 'why do you fight damn it! What are you? You are brothers! How are you going to do that?' plum!, plum!, plum!, and at the door, keeping the door was my uncle, um . . . he was raised like my dad, that's why he stayed checking the door, so no one would come in or out. And they hit them both and everything, yeah. The next day I saw them, with a black eye, and their backs covered in blood, I remember it was awful, that was the worst thing I recall ever seeing until now.
>
> (Ruben, male, 19 years old)

Another way of dealing with violence stemming from complicated family situations was building a particular version of masculinity in which young men had to show that they were able to withstand tough life and endure 'anything'. A way of showing this was to engage in extreme self-destructive behaviours, such as heavy drug consumption and alcoholism. The consequence of these behaviours was not only a negative impact on their own health, but further deterioration of the family relationships, with some families resorting to drastic measures in order to deal with the problem. Ruben, who used to work from a very early age, was expelled from his house because of his drinking problems when he was only ten years old:

AM: And you got drunk at home?

Ruben (male, 19 years old): Yes, I got drunk at home and she got angry, very angry. I also shouted to her and then she said 'well if you are going to continue like this, go away and don't come back' she told me . . . 'I'll go' I said, so I put my things together in one, two, three boxes, I got everything and I took a taxi, I took all the basics and the other things I left there, my TV, my DVD I left there.

Avoidance

Another way of dealing with violence was to try to avoid it. Some interviewees found their motivation to avoid violence in their Christian beliefs, whilst others argued that, once they had had a child, they started avoiding violence in order to stay safe for their children. This is an example of how signifiers of masculinity shift with age – between 'youth masculinities' where street credit is more important and 'adult masculinities' where the family becomes a priority. Others argued that having a 'good' girlfriend was a good way of staying out of trouble, because the girlfriend deterred them from violence. Involvement in gangs and drugs was seen as part of their natural development, as if it was a normal part of growing up and something they grew out of when they became older. Many of my interviewees told me that, with time, they realised that it was a better idea to not be violent, in order to avoid further violence:

AM:	You did before [engage in interpersonal violence]?
Rafael (male, 18 years old):	I did, when I got angry. But that's it, I'm calm now all the time, I like being like that, calm, quiet, you get more out of being quiet than aggressive.

The strategy of avoiding violence seemed to be more possible for young men with other resources, such as further education. Pedro, who was attending university, told me that other young men in his neighbourhood protected him if someone wanted to attack him, saying 'leave him alone, he studies'. Pedro did not need to build a reputation based on violence. He trained in martial arts, so he knew how to fight, but he preferred not to show off and found that keeping a low profile was a better strategy for him than fighting. Pedro had a good reputation and was respected, because he was considered intelligent and had achieved what most of them had not:

AM:	You'd rather them not know? [that he can fight]
Pedro (male, 19 years old):	In a way yes, so they pity me and say 'oh he doesn't know how to fight, let's help him, defend him' . . . In a way you avoid fights.

Sublimating violence

Another way of negotiating violence was to get involved in other activities that served to channel anger and frustration without directly engaging in socially unacceptable behaviours. Hence the violent lyrics of their music served as a – in psychological terms – sublimation mechanism, where sublimation is the defence mechanism where socially unacceptable impulses are consciously transformed into more socially acceptable actions or behaviour. One of these activities was music and, in particular, rap or hip hop:

> [Father's beatings of his mother] is something I held inside me and I needed to vent. But it's over now, it is in the past, now . . . I tell my mate and [that] music will be the most important thing.
>
> (Carlos, male, 18 years old)

Thus, for some young men in El Agustino hip hop was the way they found to vent their anger and talk about their experiences and feelings about violence, without actually getting involved in it. I learned that they called the act of rapping '*tiraera*', which means something like 'musical shoot-out'. The three interviewees who composed this kind of music told me that hip hop lyrics always talked about experiences 'on the street', daily life and included a great deal of violent content:

> What I went through, almost all my life, I talk about it there, what I have always seen, what I know, the streets, I don't lie . . . I identify with the people from the 'hood, or with . . . where I grew up, with what I've seen, violence, gangs, drugs, the streets . . . all that, that's what I talk about in my music and . . . I don't censor anything . . . Sometimes I can be angry and I take it out with the microphone.
>
> (Carlos, male, 18 years old)

Conclusions

This analysis shows that in El Agustino, and in line with results from studies on violence in similar settings (Anderson 1999; Parkes 2007), people experienced violence across layers of social relations and contexts. Violence, I found, was normalised and used as the preferred and 'common sense' way to resolve problems. Furthermore I found that violence was not a discrete phenomenon, but fluid and interconnected. The material that connected the different acts of violence was usually that of emotions. Many of the interviewees associated their violent behaviour with emotions of revenge, anger and guilt often associated with violence at home and the father figure – usually violent or absent. From these emotions, revenge in particular played a key role in the interpersonal violence among young men, with a 'tit-for-tat' logic that has been documented by others, such as Mullins (2006) in deprived urban settings in the USA. Retaliatory acts triggered an escalation of violence, and fuelled further violence.

When examining how individuals coped with violence in El Agustino I found that people could not be clearly typified as violent or not violent, victims or perpetrators. A victim of one type of violence in one context became the agent of another type of violence in a different context. Hence, the idea of a linear intergenerational causal relationship between acts of violence did not adequately explain the experience of violence in El Agustino. Actors shifted positions in relation to violence and the individual's relation to violence changed according to the context, with some young men tending to have a victim position at home but a perpetrator position at school, or vice versa. This demonstrates the situational nature of violence, and the impact context has on the way individuals can negotiate violence – by choosing to be violent or not – in certain settings. Violence, it follows, is context dependent and serves particular purposes (Messerschmidt 2004). No matter how chaotic their actions seemed, young men appeared to consider the pros and cons associated with violence before exerting it (Reilly *et al.* 2004). This semi-conscious decision was rooted in a mesh of meaning in which violence becomes a form of expression, a message for other young men and women about their own masculinity, a strategy to avoid further violence, to enact revenge, and a way of venting anger and frustration (Wood 2003). Ultimately it was seen as a way to demonstrate power and a lack of fear, hence building a strong reputation in the community and avoiding possible future violence. Self-directed violence, on the other hand, seemed to be the product of an effort to cope with stressful situations and problems. Directing violence towards themselves, in the form of misuse of alcohol and drugs, football related violent behaviours and school fights, could be seen as a way of building tough masculinities, misrecognising the broader social violence, reacting to it by directing it towards oneself and one's loved ones. In these ways, everyday violence masks the effects of structural violence, fuelling young men's engagement in risk-behaviours. On the other hand, the capacity to avoid violence altogether was associated with having other resources and access to other kinds of social capital that allowed young men to build successful masculinities based on other parameters, such as education. Finally, alternative options to violence like engaging in hip hop music, constituted a way of channelling aggression and stressful experiences in their daily lives.

When trying to understand the overall dynamics of structural violence, I found that the mechanism of misrecognition happened at different levels, with young people not identifying their parents' violence (psychological and physical) as abusive, justifying it as a 'legitimate form(s) of retributory justice' (Parkes 2007: 406), whilst adults did not recognise forms of oppression from the broader system. Despite the conditions of extreme poverty and exclusion described above, the interviewees rarely complained about the policies or the inequalities they suffered compared with other sectors of society in Lima. They were aware of the differences with other boroughs with better infrastructure; however, their main points of comparison were the other members within their community. There was also misrecognition of the violence exerted by the educational system towards students perceived as problematic or with learning difficulties, with most individuals blaming the students for not being able to keep up and stay in the system. In sum, by forming an autodepreciatory habitus that internalises a generalised feeling of neglect, these individuals misrecognise their rights and are not able to negotiate the authorities. Neither are they able to fight an unfair system that contributes nothing towards helping them emerge from poverty, and perpetuates income inequalities, and unequal access to services and opportunities with consequent imbalances of power. They blame themselves and their families and peers for not being able to change their living conditions, resulting in an everyday suffering that entails a constant fight for survival, and a generalised feeling of unworthiness and hopelessness. Hence, it becomes clear that the conditions of poverty and stigmatisation have an impact on the biographies of individuals living under these conditions at different levels, generating what Link and Phelan (2001) describe as *persistent predicament,* which 'refers to a general pattern of disadvantage that is connected to stigma processes' (p. 380).

When thinking about interventions to tackle interpersonal violence in deprived settings we need to consider the implications of actors' shifting positions from victims to perpetrators. For instance, interventions which just target perpetrators or victims need to be avoided and instead designed upon an understanding of the complex role played by violence in these young people's lives. At a practical level, I suggest that interventions should be implemented where they are most needed, for instance in the community, not only in settings such as schools, from which many of the young men had been excluded. Innovative and engaging ways of generating discussion and involvement in the interventions should be incorporated, such as through the use of hip hop, which in this setting was a popular way to express feelings and reflect on everyday life. Finally, interventions should incorporate a gender approach in which the relational dynamics of gender are stressed. Programmes should target both men and women in order to contravene traditional gender roles and work towards more equal gender interactions. Work with young women and mothers should address their own role in constructing the violent gender dynamics that affect them, recognising that 'girls and women can contribute to traditional, restrictive versions of manhood just as boys and men can contribute to traditional, restrictive versions of womanhood' (Barker 2005: 150). Of course change is needed not only at the community/individual level but also at the macro level. The education system, for instance, should not be an additional source of violence for these young men, but should help them to negotiate violence in an efficient and safe way. It is also necessary to recognise the way that broader society excludes these young men.

Finally, it seems appropriate to reflect on the multi-purpose role that violence has on the social functioning of young men in this context. Violence served as a way of asserting hierarchies of prestige and belonging, building their masculine identities and asserting moral values (Kleinman 2000; Bourgois *et al.* 2004). In addition, violence generated within the 'tit-for-tat' logic aimed to gain respect, preserve one's image on the streets, defend one's honour and fill the void left by what was considered an inefficient and abusive justice system. Violence, it seems, was a set of skills young men needed to learn while growing up in order to adjust to their context and validate their masculinity. The fact that violence served as a medium to adapt and survive should not be overlooked. In approaching the study of violence and interventions to prevent it, recognition of its adaptive function in settings such as El Agustino is needed.

Notes

1 *Habitus* is defined by Bourdieu (1990) as 'A system of durable, transposable dispositions, structured structures predisposed to function as structuring structures, that is as principles which generate and organise practices and representations that can be objectively adapted to their outcomes without presupposing a conscious aiming at ends or an express mastery of operations necessary in order to attain them' (p. 53). In other words Bourdieu defines habitus as a set of internalised dispositions that in turn generate and organise the individual's practices in a particular social context.

2 When conducting a thematic analysis of newspaper articles about El Agustino I found that El Agustino and its inhabitants are highly stigmatised. Given space constraints I do not present these results here.

3 The Shining Path (Sendero Luminoso) is a guerrilla insurgent organisation in Peru classified by the Peruvian government, the USA, the European Union and Canada as a terrorist organization.

References

Alcalde, M. (2006) 'Migration and class as constraints in battered women's attempts to escape violence in Lima Peru', *Latin American Perspectives*, 33 (6): 147–64.

Anderson, E. (1999) *Code of the Street: Decency, Violence, and the Moral Life of the Inner City*. New York: W.W. Norton.

Barker, G. (2005) *Dying to Be Men: Youth, Masculinities, and Social Exclusion*. London: Routledge.

Bourdieu, P. (1990) *The Logic of Practice*. Cambridge: Polity Press.

Bourdieu, P. and Nice, R. (1977) *Outline of a Theory of Practice*. Cambridge: Cambridge University Press.

Bourdieu, P. and Wacquant, L. (2004) 'Symbolic violence', in N. Sheper-Hughes and P. Bourgois (eds) *Violence in War and Peace* (pp. 272–4). Oxford: Blackwell.

Bourgois, P., Prince, B. and Moss, A. (2004) 'The everyday violence of hepatitis C among young women who inject drugs in San Francisco', *Human Organization*, 63 (3): 253–64.

Briceno-Leon, R. and Zubillaga, V. (2002) 'Violence and globalization in Latin America', *Current Sociology*, 50 (1): 19–37.

Burton, L. (1997) 'Ethnography and the meaning of adolescence in high-risk neighborhoods', *Ethos*, 25 (2): 208–17.

Comisión de la Verdad y Reconciliación [Truth and Reconciliation Commission] (2003) Final report. Lima.

Dixon, L., Browne, K. and Hamilton-Giachritsis, C. (2009) 'Patterns of risk and protective factors in the intergenerational cycle of maltreatment', *Journal of Family Violence*, 24 (2): 111–22.

Ertem, I.O., Leventhal, J.M. and Dobbs, S. (2000) 'Intergenerational continuity of child physical abuse: how good is the evidence?', *The Lancet*, 356 (9232): 814–19.

Farmer, P. (2004) 'On suffering and structural violence: a view from below', in N. Sheper-Hughes and P. Bourgois (eds) *Violence in War and Peace* (pp. 281–9). Oxford: Blackwell.

Farmer, P., Bourgois, P., Scheper-Hughes, N., Fassin, D., Green, L., Heggenhougen, H. and Kirmayer, L. (2004) 'An anthropology of structural violence', *Current Anthropology*, 45 (3): 305–25.

Farrer, J. (2002) *Opening Up: Youth Sex Culture and Market Reform in Shanghai*. Chicago: University of Chicago Press.

Fine, M. and Kuriloff, P. (2006) 'Forging and performing masculine identities within social spaces', *Men and Masculinities*, 8 (3): 257–61.

Iguíñiz Echevarría, J. and León Castillo, J. (2011) 'Desigualdad distributiva en el Perú: dimensiones', Lima:Fondo Editorial de la Pontificia Universidad Católica del Perú

Instituto Nacional de Estadistica e Informatica [The National Institute of Statistics and Technology] (2007) 'Censos nacionales 2007: XI de poblacion y VI de vivienda'. Available at: http://censos.inei.gob.pe/Censos2007/IndDem/ (accessed 19 Octuber 2010).

Inter-American Development Bank (2010) 'Mapa de pobreza provincial y distrital 2009: el enfoque de la pobreza monetaria'.

Kelly, P. (2000) 'The dangerousness of youth-at-risk: the possibilities of surveillance and intervention in uncertain times', *Journal of Adolescence*, 23 (4): 463–76.

Kleinman, A. (2000) 'The violences of everyday life: the multiple forms of dynamics of social violence', in V. Das, A. Kleinman, M. Ramphele and P. Reynolds (eds) *Violence and Subjectivity* (pp. 226–41). Berkeley: University of California Press.

Krug, E.G., Dahlberg, L.L., Mercy, J.A., Zwi, A.B. and Lozano, R. (eds) (2002) *The World Report on Violence and Health*. Geneva: World Heath Organization.

Lightfoot, C. (1997) *The Culture of Adolescent Risk-Taking*. New York: Guilford Press.

Link, B. and Phelan, J. (2001) 'Conceptualising stigma', *Annual Review of Sociology*, 27: 363–85.

Mercy, J., Butchart, D, Farrington, D. and Cerdà, M. (2002) 'Youth violence', in E. Krug, L. Dahlberg, J. Mercy, A. Zwi and R. Lozano (eds) *The World Report on Violence and Health* (pp. 25–62). Geneva: WHO.

Messerschmidt, J. (2004) *Flesh and Blood: Adolescent Gender Diversity and Violence*. Lanham: Rowman & Littlefield.

Mullins, C. (2006) *Holding Your Square: Masculinities, Streetlife and Violence*. Uffculme: Willan Publishing.

Newcomb, M. and Locke, T. (2001) 'Intergenerational cycle of maltreatment: a popular concept obscured by methodological limitations', *Child Abuse & Neglect*, 25 (9): 1219–40.

Parkes, J. (2007) 'The multiple meanings of violence: children's talk about life in a South African neighbourhood', *Childhood*, 14 (4): 401–14.

Reilly, J., Muldoon, O.T. and Byrne, C. (2004) 'Young men as victims and perpetrators of violence in Northern Ireland: a qualitative analysis', *Journal of Social Issues*, 60 (3): 469–84.

Scheper-Hughes, N. (1992) *Death Without Weeping: The Violence of Everyday Life in Brazil*. Berkeley: University of California Press.

Scheper-Hughes, N. and Bourgois, P. (eds) (2004) *Violence in War and Peace*. Oxford: Blackwell.

Sharland, E. (2006) 'Young people, risk taking and risk making: some thoughts for social work', *Forum Qualitative Sozialforschung/Forum: Qualitative Social Research* [Online journal], 7, Art. 23.

Thornberry, T., Knight, K. and Lovegrove, P. (2012) 'Does maltreatment beget maltreatment? A systematic review of the intergenerational literature', *Trauma, Violence, & Abuse*, 13 (3): 135–52.

Violence and Injury Prevention Programme WHO Regional Office for Europe (2007) 'The cycles of violence. The relationship between childhood maltreatment and the risk of later becoming a victim or perpetrator of violence. Key facts'. Rome: World Health Organisation.

Widom, C. (1989) 'The cycle of violence', *Science*, 244 (4901): 160–6.

Winton, A. (2004) 'Urban violence: a guide to the literature', *Environment and Urbanization*, 16 (2): 165–84.

Wood, K. (2003) 'An ethnography of sexual health & violence among township youth in South Africa', unpublished PhD thesis, University of London, London School of Hygiene and Tropical Medicine.

Wright, E. and Fagan, A. (2013) 'The cycle of violence in context: exploring the moderating roles of neighborhood disadvantage and cultural norms', *Criminology*, 51 (2): 217–49.

9 Sexuality, sexual norms and schooling

Choice–coercion dilemmas

Jo Heslop, Jenny Parkes, Francisco Januario, Susan Sabaa, Samwel Oando and Tim Hess

Much literature around the globe has discussed public control over female sexuality (Moller Okin 1999; Phillips 2007). This chapter reports on a longitudinal study undertaken with girls involved in a project addressing gender violence in schools in Ghana, Kenya and Mozambique. We explore and question the concepts of consent, coercion and choice in relation to girls, sex and schooling, and examine the role of the project in shifting discourses around gender, sex and sexual coercion.

An important strand of the international literature focuses on adolescent girls' sexuality and the contradictory expectations placed on girls. On the one hand, representations in the media and the fashion and beauty market are geared towards sexualisation of female bodies (McRobbie 2009). At the same time, ideals of virginity and innocence are still alive and well and girls' sexuality is regulated accordingly with girls seen as the bearers of sexual morality (Ringrose and Renold 2013). Girls' dress is seen as a signifier of female sexuality and is regulated accordingly, whether this is through European moral panics over child sexualisation as evidenced by 'porno-chic' dressing, or at the other end of the spectrum the debates on whether the Islamic headscarf should be banned in school as a marker of women's oppression (Duits and van Zoonen 2005). Meanwhile boys' or men's clothing is not subject to such scrutiny or regulation, nor is their sexuality, which is frequently assumed to be natural if not uncontrollable in the face of the temptation of female bodies (Gavey 2005).

In the field of international development, sexuality tends to be either ignored or framed as a problem and related to violence, disease and population control (Jolly 2007), and risk behaviours (Boyce *et al.* 2006), despite its centrality to development goals (Jolly 2010a; Jolly *et al.* 2013). Women are seen as lacking sexual agency whilst men are stereotyped as sexual predators, and this 'bad sex' discourse closes down spaces to talk about pleasure and sexuality in relation to empowerment. Susie Jolly criticises the failure to link sexuality to other aspects of life, particularly to poverty, leading to assumptions that decisions about sexual practices are made at an individual level, rather than influenced by wider societal features (Jolly 2010b).

The 'bad sex' discourse is further overdetermined in work on adolescent sexuality in relation to girls' schooling in the Global South. Sex has been associated with pregnancy and school dropout, with HIV and with sexual violence (Wilkie 2012). With sexuality often viewed in clinical health terms, education is tasked with providing information about the mechanics of sex (Humphreys *et al.* 2008). In Sub-Saharan Africa, however, even the mechanics of sex are often omitted from the curriculum, under pressure from religious authorities and the abstinence lobby – both locally (Taleb 2007) and donor led (Campbell and Gibbs 2010). Chilisa (2006) examines how sex education teaching in Botswana has been influenced by colonisation and its Western and Christian values with their emphasis on abstinence, married heterosexuality and suppression of desire. She contrasts this with 'traditional' sex education, in which she claims that desires and pleasures were acknowledged and celebrated at puberty in some African countries, although often female sexuality was still ultimately controlled by men, particularly in relation to early marriage. Vavrus, too, in an ethnographic study of sex education in rural Tanzania, traces the disconnection between sex education messages from an international NGO, school staff, families and in peer group discussions (Vavrus 2003a). For both Chilisa and Vavrus, the 'intended' curriculum is lost in a palimpsest of confusion and clashing values, and girls continue to be denied knowledge and choice.

A dominant discourse in development literature is that educating girls acts as a 'vaccine' against HIV, early marriage and pregnancy and high fertility rates. Whilst some research finds that where sex for schoolgirls is taboo, contraceptive use is low (Jemmott *et al.* 1998; Gordon and Mwale 2006), others find that being at school or doing well in school links to safer sexual practices (Grant and Hallman 2006; Marteleto *et al.* 2008). Surveying 282 former students of a school in Northern Tanzania, Vavrus (2003b) found that young people tended to associate hard work with avoiding sexual temptations, whilst 'idleness' upon leaving school (usually due to lack of employment opportunities) was linked to sexual desire and sexual risk taking. Contraceptive use was very low amongst the sexually active young people surveyed. This starts to point to a relationship between sex and schooling that is far from straightforward.

These discourses within education suppress discussion about girls' experiences of sex, and so may increase the potential for coercion in girls' sexual encounters. Coercion takes many forms in relation to girls, sex and violence. Whilst sexual assault and rape are often based on the use of physical force, less tangible but also of critical importance is the role of sexual coercion through the imposition of a power differential, whether by age, gender, position of authority, economic disparity or other forms of inequity that enable a person to wield control over another. Exchange sex for goods or grades combines a number of these differential power relations. Whilst many studies in Sub-Saharan Africa highlight asymmetry common in sexual relationships and associated risks, such as more difficulty negotiating condom use (Luke 2005), they have not tended to examine the concepts of coercion and consent closely, and particularly not in relation to schooling (though see Moore *et al.* (2007) and Heslop and Banda (2013) for exceptions). Likewise, whilst sexual violence is an increasing focus of policies and interventions internationally (Parkes 2015), what it really means is rarely questioned.

Our view of sexuality is that it is socially constructed, with taken-for-granted aspects of sexuality including desires, practices and identities shaped by normative discourse and social practices. These discourses are multiple and sometimes contradictory, contextual not universal, shared not individual, and reproduced through social institutions (Weedon 1987; Foucault 2002). What we understand as coercive, consensual or forced sex is shaped by dominant discourses around us, including those conveyed in popular media and legal definitions. However, sexual violence continues to be under-acknowledged (Gavey 2005). Whether experiences are considered violations or just normal sex will influence how these experiences are performed, resisted or responded to. These subjective dimensions have led some researchers in northern contexts to discuss sexual violence as a continuum with some sexual experience sitting in the grey area between mutually desired sex and rape (Burt 1980; Berger and Searles 1985; Kelly 1988). Gavey (2005) argues that the discourses of aggressive desiring males and passive undesiring females within normative heterosex act as the cultural scaffolding of rape. As she says: 'Violence can be thought of as a technique to enforce one person's will only when other, more subtle forms of persuasion (coercion) are not successful' (Gavey 2005: 10).

Coercion is closely related to notions of structural violence – including the institutional practices in families, schools, communities and legal, political and economic processes that reproduce dominant discourses and prohibit forms of agency and choice around gender and sexuality in poverty contexts. This constraint on agency and choice is a form of symbolic violence (Bourdieu and Wacquant 2004). Symbolic violence takes place when coercive and violent practices that perpetuate unequal social relations may be (mis)recognised by their protagonists as normal or acceptable, and can help us understand why, for example, in some contexts women may view intimate partner violence as a sign of love (Jewkes *et al.* 2001). Whilst the dictionary definition of coercion is to 'persuade (an unwilling person) to do something by using force or threats' (*Oxford English Dictionary* 2013), we question the notion of 'free will' for girls negotiating sex. In a context of poverty, for example, girls may actively 'choose' because they cannot envisage another option, or because other options may be closed to them. For example, exchange sex may be chosen to ward off hunger or to purchase resources for school (Hallam 1994). However, we also acknowledge that girls in these contexts sometimes do recognise, criticise and actively challenge some of these norms and institutions that can produce forms of violence.

From this perspective coercion is multi-dimensional, extending beyond individual acts of force to encompass the multiple intersecting inequalities that constrain choice. At times, paradoxically, the inequitable norms and institutions can also be protective. Prohibiting girls' movements outside the home may for example reduce the likelihood of their being exposed to danger. We will explore these tensions in this chapter. In our work with a project addressing violence against girls in schools, the links between coercion and intersecting inequalities have become increasingly central to our concerns, often proving particularly resistant to interventions. Below we describe this project, before investigating these coercive processes, the ways in which girls negotiate them, and the potential of an NGO to expand the sexual choices girls have and make.

The project

Our research was part of a multi-partnered project led by ActionAid in Kenya, Ghana and Mozambique. The project – funded by a Big Lottery Fund strategic grant – ran from 2008 to 2013. Its overall aim was to enable girls to enjoy rights to education in a violence-free environment, through working towards four outcomes concerned with improved legislation, more girls in school, reduced levels of violence, and girls more confident to speak out on violence. It was conceived as combining three arms which would be mutually reinforcing and enable systemic change at multiple levels: advocacy and campaigning; community-level initiatives; and research.[1] The project worked with 45 primary schools and their local communities across the three countries, each within a district locality. These were: Wenje division, Tana River District in the northern part of Coastal Province of Kenya; Nanumba North and South in the Northern Region, Ghana; and Manhiça district in Maputo Province in Southern Mozambique. The project areas in Kenya and Ghana are both remote and rural. The communities practise Islam and Christianity and combine different ethnic groups, some of whom have a history of conflict, which is often resource related. One of the groups in the Kenyan site is nomadic pastoralist, and farming is the other main source of livelihood. The project area in Mozambique is on the main road traversing the country, near the capital and therefore with better communication, including more access to mobile phones and electronic media, higher levels of mobility and migration for work (including South African mines), more diverse employment opportunities in industry and farming and higher levels of HIV/AIDS. However, all sites experience high levels of poverty, illiteracy and gender inequalities and poor access to basic services such as electricity and running water.

The baseline study, undertaken in 2009, provided a snapshot of how gender, violence and education were understood and manifested in these project communities and helped inform the design of the intervention. It found that a quarter of girls overall had experienced sexual violence in the past year, mainly in the forms of touching intimate body parts, sexual comments or peeping, but that only a very small minority took any action to challenge the violence (Parkes and Heslop 2011). It led to the design of a longitudinal study to help us to better understand the complexity of girls' lives in relation to gender, violence, poverty and education. The longitudinal study aimed to examine how girls' capacities to challenge violence and inequality changed over the course of the project, and the role of family, school and community and formal protection systems in supporting this change. A conceptual framework was developed to guide the research which, as outlined in our discussion of sexual coercion above, emphasised not just acts of physical or psychological violence, but also the interactions and institutions (or symbolic and structural violence) surrounding these acts (Parkes *et al.* 2013).

Thirty-six girls, aged 8–17 years, from four primary schools participated in the study in each country. Data was collected over four waves (October 2011, April 2012, November 2012 and March 2013). The final wave was combined with an endline study, which repeated the mixed methodology of the baseline (Parkes and Heslop 2013). For the longitudinal study, ethnographic approaches were adopted as much as possible within the timescale and resources available; for example the same researchers undertook repeated visits to build familiarity and trust with the girls and others in each community. We made conscious efforts to avoid singling out the nine girls in each school, for example including their friends in some of the activities. Activities included transect walks to elicit girls' perception of risk in their communities, and drawing 'rivers of life' as a way to discuss family backgrounds and change over time.[2] We also interviewed the girls' teachers and head teachers at each wave and spoke to their parents, boys in their class, girls out of school, and various stakeholders[3] in certain waves.

We paid special attention to conducting child-friendly research and following high ethical standards through developing a research protocol.[4] All researchers interviewing girls were female and they combined a set of qualities for under-taking this kind of sensitive research with an understanding of the local area. All teams were trained in ActionAid's child protection policy, which sets out appropriate conduct for working with children and procedures for dealing with abuse reported by children. One particularly challenging area was the relationship between the researchers and girls. While building a good rapport was critical to enable girls to speak openly about their lives, and particularly about sexuality and sexual violence, there was a risk of generating emotional dependency. On the whole we found that girls talked more openly about sexual matters in group situations, although usually in relation to 'other' people rather than themselves. Whilst this created challenges for us, we recognise the importance of paying attention to the silences as an important part of local discourses on sexuality.

Below we describe the sexual norms experienced and articulated by girls in the project communities and the role institutions played in producing, amplifying and maintaining these discourses.

Gender and sexual norms

Repeatedly, pupils, teachers, parents and community leaders involved in the research articulated a discourse of schoolgirls as non-sexual. Teenage sexual activity was therefore not spoken of, and instead excluded from the discourse of the (good) schoolgirl. Sex and schooling were seen as incompatible, as explained by these girls:

> When a man calls you, you can tell the man you are a student and run away.
>
> (Sherifa, ten years old, Ghana)

> My teachers, especially our female teachers, advise us about issues concerning sex. That sex is meant for the married people not school children.
>
> (Mwanahamisi, 14 years old, Kenya)

Chastity was emphasised in children's own comments on ideal femininities. Girls talked of the importance of being obedient, respectful, attractive and intelligent, doing duties, dressing decently and most importantly not going out with boys at night, having boyfriends or getting pregnant. In contrast, popular boys were expected to be tough, handsome, confident, in control, able to defend oneself, able to provide/have money, and do well at school. Whilst these stereotypical femininities and masculinities were evident in all three project contexts, in the Mozambique project area, where global, modernising forces are more evident, there were also allusions to alternative, 'risky' femininities and masculinities such as boys drinking and fighting and girls having boyfriends.

Both Christian and Muslim religious teaching tended to reinforce normative gender codes, with compliance, chastity and modest dressing emphasised for girls. Although the need for boys to refrain from chasing girls and abstain from sex was mentioned there was more emphasis on girls staying away from boys, with an underlying inference of a natural predatory wildness of boys:

> At the mosque and makaranta (madrasa) they have been preaching that girls should not play with boys because when you are going to school they might impregnate you and when they impregnate you and you go to the house and they won't provide your needs and will not give you money.
>
> (Nura, nine years old, Ghana)

Children tended to comply with this, often speaking positively about what they gain from their religious community, but some girls questioned the double standards given to girls and boys about sexual behaviour:

> Religion is supposed to influence children to behave positively. But I don't know what happens to the same society, as the same boys that are taught how to behave well, I hear stories of the same boys raping girls or even making some girls pregnant. This is a contradiction to the Muslim teachings. I think that they don't take their religion seriously, if religion was taken seriously most problems facing society could not be there, it is as if religion allows men to behave badly.
>
> (Hana, 15 years old, Kenya)

Schools were also key sites for reinforcing these dominant discourses of female chastity. Whilst there is a mandate in all three countries for schools to deliver a curriculum on sex and relationships, how this translates into practice is highly variable. Many girls, particularly younger girls, said they did not get any education on sex and relationships, whilst others were taught about sex in science, social studies, citizenship or 'life skills' lessons. These lessons tended to focus on information on puberty and hygiene or on girls staying away from boys, reinforcing discourses circulating about sex and gender stereotyped norms:

> We have been taught about relationships with boys, that we will get pregnant when we have been seen with boys. We were taught these in the first term.

We have been also taught on our dressing. We shouldn't wear revealing clothes because it can entice the boys. We are also taught these things since we were in class.

(Mary, 14 years old, Kenya)

Many girls talked about the disgrace, particularly of pregnancy, where the evidence of sexual interaction can no longer remain hidden, and of shame on families and social ostracism from friends:

They make fun of girls who get pregnant so that they will know what they did is not good.

(Laila, 14–17-year-old out-of-school girls' focus group, Ghana)

This has happened in my community several times to some of my friends and relatives, when my friend became pregnant last year, people did not want to associate with her, I also had to distance myself from her company because people might think that I was also involved in the same acts.

(Meresha, 15 years old, Kenya)

Such stigma is reinforced by discriminatory laws and policies, such as the policy in Mozambique of sending girls who are pregnant or mothers to night school (Wilkie 2012).

Similar messages were also reiterated in the home. Many girls spoke of family members warning of the dangers of interacting with boys:

We haven't spoken about that [sex, relationships or marriage] but my grandmother tells me that I have to run away and not to provoke people in the street.

(Natasha, 10 years old, Mozambique).

My parents don't talk about sex, relationships or marriage. They only tell me to keep off from the boys because they will make me pregnant.

(Mwanahamisi, 14 years old, Kenya)

The silences around sex education meant that many girls lacked knowledge about contraception, and pernicious myths circulated, such as tying a charm around your waist to ward off pregnancy, or grinding glass to induce an abortion. A few girls did speak about learning about safe sex, including condom usage, more commonly in the Mozambique project area. But what is clearly in evidence here is how the way girls talked and thought about sex and gender was shaped by the institutions around them. Girls, in particular, were seen as the upholders of sexual morality and responsibility was placed on them for keeping boys' untamed sexuality at bay, denying the possibility of female desire.

In the next section we see how these norms help produce coercion in girls' sexual encounters, and examine different forms of coercion that girls experience.

Sexual coercion in the project communities

Given the myriad of arguments against sex, it is not surprising that most girls in the study were reluctant to admit to having sexual relationships. Yet some girls did admit to having boyfriends. They agreed that there were a range of reasons for girls having sexual relationships, including love and desire, pressure from boys and men, and most commonly material reasons:

> It's true girls may love or desire sex but most girls go for sexual practices to access needs as to acquire sanitary towels when parents cannot provide them with that so boyfriends do.
>
> (Selina, 13 years old, Kenya)

> I know of a friend who got herself pregnant because her mother could not afford and her father was no more and a boy promised her he will help her and the day they had sex for the first time she got pregnant. This my friend was attending primary school and that brought her education to a stop but the boy continued his education.
>
> (Salima, 14–17-year-old girls' focus group, Ghana)

There were traces of both blame and sympathy in these girls' voices, with some acknowledgement of the wider structural constraints of poverty on girls' choices. Some girls made active, conscious decisions to use their relationships to help them meet goals in life, such as continuing with their education, or to gain status. Some discussions suggested that girls may have a reasonable amount of negotiating power in getting the material things they wanted, or in decisions to continue or end the relationship:

> When I date somebody who does not help me I leave him, since he doesn't help me in anything. He doesn't give me soap, doesn't dress me, should I add on my parents' expenses with a boyfriend?
>
> (Marlene, 14–17-year-old out-of-school girls' focus group, Mozambique)

However, girls also spoke about the use of force if girls refused to engage in sex, echoing Gavey's assertion about rape being used to enforce will over someone when more subtle coercive approaches fail (Gavey 2005). This suggests that girls who may be 'choosing' to have sex for material gain may actually have little choice at all:

> Yes there are intergenerational relationships. I don't know why . . . some girls only want the money that men give in exchange of sex. When some refuse, there are men who beat them up.
>
> (Carmen, 14–17-year-old girls' focus group, Mozambique)

Girls also 'chose' to have sex in the hope of marriage. Marriage was highly valued in the project communities and there were strong expectations from families for girls to marry whilst they were still young. A desirable potential husband would be able to provide financially (including paying a dowry), which can be seen as an extension of a sex exchange relationship. Girls may be 'choosing' for love, domestic or financial security, or to meet societal expectations:

> He told me that he wanted to marry me and he got me pregnant while I was still studying and lived with my parents, at that time he was 24 years old.
>
> (Florência, 14–17-year-old girls' focus group, Mozambique)

A few girls distinguished between girls who have relationships for love (with the hope of marriage) and those who have them for material gain. The latter, in their view:

> are not serious persons because they don't really love and the day the money finishes she will no longer remain with that person. My advice is for people to stay with boyfriends or husbands that your heart fancies and not your pocket.
>
> (Stélia, 14–17-year-old out-of-school girls'
> focus group, Mozambique)

However, more often our data indicated that girls' expectations of love and marriage were inextricably linked to expectations of financial security and the two were not easily separated.

Some girls explained that age differentials influenced the level of control that girls had in relationships. Although larger age gaps could place more limits on girls' agency within the relationship, they could also entail higher levels of material gain for girls, which may encourage girls into these relationships despite the disadvantages:

> If you involve yourself with someone of your father's age is because you feel you can handle it, no one is forced to. That is why I think people should not fool themselves and should find someone of their own age cohort. I am 18 years old and my husband 23, that's why I am in a position of negotiating some of the things. Even the issue of having a son just because you're in the household does not make any sense; we have to grow up a little bit. He could reach 25 years of age and myself 22, that would be appropriate because I still want to study.
>
> (Alcinda, 14–17-year-old girls' out-of-school
> focus group, Mozambique)

Occasionally, girls talked about sexual relationships with teachers. Again, they debated the amount of 'choice' girls had in entering into these relationships, though often they viewed these as coerced, as in the case of a Ghanaian teacher enticing girls to help in his home, or the teacher in Mozambique who 'grabs the small ones, he says "if you want to pass, give me what's yours"' (Maria, 14–17-year-old girls' focus group, Mozambique). Girls could agree to sex with their teachers because they were aware that there could be favourable consequences such as improved grades, material rewards, or to gain status (a teacher being seen as having good credentials for marriage). More often, girls found it difficult to say no or were worried about the consequences, such as being failed in their exams or other punishments that the teacher was able to enact. Teacher–pupil relationships illustrate a combination of power differentials based on age, authority, status and economic resources.

Some girls in Ghana talked about coercive supernatural forces in them engaging in sex:

> There are some boys in the class and when they befriend you and you refuse they will lock you in a padlock. You fall in love with them and when they don't need you they will unlock you.
>
> (Asibi, 14 years old, Ghana)

The taboos around schoolgirls having sex made it almost impossible for girls to acknowledge sexual desire. As a result it is difficult to know whether reasons such as fear of witchcraft were sometimes used as a smokescreen for mutually desired sex. And in a context of poverty and where exchanging sex for goods or money is a norm, defining the boundary between consenting and coercive sex, and how much agency girls have in these relationships, is extremely difficult. However, clearly evident in this murky grey area that falls between forced and consenting sex are forces of structural violence (such as poverty) and symbolic violence (such as expectations of men as providers or lack of acknowledgement of girls' sexual desires). The murkiness of the boundaries around sexual coercion make intervention immensely challenging.

Disrupting discourses? The role of the intervention

The project worked at multiple levels to address issues related to gender, violence and sexuality, but with uneven success (Parkes and Heslop 2013). Working directly with girls and boys, the project instituted girls' clubs and boys' clubs in schools. Reflect circles[5] and advocacy activities[6] encouraged community members to discuss and deliberate on gender, rights and violence. Workshops and training sessions involved teachers, community members and district officials, and the project promoted the development of school level policies on gender-friendly schooling. The project also worked at national level to strengthen clarity and consistency in national laws and policies, and at local level to support the enactment of laws and policies on gender, violence and education, through for example strengthening the ways formal and informal justice systems worked together on violence against girls.

This project work helped to strengthen girls' capacity to challenge violence, in for example heightening awareness of laws and response mechanisms. Girls' clubs were key sites where girls learned what actions to take in cases of violence:

> They told us that when something happens to us we can come to them so that they will report the case to the police. If a boy rapes you or he is disturbing you, you can come and report to CAT[7] and when your house people are disturbing you, you can go and report to them.
>
> (Laminu, 15 years old, Ghana)

> I learn things about domestic violence. I learn that when somebody meets you in the street saying 'I want to marry you', you should say NO and afterwards stop using that path. Now that I am in the club I learn to read and answer questions, make drawings of a person beating the other. The meaning of the drawing is that the one beating will go to jail.
>
> (Maira, 8 years old, Mozambique)

As well as increasing girls' confidence to challenge violence, the girls' clubs seemed to have been instrumental in generating female solidarity and a discourse emphasising the importance of girls' education. Project work with parents also influenced family dynamics, with some girls talking about how their labour in the home reduced:

> These days I come to school every day, I don't absent myself from school on market days and my father told my mother not to let me sell things in the market during school hours. I have also learnt a lot from the girl's club and I was part of the advocacy team which went to the market to talk to parents who keep their girls in the market during school hours and so I am happy.
>
> (Issah, 12 years old, Ghana)

However, the emphasis on violence in the project tended to steer the discussions towards how to deal with sexual aggression and reinforced the emphasis on how to say no to sex, rather than how to make and communicate decisions about sex and ensure that any sex is safe and wanted. The risk is that the project, with its emphasis on child protection and challenging violence, ends up reinforcing discourses of the chaste schoolgirl, who is responsible for maintaining her own chastity and keeping boys at bay. However, girls in Mozambique were sometimes taught about condoms, and in this more modernised context, with broader networks of information and communication, girls' clubs appeared to be more effective at enabling girls to break silences on taboos around sex and sexual violence, and to report violence with more confidence than in the more remote, rural areas of Kenya and Ghana (Parkes and Heslop 2013).

When asked how girls and boys can be helped to have safe, healthy relationships, some girls also acknowledged the importance of working with boys, which had been largely missing from discourses circulating in project communities. The project may have had some influence there, as activities with boys increased towards the end of the project, with the development of boys' clubs possibly influencing ideas about male responsibility. Sometimes, however, there was criticism of the project's tendency to protect girls through positioning boys and men as perpetrators.

> You people of ActionAid should stop making boys and girls enemies and thinking that having boyfriends is bad. I have boys and girls as my friends.
>
> (Dusila, 12 years old, Kenya)

The focus on violence, punishment and on acts of violence involving (male) perpetrators and (female) victims can all too easily reinforce the criminalisation of teenage sex. It seems that girls were helped with some very useful strategies to avoid unwanted sexual advances, but in doing this desire on the part of girls was denied.

Whilst the project had some success through national and district advocacy work, with data indicating increasing action to challenge violence against girls by government officials over the course of the project, a recent speech by an education official at an inauguration of girls' club executive suggests that there is still a long way to go:

> Basic school girls who get pregnant should be punished severely to serve as a deterrent to their peers. She said that the government was investing so much in education of the girl-child and that any girl who decided to waste such resources through loose morals should be made to re-pay such investment.
>
> (Deputy Director of Education and Head of the Inspectorate at the Ghana Education Service, World News.Com 2013)

At all levels, there is a clear need to challenge the blaming of girls as well as boys, and to consider the bigger picture of intersecting inequalities and structural violence.

Conclusion

> If we don't provide a cultural context which clearly spells out that sexual relationships should be built around women's sexual desires just as much as men's, then heterosex is doomed to be a site conducive to coercion of women.
>
> (Gavey 2005: 12)

The 'cultural contexts' discussed in this chapter are complex, variable and fluid, but although the project has shifted some attitudes, knowledge and practices on gender and violence, it has clearly not provided a context for teenage sexual relationships built around women's sexual desires. Sexual coercion in these contexts is shaped by structural and symbolic violence, in particular poverty, expectations of marriage and males providing in relationships, and age and authority asymmetries in sexual relationships or encounters blur the boundaries around sexual consent. Discourses emphasising female chastity (particularly in relation to schoolgirls) feed into sexual coercion, and are articulated through schools, families and religious institutions. The denial of female desire and sexual agency in discourse makes discussion around (and identification of) consent, coercion and force particularly difficult. In promoting a discourse of girls' empowerment and education and in helping girls to recognise and challenge sexual violence, the project may have unwittingly exacerbated silences around sexual relationships and a pre-existing discourse of sex as automatically violent, closing down space to discuss the complexities of sexual coercion, agency, decision-making, bodily integrity and safe sex.

Interventions need to find ways to open up discussions with girls and others about how institutions and taken-for-granted norms shape sexual coercion and how they can be disrupted. This is particularly challenging given the strength of taboos around teenage and particularly adolescent girls' sexuality. Success in increasing support for girls' empowerment could be built on by expanding this concept beyond education, economic success and female solidarity to include bodily empowerment. Project staff need to build specialist skills in these areas. There have been some successful interventions that are framed around adolescent sexual and reproductive health and rights and closer working between education and health programmes could help to develop this area. At the same time, the variations between contexts in this project caution against one-size-fits-all approaches, and show how projects need to be tailored for and responsive to specific contexts. Particularly in more remote and rural communities, there can be deeply entrenched taboos around openly discussing sexuality, particularly in relation to girls and young women. Faced with such challenging contexts, NGO staff can lack the skills and understanding of how to effectively create safe spaces where norms around gender and adolescent sexuality can be openly discussed and reflected on. Further, conservative attitudes among project staff themselves can create additional barriers to addressing these sensitive issues.

Notions of structural and symbolic violence expand the ways research is able to conceptualise coercion, but there is a continuing need for research to explore the dynamics of coercion and mutuality in specific contexts, including the complex and active ways in which girls – as well as boys – resist and rework their positioning within constraining discourses around gender and sexuality. Disrupting discourses, we believe, is about reflecting in research and practice on our own attitudes, and creating discussions in schools, communities, government departments and the media, as well as listening to young people themselves, and working with them to analyse, question and reframe the discourses around sexuality and schooling.

Notes

1 Seven different partner organisations had responsibility for these areas of work in the three countries, working with ActionAid, who had management oversight of the project in country and internationally. The research was carried out by national research partners (Eduardo Mondlane University in Mozambique, Catholic University of East Africa in Kenya and Child Research and Resource Centre (CRRECENT)/Ghana National Education Campaign Coalition (GNECC)) and coordinated by the UCL Institute of Education.
2 The transect walk is a participatory research method that involves walking with research participants whilst asking questions about physical and social features of the locality; in this case researchers accompanied schoolgirls on their walk home from school.
3 These included school committee members, government community leaders, traditional leaders, religious leaders, women's group leaders, activists connected to the project such as Community Advocacy Team members (CATs – see note 7).
4 See Parkes and Heslop (2013: Appendix 1) for the Research Protocol, which discusses research design, ethics and safety, and researcher selection, training and communication. The research was also awarded ethical approval by the Institute of Education's ethics committee and followed local protocols in the three countries.
5 Reflect is an adult literacy approach developed by ActionAid as a key element of its development programmes. It is based on Paulo Freire's thinking on political consciousness raising about inequalities and incorporates practical social action on issues concerning group members. In this particular project Reflect circles are run with parents and discussion centres around issues of gender, violence and education.
6 Advocacy activities include members of girls' clubs talking to other girls and community members in marketplaces about violence in schools and girls' education, and parents committed to the issues becoming Parent Peer Educators and visiting other families' homes to discuss how parents can help protect girls from violence and support their education.
7 Community Advocacy Team members (CATs) are community members supported by the project to respond to cases of violence, in particular by linking communities with formal reporting and support systems.

References

Berger, R. and Searles, P. (1985), 'Victim-offender interaction in rape: victimological, situational, and feminist perspectives'. *Women's Studies Quarterly*, 13 (3/4), 9–15.

Bourdieu, P. and Wacquant, L. (2004), 'Symbolic violence'. In N. Scheper-Hughes and P. Bourgois (eds), *Violence in War and Peace: An Anthology* (pp. 202–4). Oxford: Blackwell.

Boyce, P., Huang Soo Lee, M., Jenkins, C., Mohamed, S., Overs, C., Paiva, V., Reid, E., Tan, M. and Aggleton, P. (2006), 'Putting sexuality (back) into HIV/AIDS: issues, theory and practice'. *Global Public Health*, 2 (1), 1–34.

Burt, M. (1980), 'Cultural myths and supports for rape'. *Journal of Personality and Social Psychology*, 38 (2), 217–30.

Campbell, C. and Gibbs, A. (2010), 'Gender, poverty and AIDS: perspectives with particular reference to sub-Saharan Africa'. In S. Chant (ed.), *The International Handbook of Gender and Poverty* (pp. 327–32). Cheltenham: Edward Elgar.

Chilisa, B. (2006), 'Sex education: subjugated discourses and adolescents' voices'. In C. Skelton, B. Francis and L. Smulyan (eds), *The Sage Handbook of Gender and Education* (pp. 249–61). London: Sage.

Duits, L. and van Zoonen, L. (2005), 'Headscarves and porno-chic: disciplining girls' dress in the European multicultural society'. *European Journal of Women's Studies*, 13 (2), 103–17.

Foucault, M. (2002), *The Archaeology of Knowledge*. London: Routledge.

Gavey, N. (2005), *Just Sex? The Cultural Scaffolding of Rape*. London: Routledge.

Gordon, G. and Mwale, V. (2006), 'Preventing HIV with young people: a case study from Zambia'. *Reproductive Health Matters*, 14 (28), 68–79.

Grant, M. and Hallman, K. (2006), *Pregnancy-related School Dropout and Prior School Performance in South Africa*. Policy Research Division Working Paper No. 212. New York: Population Council. Available at: http://r4d.dfid.gov.uk/PDF/Outputs/ABBA/Working_Paper_212.pdf (accessed November 2013).

Hallam, S. (1994), *Crimes Without Punishment: Sexual Harassment and Violence Against Female Students in Schools and Universities in Africa*. Discussion Paper No. 4. London, Africa Rights.

Heslop, J. and Banda, R. (2013), 'Moving beyond the "male perpetrator, female victim" discourse in addressing sex and relationships for HIV prevention: peer research in Eastern Zambia'. *Reproductive Health Matters*, 21 (41), 225–33.

Humphreys, S., Undie, C. and Dunne, M. (2008), 'Gender, sexuality and development: key issues in education and society in Sub-Saharan Africa'. In M. Dunne (ed.), *Gender, Sexuality and Development: Education and Society in Sub-Saharan Africa* (pp. 7–40). Rotterdam: Sense.

Jemmott, J., Jemmott, L. and Fong, G. (1998), 'Abstinence and safer sex hiv risk-reduction interventions for African American adolescents: a randomized controlled trial'. *The Journal of the American Medical Association*, 279 (19), 1529–36.

Jewkes, R., Vundule, C., Maforah, F. and Jordaan, E. (2001), 'Relationship dynamics and teenage pregnancy in South Africa'. *Social Science and Medicine*, 52, 733–44.

Jolly, S. (2007), *Why the Development Industry Should Get Over its Obsession with Bad Sex and Start to Think About Pleasure*. IDS Working Paper 283.

Jolly, S. (2010a), *Poverty and Sexuality: What are the Connections? Overview and Literature Review*. Stockholm: Swedish International Development Cooperation Agency.

Jolly, S. (2010b), 'Sexuality and poverty: what have they got to do with each other'. In C.O. Izugbara, C. Undie and J.W. Khamasi (eds), *Old Wineskins, New Wine: Readings in Sexuality in Sub-Saharan Africa* (pp. 139–55). New York: Nova.

Jolly, S., Cornwall, A. and Hawkins, K. (2013), 'Introduction: women, sexuality and the political power of pleasure'. In S. Jolly, A. Cornwall and K. Hawkins (eds), *Women, Sexuality and the Political Power of Pleasure* (pp. 1–41). London: Zed Books.

Kelly, L. (1988), *Surviving Sexual Violence*. Oxford: Blackwell.

Luke, N. (2005), 'Confronting the "sugar daddy" stereotype: age and economic asymmetries and risky sexual behavior in urban Kenya'. *International Family Planning Perspectives*, 31 (1), 6–14.

McRobbie, A. (2009), *The Aftermath of Feminism: Gender, Culture and Social Change*. London: Sage.

Marteleto, L., Lam, D. and Ranchhod, V. (2008), 'Sexual behavior, pregnancy, and schooling among young people in urban South Africa'. *Studies in Family Planning*, 39 (4), 351–68.

Moller Okin, S. (1999), *Is Multiculturalism Bad for Women*. Princeton: Princeton University Press.

Moore, A., Biddlecom, A. and Zulu, E. (2007), 'Prevalence and meanings of exchange of money or gifts for sex in unmarried adolescent sexual relationships in Sub-Saharan Africa'. *African Journal of Reproductive Health*, 11 (3), 44–61.

Oxford English Dictionary (2013) Oxford: Oxford University Press.

Parkes, J. (2015), 'Gender-based violence in education'. Background paper for Education for All Global Monitoring Report 2015. Paris: UNESCO.

Parkes, J. and Heslop, J. (2011), *Stop Violence Against Girls in School: A Cross-Country Analysis of Baseline Research from Ghana, Kenya and Mozambique*. London: ActionAid International.

Parkes, J. and Heslop, J. (2013), *Stop Violence against Girls in School: A Cross-Country Analysis of Change in Kenya, Ghana and Mozambique*. London: ActionAid International.

Parkes, J., Heslop, J., Oando, S., Sabaa, S., Januario, F. and Figue, A. (2013), 'Conceptualizing gender and violence in research: insights from studies in schools and communities in Kenya, Ghana and Mozambique'. *International Journal of Educational Development*, 33 (6), 546–56.

Phillips, A. (2007), *Multiculturalism Without Culture*. Princeton: Princeton University Press.

Ringrose, J. and Renold, E. (2013), 'Slut-shaming, girl power and "sexualisation": thinking through the politics of the international SlutWalks with teen girls'. *Gender and Education*, 24 (3), 333–43.

Taleb, H. (2007), 'Sexual education from an Islamic perspective'. In E. Maticka-Tyndale, E. Tiemoko and P. Makinwa-Adebusoye (eds), *Human Sexuality in Africa: Beyond Reproduction* (pp. 29–52). Auckland Park, South Africa: Fanele.

Vavrus, F. (2003a), '"Condoms are the devil" and the culture-as-cure conundrum'. In F. Vavrus (ed.), *Desire and Decline: Schooling amid Crisis in Tanzania* (pp. 66–88). New York: Peter Lang.

Vavrus, F. (2003b), 'The "Acquired Income Deficiency Syndrome": school fees and sexual risk in Northern Tanzania'. *Compare*, 33 (2), 235–50.

Weedon, C. (1987), *Feminist Practice and Post Structuralist Theory*. Oxford: Blackwell.

Wilkie, M. (2012), 'Policy enactment in Kenya and Mozambique: education for pregnant schoolgirls and adolescent mothers'. Unpublished MA dissertation, Institute of Education, London.

World News.Com (WN.Com) (2013) 'Pregnant school girls should be punished'. Available at: http://article.wn.com/view/2013/11/08/Pregnant_School_Girls_Should_Be_Punished (accessed 6 November 2013).

Part IV
Policy and interventions

10 From assets to actors

Reassessing the integration of girls in anti-gang initiatives in Rio de Janeiro

Polly Wilding

Increasing attention is being paid internationally to the nexus of development, youth and poverty and, in particular, there is rising concern in many international institutions about a perceived 'crisis of youth' and connections between youth unemployment and crime, violence and social unrest (Jones and Chant 2009: 185). Exacerbated by fear surrounding the idea of a demographic 'youth bulge' in many developing countries, which focuses on 'too many young men with not enough to do' (Mabala 2011: 161), NGO and government interventions all too often aim to simply 'contain or entertain' young people (Mabala 2011), providing distraction for young men who are assumed to be vulnerable to quick thrills, risk taking and violence. This chapter challenges the a priori focus on young men as victims and perpetrators of insecurity and suggests that youth-violence reduction initiatives need to broaden their focus to incorporate young women and girls in a more thoughtful way, informed by consistent gender analysis. Drawing on Risley's critique of the 'gender gap' in Argentinean research and practice (Risley 2006), I highlight the disjuncture between treatment of violence that occurs in the public sphere in Brazil and that which occurs in 'private', with the former privileged and prioritised in social justice discourse and activism.

The *favelas* (slums) of Rio de Janeiro, Brazil, form the backdrop to this chapter, spaces that are associated with urban violence, crime and the stigmatisation of young, black men (Htun 2004; PNUD 2005; Penglase 2009; Fernandes 2012). At their height in the mid 1990s, rates of violence in the city reached the levels of conflict zones. Driven by turf wars between gangs, and with gun battles between gangs and the police, young poor black men carried the heaviest burden of casualties and lives lost in these street wars (Cano and Santos 2001; Dowdney 2003). This explosion of violence has resulted in social projects explicitly focusing on young men and their needs, aiming to discourage involvement in illicit and violent networks. A persistent policy response has been to improve employability through education and/or skills training (e.g. World Bank 2006), despite the trickiness of the pathway between education and work, which is highly dependent on context, identity and opportunity (Jones and Chant 2009). In contrast, there are some interventions that go beyond education, vocational training and cultural activities. This approach, which I refer to as holistic, aims to improve interpersonal skills and reflexivity, encourage participants to question moral codes, examine gendered identities, identify personal goals, and evaluate alternative life choices. It is hoped that promoting a more questioning attitude amongst participants will not only deter them from getting involved in violent networks and related criminality, but also strengthen their ability to make positive decisions and, ideally, equip them with the confidence, knowledge and skills to challenge structural barriers. However, by applying a gender lens to the examination of two holistic projects, I argue that even progressive, transformative approaches tend to neglect, overlook and trivialise young women's roles and experiences in the context of chronic violence. This chapter explores the practical limitations inherent in this perspective, in particular the failure to acknowledge the highly complex reality that encompasses overlapping forms of violence and gendered power hierarchies.

In the next section of this chapter I introduce the theoretical approach to gendered analysis applied in my research. Then I will discuss two anti-violence initiatives, chosen for their holistic approach to working with young people, and I will explore the extent to which gender is considered in the work of these projects. I will conclude with a framework for incorporating the needs of both young men and young women into programmes aiming to tackle urban violence and insecurity.

Gendering urban violence in Brazil

Public concern about violence in Brazil is most closely associated with violence that occurs in public spaces, committed largely by groups or associated with institutional and/or criminal networks. This association is not exclusive to Brazil, but is exacerbated by the extreme levels of violence found in Brazil's urban centres, which are at once very real, but also magnified by media reporting and a climate of fear (Caldeira 2000; Holston 2009). The street has various and sometimes contradictory associations; seen as both a place of social activity, excitement and opportunity, and a source of danger and confusion – both images having corresponding gendered associations attached to them. The primary source of danger is commonly perceived to be crime committed by strangers, such as mugging or carjacking in public spaces. Young men and boys, in particular, are seen to be vulnerable to the temptations of shady individuals and the highs offered by drugs, fast money and excitement; whereas young women and girls are considered vulnerable to sexual exploitation and the lure of men with money. In contrast to these relatively visible risks, the home is seen to be a safe place away from the risks of the street, a refuge from crime, violence and corruption despite the fact that such forms of public violence do not stop at the front door (Wilding and Pearson 2013). A contradiction lies in the fact that although public violence in general receives more attention than 'private' violence, violence in the home is assumed to be private in nature, and thus little policy and media attention is given to the reverberation of public violence in the private sphere. Secondary effects of urban violence may result in tangible impacts on women's lives, such as when they are left to care for the sick and injured, or forced to assume the responsibility of the main breadwinner.

The separation between that which goes on in the private and public spheres is also echoed in the academic literature on violence and in the fault line between different areas of activism against violence (Wilding 2010, 2012). As Risley demonstrates in the context of Argentina, this 'gender gap' results in a failure to integrate gendered discourse with class-based discourse. Activists who focus primarily on the poor and marginalised only rarely draw 'attention to the gender dimensions of either police brutality or social exclusion' – ranging from rape committed by the police, to the abuse of women in destitute households (Risley 2006: 591). Risley therefore argues for the need to address 'the asymmetries of power and gender violence' (2006), which allow this to continue. Similarly, in Brazil, NGO discourse prioritises direct and indirect forms of institutional violence, at the hands of the police and structural discrimination, alongside gang violence – drawing on the discourse of the criminalisation of the poor (Wacquant 2003). The gender gap in Brazil also has a spatial component, as the different areas of activism and research concentrate on different geographical spaces (Wilding and Pearson 2013). Those that address class-based urban violence concentrate on *favelas*, as spaces of poverty and marginalisation. Those that address gender-based violence tend to focus on formal areas of the city – including middle-class women and working-class residents of the formal city, in part due to the security concerns that deter research and support services in *favelas*. This has the consequence that there has been little research into the gendered implications of urban violence (Wilding 2012).

In reality, while young women are not usually the primary actors in illegal, gang-related activities, their roles are complex and not easily defined; often strategic, but not necessarily of lesser importance, young women carry guns, messages and infiltrate rival groups (Gay 2005; Wilding 2012). Gender norms and restrictions, as well as the gendered nature of fear and risk, impact on the choices women are able to make. Women are still more likely to be the victims of private violence at the hands of partners, but they may also fall victim of direct gang violence – as a result of involvement, association, punishment or stray bullets. In some contexts girls are less at risk than boys, such as when crossing gang boundaries or when confronted by the police, protected in part by the perception that they are less active in gangs. However, their roles are not confined to secondary ones, with increasing numbers of women being charged for drugs related offences in recent years (from 32.6 per cent of all convictions in the state of Rio in 1988 to 56 per cent in 2000 (Soares 2002: 1)). Of course, rises in arrests can indicate increasing police repression as well as greater awareness of women's roles, not simply rising female criminality. Moreover, the fact that women generally occupy lower status positions in gang hierarchies implies their limited financial ability to negotiate release (Soares 2002: 2). Women tend to be restricted to certain roles within gang structures, and the lack of status also increases their vulnerability to violence perpetrated by boyfriends or in the name of punishment (Gay 2005; Wilding 2010). By ignoring the complexity of women's roles and experiences, the gender gap reproduces the conceptualisation of violence as predominantly a male problem.

In contrast, using gender as a cross-cutting analytical lens provides insight into the intersecting identities that leave girls and young women in the *favelas* at risk, without trivialising men's gendered suffering. Applying a gendered analysis foregrounds how women and girls come into contact with violence, in their roles as girlfriends, wives, mothers, sisters, friends, and how these gendered relationships shape their desire and opportunities to protect, support and care for others, and whether they provoke or discourage, mitigate or engage in violence. In order to situate my own gendered analysis, I turn now to a brief description of the two projects that were the focus of my research.

Attempts at transformation: two projects working with young people

Approaches to tackling youth unemployment, and consequently the perceived problem of young men with 'nothing to do', often focus on improving access to education and vocational training (World Bank 2006). The more simplified iterations of such approaches see education and training as a solution, without examining the complexities of local labour markets and social relations. In contrast, a more nuanced educational approach would consider a wide range of factors that shape individual decision-making – such as the social and economic costs associated with educational achievement, the quality and range of formal and informal labour market opportunities, and the comparative benefits of licit and illicit income-generating activities. Furthermore, high levels of schooling are unlikely to equate with improved employment chances unless accompanied by the relevant social capital. Going a step further to assume a direct link between improvements in education and training and reductions in youth crime is yet more tenuous. The holistic projects discussed here attempt to tackle some of the individual factors related to education, employment and gang involvement, as well as to lobby for broader social change.

Although the pervasive control of gangs over residents' movements and interactions in gang-controlled *favelas*[1] means that projects are often discrete about their focus on youth violence, two projects in Rio de Janeiro were comparatively open about their goals of engaging young people at risk and discouraging involvement in gang structures. The holistic approaches they apply go beyond entertaining or containing young people, to promote critical thinking, reflection and interpersonal skills, with the ultimate goal of deterring participants from getting involved in violent networks and related criminality. These two projects applied a relatively bottom-up way of working, involving participants in identifying issues of concern. Luta pela Paz (Fight for Peace, henceforth LPP) did this through a Youth Council, which liaised between beneficiaries and management. Rotas de Fuga (Escape Routes, henceforth Rotas) consulted gang-involved young people about the project focus and activities from the start. The ambitious goals of these two projects make them particularly interesting to study: both ultimately aimed to bring about changes in participants' life choices, facilitated through action at the individual, community and state levels. This transformative approach aspires to contextualise participants' personal situation through psychological, professional and academic support, whilst acknowledging the structural barriers to making these choices work.

LPP was launched in 2000 and continues to involve between 100–200 young people in its activities. Initially designed as a boxing academy, its primary aim was to provide a positive physical outlet for boys and young men, as a distraction from crime and armed violence, while instilling discipline and routine. Since then it has expanded to include young women and girls as members and broadened its remit to offer other sports training (e.g. capoeira and martial arts), alongside transferable skills and social development. It offers professional training, educational assistance, individual psychological and social support, citizenship classes, provision of food parcels and family support. The project aims to provide alternatives to involvement in the drugs trade, transforming aggression into positive energy and encouraging a culture of peace (LPP 2004). The international acclaim it has received (Waldherr 2012; Wiener 2012) paved the way for its first sister academy opening in London in 2007. Project documents identify the reason for its success as the methodology, which includes project members' active involvement in running the project, and the promotion of a critical attitude towards violence and other social issues, such as sexuality, family and culture (LPP 2004). Thus, this project tackles both the practical impacts of poverty and inequality, through the provision of food parcels, for example, but also attempts to make inroads into long-term structural disadvantage, by reducing the education gap, and equipping participants with a variety of life and vocational skills.

The NGO Observatório de Favelas is primarily interested in knowledge production, research and stimulating policy debate and design based on empirical evidence. As part of this work, it engages in some direct service provision, including the Rotas pilot project, which ran for two years (2005–7). It targeted young people at risk of involvement with the drugs trade; having a cohort of approximately 30 adolescents at any one time. Its overarching aim was to design a methodology for wider replication, which could help prevent youth involvement in illicit activities and promote alternative life choices. This involved assisting those wanting to leave trafficking networks by exploring alternatives for future work possibilities, widening perspectives and providing training. Similar to LPP's citizenship classes, it held discussion sessions, or 'thematic workshops', which aimed to foster social development and personal reflection. It also provided practical and professional skills, through access to courses on digital photography and communications, and partnerships with local employers. A core aspect of its work was to raise awareness about structural barriers among the general public, professionals and policy-makers, including stigma and institutional practices that marginalise young people and limit their long-term life chances.

Researching responses to violence in the *favelas*

Drawing on fieldwork carried out between 2005 and 2009 in Rio de Janeiro, my research explored the ways in which men and women's lives were affected by contexts of high levels of violence. Its central thesis was that the focus on male perpetrators and actors overshadowed women's and girls' experiences, to the detriment of a complete understanding of how forms of violence overlap and reinforce one another, and how networks of violence function (Wilding 2012). One question that arose from this research was the ways in which projects were gendered. This chapter addresses this question, by exploring the ways in which NGOs considered girls within the remit of their interventions, how they viewed girls' involvement in the project work, as well as their wider roles in the community. Material comes mainly from the NGOs' grey literature and interviews with project workers, supplemented by interviews with young people.

The research was located in 17 *favelas* in the north-east of Rio de Janeiro, Complexo da Maré, an area that has undergone several urbanisation projects in the last 30 years. Despite significant disparities in social indicators between the communities, by the early 2000s the majority of the 132,000 residents lived in concrete or brick houses, with access to basic services and infrastructure, 11 NGOs, 68 churches and some limited state social projects (CEASM 2004). As in most of Rio's *favelas*, urbanisation policies have resulted in increased visibility of the state (Souza e Silva 2003: 2), particularly in areas recently targeted for 'pacification' in preparation for the 2014 World Cup and 2016 Olympics (see endnote 1). Nevertheless, social projects run by government institutions remain relatively scarce in gang-controlled communities (Goldstein 2003; Leeds 2007), whereas NGOs, churches, political organisations, researchers and activists tend to be more accessible, providing hands-on assistance and activities. Consequently, projects and NGOs are widely considered to constitute some of the more positive aspects of *favela* life. NGOs[2] acted as my gatekeepers, helping to identify potential research participants, who were primarily members of social projects. In the next section, I am drawing primarily on 19 individual interviews between the ages of 13 and 20, 12 of whom were young women, who were participants in these two holistic initiatives, alongside the views of project workers.

This data was collected as part of the broader research project described above, which used qualitative, participatory methods, such as community mapping and problem trees, prior to more in-depth discussion in semi-structured interviews and discussion groups. Topics included their perceptions of the acceptability of different forms of violence (as punishment, as discipline, etc.), recent experiences of violence, and attitudes towards the NGOs and projects. The interviews with professionals mainly focused on their work with young people and at-risk groups, and their understanding of networks of violence and wider social problems affecting these communities.

Benefits of participation

Interviewees from Rotas cited a range of benefits of participation, with Marilia (aged 13) stating that the project was the best thing in the community and that, since attending, she was now no longer 'living out on the streets' but spending all her spare time at the project instead. Regina (aged 17) observed how project workers at Rotas did their best to seek solutions to participants' problems, taking time to explain things properly and helping her become calmer and better able to communicate at home. Zeca (aged 15), who had been at the project for five months, said he liked the thematic workshops because they helped him talk about personal issues, exchange experiences and form opinions. Elza (aged 20) also referred to communication, explaining how her confidence had grown, alongside the sense of belonging and trust within the group:

> When I started, I think I was half-lost. It wasn't one group, it was all divided. No one talked straight. The students started to change and now I identify more with this [new] group. I feel more comfortable talking . . . Everybody talks together, we all talk about the same things; everyone talks about everything and gives their opinion.

Interviewees from LPP referred to a similar range of benefits, with many identifying the project as one of their most important places in the community. Milton (aged 14) thought that LPP had influenced 'lots of young people to keep off the streets, even to [leave] the drugs gangs', while Oscar (aged 16) admitted that he initially joined the project in order to learn how to fight, but as a result of attending he had become 'calmer and less aggressive', adding that he had 'grown a lot since then'. Marcello (aged 18), who was on the Youth Council, was even more effusive in his praise, likening the space to 'heaven for us', stating that he spent more time at the project than at home. Similarly, adolescent girls stated they spent a lot of time at the project, viewing it as their second home, and that it had helped them personally, with Maitena (aged 13) describing it as more than a project, but somewhere you learn to deal with sensitive issues, such as learning about safe sex.

Involvement in these projects appears to provide young people with the opportunity to explore new roles, challenge social expectations, build their confidence and rethink future options. These snapshots suggest a level of success for LPP and Rotas in going beyond simply providing a distraction from the risks of criminal involvement, to fostering more fundamental change in behaviour, social interaction and self-reflection. Given the shortage of comparable spaces, these opportunities were attractive and in demand by young people in the area. However, although girls have claimed a space in these initiatives, it is less clear that all their needs are addressed, a question which the next section explores by examining the ways in which female participants are integrated into project goals and activities.

The absence of gender in project design

Despite the take-up by girls and young women, neither project included girls' involvement in the initial project design, nor was their presence seen as automatically desirable by project workers. On the one hand, prior to the launch of Rotas, researchers interviewed over 200 young people involved in gang networks, including only six young women. Consequently, when the project was launched it was anticipated that a similarly low percentage of participants would be female, reflecting the perception that women were in the minority and on the periphery of gang structures. In practice, the scale of the take-up by girls was much larger, constituting nearly half of all participants. On the other hand, LPP began explicitly as a male-only project. Luke Dowdney, the project founder, justified this initial decision, stating that the project goal was to work with young people involved in gun violence, 'of which 99% were boys', complemented by his view of the gym as traditionally 'a very male reserve'. However, in response to the demands of male project members, the project was opened up and now a significant number of girls and young women participate. Luke described this change as having an extremely positive impact on the club as a whole, citing benefits that rely on gendered notions of femininity, such as their diligence, adherence to rules and tendency to greater social cohesion.

Despite Luke's verbal enthusiasm, LPP's written material and the talk of project workers are dominated by gender-neutral language, with scant reference made to gender or gender-specific issues. For example, one of its annual reports documents the number of female participants (31 per cent in 2009 (LPP 2010: 5)), and the fact that there are male-only, female-only and mixed sport classes, but without any indication of the rationale for this. An independent review of the project refers to some gender issues, such as domestic violence (CLAVES 2006). However, the project's documentation does not discuss the problem of violence in terms of its gendered dynamics or impacts.

The fact that Rotas brings together research and practice elements, and draws on the views and experiences of its participants (Observatório de Favelas 2003: 12), might suggest fertile ground for gender awareness. The original baseline study cites the need for 'adequate comprehension' of the experiences of those involved as a key to developing appropriate interventions for 'young people [*jovens*] who live through such a dramatic experience [of involvement in violent networks]' (Observatório de Favelas 2003: 15). However, there is a discrepancy between the knowledge base gained from Rotas' initial research, which included few female voices, and the practical experience of working with large numbers of girls in mixed-sex groups. In part this disjuncture can be located in the distinct methodologies used to identify participants for the research, who were mainly gang members, and for participation in the project, which included a broader range of participants, not only gang-involved young people, and many self-referred. Consequently, the project itself had an almost equal split of young men and women – far outstripping girls' active roles in drug trafficking networks. Through their active engagement, girls had become key actors, welcoming the space to gain new skills and to reflect on their experiences. Yet in their dissemination material, the call to adequately comprehend young people's experiences was not extended to women's and girls' experiences. For example, the initial research report refers to the importance of masculinity, and the role of a 'sense of virility with regards to the boys' and 'male honour', without exploring the link between these masculinities and norms of femininity. Thus, Rotas' holistic approach falls short in its omission of a discussion of gender issues, gendered group dynamics and female involvement in illicit networks, and this shortcoming is obscured by terms such as 'young people' which belies their primary interest in young men. By failing to adopt a gendered analysis, Rotas and LPP miss the opportunity to explore the mutually constitutive nature of gang masculinities and femininities – such as the cost involved when women involved with gang members fail to conform to submissive models of femininity (Gay 2005).

Girls as assets: countering aggressive masculinities

Project workers from LPP and Rotas discussed several positive outcomes of female involvement in their projects, including an enhanced atmosphere of reflective change. Their active participation also challenged the prevalence of certain norms associated with violent masculinities. For example, Luke suggested that the engagement of young women in the boxing academy had resulted in a change in attitudes and organisational culture that benefited the club as a whole. Although he argued that girls' sporting achievements were the primary consideration, when reflecting on their involvement he commented:

> It has had a secondary effect of helping the aims of the project to work with kids involved in violence and gun violence, because it's about readdressing the social roles of young people. Especially those that young boys fulfil, because they believe that they're supposed to fulfil them because that is what they are taught at street level.

This belief that girls' involvement can counter some of the more destructive elements of hegemonic masculinity, was mirrored in the comments of Andrea Rodrigues, social worker and psychologist, at Rotas:

> The girls make the boys think, so in truth they help us. Apart from this, the girls in the group provide another atmosphere. You know, the young men tend to be more aggressive, swearing, one will be trying to impress the others, so they end up reinforcing the issue of having to rob, but the girls put a stop to this. The boys are ashamed when the girls are there, so they change their stance.

Andrea's comment shows how the gendered socialisation of girls means that, despite the milieu that they are moving in, it is relatively acceptable for them to raise moral issues and question cultural values that prioritise easy money and quick thrills. Andrea maintains that young women act as a counterpoint, arguing with the boys and providing 'the voice of justice', questioning the boys' actions: 'they say, why do you have to kill, why do you have to rob, why don't you get a job?' Moreover, the girls sometimes challenged the sexist and macho ideas more directly than Andrea herself felt able to do, for fear of alienating the young men and thus jeopardising the goals of the project. However, the willingness of girls to conform to the dominant project discourse on violence and crime does not preclude them from expressing different views in and beyond the project. Moreover, girls and young women exert influence on young men in contradictory ways. In the UK, for example, research into youth violence suggests that girls may encourage boys to engage in violent or destructive activities when they feel unable to exert a more positive influence over boys' behaviour (see Firmin 2010). In Maré, a perceived benefit of associating with young men involved in criminality was material gain. As one focus group of young women described, if a girl goes out with a gang member, he will 'buy her everything', but this comes at the cost of knowing that she is never the only girlfriend. The subsequent wish to experience a level of power in relationships where they otherwise feel relatively powerless, counters the dominant gender narrative that girls are more inclined to observe social rules and norms instead of acting in accordance with their own interests and the situation at hand. Girls may also feel the same desire as boys to live for the moment, seeking thrills and excitement when the opportunity arises. Camila (aged 15) describes how she rails against restrictions, such as her mother wanting her to stay in:

> But I want to go out with my girlfriends because, listen, today is the 23rd. I'm not going to have another 23rd [of June] in 2009. It's only going to be this year, you know, I won't be born again. So I want to make the most of every moment.

Alongside acting as a counterpoint to moral norms associated with violent masculinities, a second benefit of the presence of girls in LPP was perceived to be a more open atmosphere, allowing for the discussion of personal and sensitive issues such as parenting, as Luke Dowdney stated:

> Especially when we are talking about teenage pregnancy and that kind of stuff, which was one of the issues that was identified as being key to our work . . . I think that it was important to bring the boys into that as much as anything else, the theme would not have been dealt with the way it has been if we didn't have the girls in the class, so that's been important.

Luke stressed that the girls' presence changed how the boys responded to the topic, but did not question whether girls' and boys' gender needs might be overlooked within a mixed-sex environment, or whether certain issues, such as domestic violence or being left a single parent by gang violence, might require some single-sex discussion to create safe environments for participants to express themselves freely. Gang-related problems experienced by female participants tended to be dealt with in isolation, rather than a structured response being provided. At the time of this research, there were some incipient initiatives to develop partnerships with other organisations – to refer girls for teenage pregnancies for example (Magnavita 2005), and to develop work with Promundo on positive constructions of masculinity (LPP 2009). However, the secondary victimisation effects of male-on-male violence, the complications that arose from girls taking active roles in gang activities, and the silencing effect of gang punishment on hidden forms of gender violence (Wilding and Pearson 2013) were dealt with on a one-to-one reactive basis.

A third perceived benefit of girls' involvement was that they were believed to act as conduits of information to their wider social networks. According to Luke, girls' involvement helped young men to question the negative aspects of the social roles that they were encouraged to fulfil. Andrea went further to claim that girls' engagement in Rotas had a knock-on impact on male relatives and friends, disseminating messages beyond direct participants. The overall suggestion that the presence and participation of young women in violence reduction initiatives might have a positive impact on the attainment of wider project goals of reducing (male) violence is of itself not inherently problematic. However, it raises some important questions about the nature and sustainability of their involvement.

On the one hand, the focus on girls' positive influence is troublesome when considered in the light of how instrumental arguments are often taken up by agencies with alternative agendas. Feminist analysis, for example, has highlighted the links between education and fertility reduction, messages which have been readily adopted by international agencies concerned with population control, not women's equality (Jeffery and Jeffery 1998). Alongside the risk of exploiting women's engagement for alternative goals, an additional danger of instrumental arguments is the fact that they are vulnerable to counter-evidence: if the impact of the girls' involvement proves to be more complicated or costly than reverting to a male-only project design, would their involvement be secured? Would their sporting merit or the girls' personal benefit from participation be sufficient to ensure their continued participation? It is not clear that, if the girls' presence had been less overtly positive or even divisive, they would have been allowed to remain, given the uncertain basis for their inclusion. The fact that their participation is not generally framed in terms of the young women's own rights or needs in the context of violence implies their participation is at least to some extent conditional on their contribution to the goal of reducing male-on-male violence.

On the other hand, this approach raises complex issues about the reliance on models that are attractive to young men involved in gang networks. Gang identity is closely associated in the public imagination with hyper-masculinity, which includes, among other aspects, the association with violence against women (Wilding 2010, 2012). There may therefore be a pragmatic trade-off, attempting to tap into, and not threaten, models of aggressive masculinity, and tolerating certain attitudes so that beneficiaries do not feel alienated or prejudged. Luke's reflection that the gym is a 'male reserve' touches on the tension between playing on the link between masculinity and physical prowess as a means to attract those involved in violence, and channelling aggression in a constructive and controlled environment to lure members away from gangs. Therefore, projects may fear that promoting overtly progressive and alternative models of masculinity might fail to attract the target group of those who are most vulnerable to involvement in violent networks. Seen in this light, Andrea's reluctance to challenge destructive and abusive attitudes can be understood as pragmatic, although also risky in that these masculinities lie at the heart of the cycles of behaviour that they wish to challenge. As Pearce argues, if it is accepted that different forms of violence are interlinked, with violence against women and girls central to the reproduction of all forms of violence, then violence against women cannot be a luxury to be dealt with once more 'serious' forms of violence are addressed (Pearce 2006).

Conclusion: bringing girls as actors into focus

This chapter builds on Risley's argument that the separation of different fields of expertise and intervention, and the failure of gender experts and social-justice advocates to talk to one another, is detrimental to the development of a more holistic and grounded understanding of overlapping forms of violence. The two NGO projects explored here are in many ways exemplary and innovative in the way they attempt to transform the behaviours of their young participants. Although translating new ways of talking into new ways of interacting can be challenging, and the mantra that all violence is wrong is tested by the pressures and tensions of everyday social interaction beyond the learning environment, their holistic approaches – integrating social support, family engagement and informal learning spaces, alongside more targeted activities and skills – were attractive to young people and had positive outcomes (CLAVES 2006). One of the strengths of the projects was that they engaged to an extent with intersecting inequalities – with socio-economic concerns, structural and social stigma around class and race. Although gender concerns were not entirely overlooked, gender was viewed in quite a narrow way, primarily as a link between masculinity and violence. Both projects acknowledged the gendered identities of young men, but there was limited understanding of how the gendered identities of young women influenced their engagement with violence and gangs, or indeed with the projects themselves. In the examples explored here, female participants were welcomed as they were seen to introduce a different set of morals and values and have a moderating effect on boys' behaviour. Considering girls primarily as a means to achieve project aims for men and boys, however, risks sidelining their specific needs and concerns and minimising their potential benefit from involvement. Thus, I argue that what is needed is an approach that goes beyond engaging young people in project management to one that puts gendered power relations at the core, and propose three ways forward for violence prevention initiatives.

First, if projects tackling urban violence are to broaden their understanding of the gendered power dimensions that underlie violence, an important step is to widen the perspective, from one which primarily targets young men as potential actors and victims, to one that also includes girls as primary beneficiaries. While resource constraints should not be underestimated, if gender is considered in the early stages of planning and analysis, this may lead to a different allocation from the start. Moreover, a range of methodologies are needed, some of which might entail separate spaces and others which involve young men and women working together. Spending money on some female-only activities should not mean diverting funds from the primary goal, but has the potential to contribute to the overall success of the project, as well as benefiting girls and women individually. Second, developing partnerships between feminists and urban violence specialists, across the 'gender gap', would open up dialogue and exchange between experts in different areas, and produce innovative approaches that tackle a diversity of issues (Soares and Ilgenfritz 2002; Moura 2007). Finally, a more thorough gender approach should include opening up spaces for male-specific gender issues to be addressed sensitively. After all, it is no use dismantling certain forms of destructive or aggressive masculinities if they are not replaced with alternative models that allow young men 'to conceptualize manhood in more positive and constructive ways' (Gilbert 2006: 361). Alternative narratives need to move beyond traditional hegemonic models of protector and provider if this relies on male competition, aggressiveness and power – models that tend to place women in submissive roles (Froyum 2013). Young men need to be able to articulate the problems they experience with the current models of masculinity and define their own alternatives that do not reproduce gender hierarchies, allowing them to experiment with alternative gendered identities and behaviours.

Recognising the advantages of a more thorough gendered approach for both young men and young women would contribute to a genuinely holistic approach in project design and implementation, tackling intersecting forms of inequality and poverty that provide fertile ground for criminality and violence. Supporting positive shifts in attitudes and understanding and listening carefully to how young men and women express their concerns and their ideas to overcome obstacles is a good place to start.

Notes

1 In the past, research claimed that all of Rio's *favelas* were under the control of one of the city's three rival drugs factions, and the local gangs affiliated to them, but in the last few years there has been an increase in the ousting of gangs by militias, who are made up of off-duty police and other security sector workers, but security in advance of the 2014 World Cup and 2016 Olympics have included the 'pacification' of strategically located *favelas*, by removing the gangs, introducing community policing and social programmes (Jones and Rodgers 2011).
2 I worked with several NGOs, some of which provided education and vocational training, some provided sport and cultural activities, while others acted to supplement formal education for children who were at risk of being excluded. I also worked with two churches and a women's organisation that focused on domestic violence.

References

Caldeira, T. (2000). *City of Walls: Crime, Segregation, and Citizenship in São Paulo.* London: University of California Press.
Cano, I. and Santos, N. (2001). *Violência letal, renda e desigualdade no Brasil.* Rio de Janeiro: 7Letras.
Centro de Estudos e Ações Solidárias da Maré (CEASM) (2004). *Instituições do Bairro Maré: Dados Gerais.* Rio de Janeiro: CEASM.

Centro Latino Americano de Estudos sobre Violência e Saúde (CLAVES) (2006). *Avaliação do Projeto Luta pela Paz-Maré – Rio de Janeiro*. Rio de Janeiro: CLAVES.

Dowdney, L. (2003). *Children of the Drug Trade: A Case Study of Children in Organized Armed Violence in Rio de Janeiro*. Rio de Janeiro: Viveiros de Castro Editora Ltda.

Fernandes, F. (2012). 'Os jovens da *favela*. Reflexões sobre controle e contenção sócio-espacial dos párias urbanos de Rio de Janeiro'. *Revista de Ciencias Sociales*, 19 (59), 159–86.

Firmin, C. (2010). *Female Voice in Violence: Introductory Report*. Phase 1: a cross-regional study on the impact of gangs and serious youth violence on women and girls. London: ROTA.

Froyum, C. (2013). 'Leaving the street alone: contesting street manhood as a gender project'. *Journal of Gender Studies*, 22 (1), 38–53.

Gay, R. (2005). *Lucia: Testimonies of a Brazilian Drug Dealer's Woman*. Philadelphia: Temple University Press.

Gilbert, J. (2006). 'Boys becoming men'. In A. Jones (ed.), *Men of the Global South* (pp. 376–81). London: Zed Books.

Goldstein, D. (2003). *Laughter Out of Place: Race, Class, Violence, and Sexuality in a Rio Shantytown*. London: University of California Press.

Holston, J. (2009). 'Dangerous spaces of citizenship: gang talk, rights talk and rule of law in Brazil'. *Planning Theory*, 8 (1), 12–31.

Htun, M. (2004). 'From "racial democracy" to affirmative action: changing state policy on race in Brazil'. *Latin American Research Review*, 39 (1), 60–89.

Jeffery, P. and Jeffery, R. (1998). 'Silver bullet or passing fancy? Girls' schooling and population policy'. In C. Jackson and R. Pearson (eds), *Feminist Visions of Development: Gender Analysis and Policy* (pp. 235–54). London: Routledge.

Jones, G.A. and Chant, S. (2009). 'Globalising initiatives for gender equality and poverty reduction: exploring "failure" with reference to education and work among urban youth in The Gambia and Ghana'. *Geoforum*, 40 (2), 184–96.

Jones, G. and Rodgers, D. (2011). 'Policy arena: the World Bank's world development report 2011 on conflict, security and development: a critique through five vignettes'. *Journal of International Development*, 23 (7), 980–95.

Leeds, E. (2007). 'Rio de Janeiro'. In K. Koonings and D. Kruijt (eds), *Fractured Cities: Social Exclusion, Urban Violence & Contested Spaces in Latin America* (pp. 23–35). London: Zed Books.

Luta pela Paz (LPP) (2004). *Methodology Manual: Fight for Peace Project*. Rio de Janeiro: Viva Rio.

Luta pela Paz (LPP) (2009). *Luta pela Paz: Relatório 2008/9*. Rio de Janeiro: Luta pela Paz.

Luta pela Paz (LPP) (2010). *Luta pela Paz: Relatório 2009*. Rio de Janeiro: Luta pela Paz.

Mabala, R. (2011). 'Youth and "the hood" – livelihoods and neighbourhoods'. *Environment and Urbanization*, 23 (1), 157–81.

Magnavita, C. (2005). *Projeto 'Ana e Maria' será lançado no Dia Internacional da Mulher*. Available at: www.vivario.org.br/publique/cgi/cgilua.exe/sys/start.htm?infoid=941&sid=16&UserActiveTemplate=_vivario_e n&from_info_index=291.

Moura, T. (2007). *Rostos Invisíveis da Violência Armada: Um estudo de caso sobre o Rio de Janeiro*. Rio de Janeiro: 7 Letras.

Observatório de Favelas (2003, unpublished). *'Rotas de Fuga', Ações integradas para crianças e jovens que trabalham no tráfico de drogas e seus familiares.* Rio de Janeiro: Observatório de Favelas.

Pearce, J. (2006). 'Bringing violence "back home": gender socialisation and the transmission of violence through time and space'. In M. Glasius, M. Kaldor and H. Anheier (eds), *Global Civil Society 2006/7* (pp. 42–62). London: Sage.

Penglase, B. (2009). 'States of insecurity: everyday emergencies, public secrets, and drug trafficker power in a Brazilian *favela*'. *PoLAR: Political and Legal Anthropology Review*, 32 (1), 47–63.

Programa das Nações Unidas para o Desenvolvimento (PNUD) (2005). *Relatório de Desenvovimento Humano: Racismo, Probreza e Violência.* Brasília: PNUD.

Risley, A. (2006). 'Framing violence: Argentina's gender gap'. *International Feminist Journal of Politics*, 8 (4), 581–609.

Soares, B.M. (2002). 'Retrato das Mulheres Presas no Estado do Rio de Janeiro - 1999/2000'. *Boletim Segurança e Cidadania*, 01 (01). Rio de Janeiro: Centro de Estudos de Segurança e Cidadania – CESeC.

Soares, B.M. and Ilgenfritz, I. (2002). *Prisioneiras: vida e violência atrás das grades.* Rio de Janeiro: Garamond.

Souza e Silva, J.d. (2003). 'Adeus, "Cidade Partida"'. *Boletim 'Rio de Janeiro: Trabalho e Sociedade'.* Available at: www.iets.org.br/biblioteca/Adeus_cidade_partida.pdf (accessed 20 August 2007).

Wacquant, L. (2003). 'Toward a dictatorship over the poor? Notes on the penalization of poverty in Brazil'. *Punishment and Society.* 5 (2), 197–205.

Waldherr, G. (2012). 'Fighting the good fight: a Laureus special report'. *Laureus News.* Available at: www.laureus.com/news/fighting-good-fight-laureus-special-report (accessed 19 April 2012).

Wiener, L. (2012). 'Cameron visits Brazil boxing project'. *ITV News.* Available at: www.itv.com/news/story/2012-09-27/david-cameron-in-brazil/ (accessed 28 September 2012).

Wilding, P. (2010). '"New violence": silencing women's experiences in the *favelas* of Brazil'. *Journal of Latin American Studies*, 42 (4), 719–47.

Wilding, P. (2012). *Negotiating Boundaries: Gender, Violence and Transformation in Brazil.* Basingstoke: Palgrave.

Wilding, P. (2014). 'Gendered meanings and everyday experiences of violence in urban Brazil'. *Gender, Place and Culture: A Journal of Feminist Geography*, 21 (2), 228–43.

Wilding, P. and Pearson, R. (2013). 'Gender and violence in Maré, Rio de Janeiro: a tale of two cities?' In L. Peake and M. Rieker (eds), *Rethinking Feminist Interventions into the Urban* (pp. 159–76). London: Routledge.

World Bank (2006). *World Development Report 2007: Development and the Next Generation.* Washington, DC: World Bank.

11 Violent lives and peaceful schools

NGO constructions of modern childhood and the role of the state

Karen Wells

This chapter explores how children have become a central, if not the central, figure of (international) development, and girls the ideal subject of development. It analyses the role of non-governmental organisations (NGOs) and international non-governmental organisations (INGOs) in discursively constructing girls this way. In this construction interventions on gender violence are largely reduced to interventions on access to schooling on the assumption that the integration of girls into a particular kind of modernity will reduce gender-based violence and gender inequality more generally. INGOs and NGOs thereby construe issues of political struggle as technical problems amenable to expert intervention and programming.

There is considerable academic disagreement, largely ideological, about the role of NGOs vis-à-vis civil society and the state (Kamat 2004). The position I adopt in this chapter is that INGOs, regardless of the discourses through which they legitimate themselves, are part of the structure of international governance. Through a discourse analysis of two exemplary texts, Save the Children's *The Future is Now* (2010) and Plan International's *Because I am a Girl: Learning for Life* (2012), I show how NGOs legitimate or establish their right to govern in the Global South through claims about their ability to increase the health and welfare of the population, and I locate education as a technology through which this work gets done. The chapter begins with an account of governmentality theory to establish the theoretical framework of the discourse analysis that follows. After a brief description of the method the chapter turns to elaborating the key themes that emerged from this discourse analysis: development as a concept of the gradual unfolding of immanent potential of both girls and nations; school as a zone of peace in a wider cultural context of presumed violence; and gender equality as an effect of modernity rather than a site of political struggle.

Governmentality, the politics of life and the emergence of rights discourse

Government, as a Foucauldian concept, means something far more than the institutions of political power. The shift from sovereignty to bio-politics, according to Foucault, describes a shift from government as a limited relationship between the sovereign and the populace to government in the wider sense of all those mechanisms and institutions, including school, police, hospitals and prisons, that constitute a field of power (Dean 1999; Inda 2005; Gallagher 2008: 401–2; Foucault 2008). Sovereignty is the power to 'take life or let live'. It is a power of 'deduction'; of taking things away from the population – taxes, land, conscripts – or leaving them alone. Sovereign power waned as liberal government replaced it and, in this new political regime, the power to 'take life or let live' was steadily replaced by the power to 'give life or let die'. No longer was power content to simply take from the populace, rather the population itself became the object of government. The rationale of government is no longer its own self-aggrandisement, materially and symbolically. Instead, the aim of government is to secure the health and welfare of its population or the exercise of power through the giving of life (Foucault 1978: 142).

The objectives of a regulatory government focused on 'the mechanics of life' and on securing increases in the health and welfare of the population are clearly relevant to the modern governing of childhood and, relatedly, of motherhood, in the Global South. Foucault located the emergence of a contemporary rights discourse, one centred on claims about the right to health, happiness and satisfaction of needs to the emergence of a politics of life as the central problem and justification of government (Foucault 1978). In a liberal polity the right of the state to intervene in the lives of citizens is constrained by the legitimating principle of limited government. This constraint however can be set aside if the objective is to secure the expansion of other 'rights' – the right to health and the improvement of welfare. The justification for the expansion of government powers rests on the maxim that *Society Must Be Defended* (Foucault 2003).

The classic focus of human rights claims was to protect subjects from encroachments by the sovereign. In contrast, contemporary human rights claims expand the state's prerogative to rule in the name of securing life. In the frame of liberal bio-politics rights are concerned with health and welfare and this is especially true of children's rights, particularly in the Global South. The expansion of education, which has become a cornerstone of children's rights, is primarily directed towards ensuring the expansion of the health and welfare of the population. The right to education is compulsory not only on governments to provide access to education but on children to be in school. This almost entirely reverses the meaning of rights in the classical sense in that, rather than protect citizens from the reach of the state, it obliges them to subject themselves to the state's authority. The different kinds of injunctions and exhortations in the United Nations Convention on the Rights of the Child (UNCRC), ranging from the right to clean drinking water and nutritious food to the abolition of harmful 'traditional practices', are not the kinds of claims that would be called 'rights' in the classic tradition. Their inclusion in the UNCRC supports Foucault's contention that a politics of life, which is the justification and object of modern liberal government, has become at the same time the site of political struggles.

Childhood is emblematic of the politics of life because of the centrality of development discourse to bio-politics; to deliver increases in health and welfare, to deliver progress, is to develop and childhood is the quintessential site of development. The idea of the child as a gradually unfolding potential, notwithstanding the attempts of childhood studies scholars to disrupt this construction, is deeply embedded in modern European culture (James and James 2004: 142). The project of modern government is one of securing knowledge about the child in order to ensure his or her transformation to a fully mature, healthy, civilised adult. Modern education and health care are shaped by psychologically informed ideas about the unfolding of the child's moral and intellectual potential and the kinds of practices that might block or divert the normal trajectory from immaturity to maturity. The school is perhaps the most important site for the governing of 'the conduct of conduct' of children (Valentine 2010: 26). This not only involves learning subject knowledge but also includes the design of the school, the arrangement of children into age-cohorts and ability groups (Srivastava 1998; Kress and Jewitt 2005), and into school timetables that inculcate in the child the importance of punctuality and regularity (Thompson 1967). Childhood is a particularly powerful site for regulating the conduct of conduct because interventions made on the grounds of being 'in the best interests of the child' are difficult to contest whilst maintaining a claim to moral action. Furthermore compliance with these technologies promises for both children and parents the possibility of a good childhood that has itself become the leitmotif of modernity.

Child-saving or the intervention of the state and other governing agencies (including NGOs) in securing improvements in the health and welfare of the child-population has been a key motif of the governing of childhood from the onset of modern government. In the nineteenth century, when the idea of modern childhood as a period of life deserving of special government protection was first established, there was a racial bifurcation of the governance of childhood. In this period, colonial children, African-Americans in the USA and indigenous children in the settler colonies were excluded from the modern idea of childhood and the special protections it intended to afford to children. NGOs and missionaries were significant actors in forcing colonial governments to extend the norms of the governance of modern childhood to the regulation of childhood in the colonial countries, e.g. Save the Children convened the first international conference on the 'African child' in 1931 (Marshall 2004). The focus of NGO and missionary activity was in the areas of health and education since it is in these spheres that the apparatus of government can be brought to bear on the reshaping of subjectivities and the reformation of cultures in the name of saving bodies and souls. This was then, and remains today, a complex project. As the expansion of primary enrolment shows, parents in developing countries and children themselves are increasingly convinced that children belong in school and that school will be the means through which their future lives will be made easier and more secure.

Analysing INGO texts on gender, violence and schooling

The NGOs included here were selected because they are two of the largest INGOs focusing specifically on children and primarily in developing countries.

Together with CARE International, MSF (Médecins Sans Frontières), Oxfam, World Vision, ACORD (Agency for Cooperation and Research in Development) and the Steering Committee for Humanitarian Response they account for 20 per cent of the entire international NGO sector (Salm 1999: 87). In their focus on childhood they are different from other INGOs who resolve the problem of legitimation through various discourses, e.g. human rights (Oxfam), solidarity with the poor (ActionAid), Christian charity (Christian Aid). INGOs whose focus is children benefit from the exclusion of the figure of 'the child' from political and economic calculation. Saving children by any means necessary is an irrefutable trope that overrides the usual prohibition on the constraints placed on governance by the rule of law and democratic politics. The figure of the child (as opposed to the real lives of real children) represents that permanent state of exception that Agamben (2005) argues state sovereignty is founded on. In order to analyse the work of these two NGOs I chose two reports that are emblematic of their approach. For Plan, their annual survey of girls and development: *State of the World's Girls 2012: Learning for Life* and for Save the Children *The Future is Now*, which is the final evaluation of their campaign linking conflict and violence eradication and prevention and education: *Rewrite the Future*.

The Future is Now is the most lengthy of a series of reports and other outputs from the campaign,[1] and comprises a 70-page report, including five pages of endnotes. It is divided into chapters: overcoming the barriers to education; improving educational quality; schools as sites of conflict or agents of peace; education as an essential emergency response; financing education in conflict-affected fragile states; and conclusion and recommendations.

Learning for Life is the latest 200-page report[2] in a series that Plan publishes each year on different aspects of girls' lives in developing countries, linked to Plan's *Because I am a Girl* campaign. It has a foreword by the UN Women Executive Director and consists of three sections. The first section is a report divided into four chapters and interspersed with case studies. The second section is an update of Plan's cohort study on girl's lives in eight developing countries plus Brazil. The third section consists of reference material including nearly 20 pages of endnotes.

The themes that are discussed in the rest of this chapter emerged out of my coding of the reports. This approach to discourse analysis starts with a deep familiarity with the documents based on repeated reading. I then identified a series of codes from recurring motifs, words and phrases in the report. I had electronic copies of both reports and so was able to highlight words and phrases electronically and then explore the surrounding text in detail. I then organised these codes into groups under a meta-code ('development', 'violence/peace' and 'gender equality') which are the headings of the following sections. I also attended to the silences or absences in the text; the stories or information the reader might expect to find in these reports but which was absent. In thinking about how the school is represented, for example, one might expect some attention to the curriculum or teaching but in fact there is very little said about pedagogy or bodies of knowledge. My analysis of the work that these words and phrases do, as well as their positioning in relation to other parts of the text, figures and images was also informed by the theoretical framework outlined above.

Developing girls and developing countries

In Save the Children's *Rewrite the Future* campaign and Plan International's *Because I am a Girl* campaign, school is axiomatically the space in which children belong and flourish. It is in school that they will learn the habits and aspirations of capitalist modernity. Children quoted in these NGO materials reveal remarkably similar dreams of returning to school and then getting a better life:

> 'Maybe one day when my siblings are a bit older I could go back to school. I would learn and pass all my subjects, and then I could have a better job and a better life. Sometimes, I dream about becoming a teacher or maybe a nurse.' Talent, 14, Zimbabwe.
>
> (Plan International 2012: 12)

In Plan's report a diagram in the scientific genre of an evolutionary chart is used to show how the school will change a girl's future from one in which 'the cycle of poverty continues' (p. 13) to one in which Nargis (the seventh billion child to be born) 'finishes school and gets a good job'. A fuller elaboration of the chart imagines the alternative outcomes for Nargis at each juncture when she either drops out of or continues in school from Early Childhood Care and Development (ECCD) through to secondary school. The Nargis who does not go to school simply 'doesn't learn' she is married off at age 12, and pregnant at age 14. Her life is coloured in grey. In the alternative route, a pink figure progresses along an orange route through primary school and secondary school until she simply 'gets a good job' (p. 13). Leaving aside the simple-mindedness of the claim that school qualifications lead inexorably to a better life, materially or otherwise, Plan's use of the science communication genre of diagrammatic representation of evolutionary development is indicative of the prevalence of a discourse of development in NGO representations. This is a kind of double discourse, where development refers to both the developing child and the developing country.

Plan's 2012 report, *Learning for Life*, focuses on adolescents, recognising that whilst the MDG 2 (full universal primary school enrolment) has led to significant increases in expanding school enrolment, once children, and particularly girls, reach adolescence they and their families are less likely to see school as the best use of children's time and effort. Centres for ECCD extend the reach of governance into the lives of children and their families. The discourse supporting this has increasingly relied on scientific claims about how early children's brains are 'hard-wired' and how important early intervention is to ensure that neurological development happens before the child's brain loses its plasticity. Despite the complexity of neurological science, these claims about brain development have already become part of development (child development and economic development discourse) and it is asserted that the failure of early intervention will reduce children's capacity to learn and progress intellectually and in a range of psycho-social or 'non-cognitive' skills as they grow up (Dercon and Sanchez 2011).

Plan's *Learning for Life* report extends the scientific claims about development to teenagers. Through a scientific discourse of knowledge about adolescent development, unsupported by any references to research, Plan insists that school is where adolescents 'ought to be' (p. 17). In a section of the report title 'from child to married woman overnight' Plan explains that:

> Adolescence is a life-cycle period whereby children are learning to think abstractly and better able to connect values to actions and actions to consequences. It is a period of physical, emotional, psychological and cognitive development during which experimentation and risk-taking are both normal and a fundamental part of developing decision-making skills.
>
> (p. 22)

It is unclear what the 'experimentation' and 'risk-taking' are that are a 'fundamental part of developing decision-making skills' or how adolescent girls who are out of school are denied the scope for either. Nor is it clear why experimentation and risk-taking will be experienced by girls through staying in school. Is it that school is the experiment here and that risk-taking is the risk of staying in school and defying traditional expectations? The report continues:

> However, these experiences are denied to girls in rural Pakistan who change, almost overnight, from being 'children' with extremely limited access to information relating to sexual reproductive health to being married women with all the responsibilities that entails.
>
> (p. 22)

It seems then that the experimentation and risk-taking refer partly to sexuality and partly to a broader idea of an ideal human subjectivity that is flexible, adaptable and innovative. This analysis is supported by the statement that education 'helps promote the awareness, independence and understanding of participation necessary for a citizen' (p. 22).

In addition to scientific discourses about the normally developing brain and its needs, justification for the claim that school is axiomatic of a good childhood is made through the citing of statistics about the impact of education on girls' future lives. However, as so often with NGO sources, the evidence for these claims is circular; the sources cited to verify them are themselves from Save or Plan's own research, much of it unpublished internal documents, and that of other NGOs and UN agencies. Although on occasion these kinds of evidential support for NGOs educational policy have been adjusted for the effect of class on outcomes, given that entry into secondary school education remains a middle-class attainment across the developing world it is not clear how reliable these adjustments can be. The statistics are used, along with vignettes or case studies of girls' experiences, to establish the importance of education to securing the future health and welfare of girls. School is what will enable adolescent girls to:

> obtain skills . . . earn more income in the future, marry later, and have fewer, and healthier, children. In the longer term, secondary education protects girls against HIV and AIDS, sexual harassment and human trafficking. In short, secondary education, in combination with financial assets and life skills, is essential for adolescent empowerment, development and protection.
>
> (Plan International 2012: 22)

This is an extraordinary paragraph which in two sentences gathers together all the current tropes about developing countries (HIV/AIDS, sexual harassment, human trafficking) as sites of disease and violence and the tropes about the development project (empowerment, development, protection) as the foundation of human liberation and distributes them according to whether girls stay in or leave school.

Plan recognises that as children transition to adulthood, their families and wider social recognition demand more of their time and that they learn new skills and bodies of knowledge commensurate with emerging adulthood. Clearly, for Plan this is a problem because school is the site which children need to grow up in to learn gender equality, non-violence and the management of reproductive and physical health. In *Learning for Life*, adolescence is the mechanism through which successful transitions to adulthood are accomplished.

In these reports and other materials produced in support of these campaigns, the site of the school itself is curiously empty. There is little or no sense of what goes on in the school in relation to curriculum, pedagogy, qualifications and the acquisition of knowledge and skills. In place of any account of the space, time and pedagogy of the classroom, both Save and Plan use visual evidence of children's enjoyment and engagement with learning. There are key tropes deployed in these photographs and four themes are predominant: children concentrating, children writing, children laughing, and children raising their hands. In these last images the significance of this gesture is instantly recognisable to anyone who has been a teacher or a student. It is perhaps one of the most simple gestures that reveal the pedagogical space of the classroom as one in which knowledge is distributed, digested and returned as evidence of learning. There is no space here for anything resembling a critical, discursive pedagogy. These images are clearly intended to convey the pleasure that children take in learning within the school and the incontrovertible connection between being in school and having a good childhood or, indeed, a recognisable childhood. These images suggest the significance of the school as a site in which childhood is regularised and globalised. But more than that the absence of any content to the learning that goes on in school also suggests that the NGO interest in schools is as a site of governance, a site for the regulation of childhood through the inculcation of particular norms and dispositions concurrent with the reformation of subjectivity, which returns to the problem of developing countries as spaces saturated with risk and violence.

Violent lives and peaceful schools

If development of the child and their potential and the linking of this to economic development is one key theme in NGO discourse on schools, a second key theme is that school is the space within which children will learn how to become peaceful, tolerant people. Numerous references are made in reports and campaign summaries to how children learn in school to resolve conflict through discussion and are tolerant of differences. School is offered as the site in which conflicts outside the classroom are left at the door and children enter a new space in which dialogue and goodwill flourish. The images of children sitting at their desks laughing similarly convey the same message of school as a site insulated from wider conflicts and violence.

Save the Children's *Rewrite the Future: Three Years On* is a short evaluation of the campaign, which illustrates well this discourse of the wider space of society and culture as a space of unremitting violence which can only be interrupted by the school as an insulated space and education as a redemption from the violence of tradition. In the following quote, the authors' citation of a respondent illustrates very effectively the symbolic violence of the circulation of a discourse of inadequacy between INGOs and the children involved in their projects:

> In the beginning, especially in the south, we weren't educated . . . people just went to the bush and fought. But now we are in school. Without education we would still be in the bush.
>
> (Save the Children 2009: 7)

Similarly in *The Future is Now*, Save identifies education as necessary to return countries to peace, 'Without education . . . countries remain on the brink of returning to conflict' (2010: 30). *Rewrite the Future*'s campaign and its various reports are premised on the claim that education reduces violence and teaches people how to resolve conflict by non-violent means. The very title of the campaign suggests that without school education the future will be a simple projection forward, a repetition of the predictable and atavistic space of the present. Teacher training should focus on showing teachers how to 'help children solve problems through discussion and negotiation rather than through violence' (2010: 20). The school is represented as a kind of alchemical space in which adults' and children's experience of violence in conflict and fragile states 'can be used – with mutual trust and respect – to transform lives and build peace' (2010: 20) In contrast to the space of violence outside of the school, school is 'protective – safeguarding children from exploitation, abuse, violence and conflict' (2010: 18).

In Plan's report the role of school in reducing violence is discussed in a case study entitled 'The Protective Role of Education' and presented as 'primary research' by the Institute of Education. The academic credibility of the inset is established in the opening paragraphs by the reference to the Institute of Education and the citation of research, including research by Plan, showing that girls are exposed to violence on the way to school, at school and because of being educated. It also notes the limits to the protection against violence that school provides. Having established the credibility of its claims through this balanced approach, it then says '[n]ot only are women who are educated to secondary level or higher less likely their non-educated or primary-educated counterparts to experience violence, but men who are educated to [these levels] are less likely than their non-educated or primary-educated counterparts to perpetuate violence' (2012: 100). These are not proxies for class or employment: 'the data suggests that secondary education has a bigger impact on gender-based violence than . . . [does] high family wealth or female employment' (2012: 100). Why? Because 'Education seems to shift attitudes, and cycles of violence can be broken as women become more likely to report it, or to join together to fight against gender-based violence and to campaign for progressive laws' (2012: 101).

Within this text are two tables correlating experience of violence to primary and secondary education in 14 selected countries for ever-married women aged 15–49. However, in eight of these 14 countries women's experience of violence by *men's* education level is lower for no education than for primary education (Cambodia, Ghana, Liberia, Nigeria, Tanzania, Uganda, Zambia and Zimbabwe). This evident contradiction between levels of education and protection against violence is simply elided by the supporting text which says: 'For men in most countries, continuing schooling beyond the primary level decreases the risk of committing violence' (2012: 101). A more accurate recounting of the two tables would note that in many countries women experience less domestic violence if they and their husbands have no education. This is the case in Liberia, Malawi, Nigeria and Uganda where, according to the statistics cited in the report, women's experience of violence is also lower when their husbands have no education than when they have secondary education. When experience of violence is correlated to women's level of education, the percentage of women who have ever experienced violence is lower for no education than for primary educated in Ghana, Malawi, Nigeria, Philippines, Rwanda, Tanzania, Uganda and Zambia; and lower than secondary educated in Liberia, Malawi, Nigeria and Zambia. The table does not then, in fact, support a simple correlation between education and the diminishment of violence against women and girls. The case study also excludes Latin American countries, in which, as noted elsewhere in *Learning for Life*, gender parity in secondary education has been achieved and girls often do better at school than boys do, and yet violence against women has not reduced. Other research suggests that education, age and marital status do not account for the difference in levels of intimate partner violence that women are subjected to and that the key difference in prevalence and severity is between rural and industrialised areas (Garcia-Moreno *et al.* 2006: 1267).

So, the report correlates school enrolment to reduction in violence, not entirely accurately but also without any explanatory elaboration of why school education might or should lead to reductions in violence; like the idea of a good childhood being a schooled childhood, it is taken as axiomatic that school education is where people learn to be tolerant and non-violent and are protected from the violence space outside of school. The idea that school education and, particularly the acquisition of literacy, makes people less violent and more co-operative and tolerant of difference can be traced to modernisation theory and, prior to that, to the denigration of oral cultures in the colonial period. It points to the role of schooling and the learning of literacy as a 'moral technology' in the Foucauldian sense. Literacy is not simply the learning of the technical skills of reading and writing but also, as the 'new literacy studies' argue, a practice through which (new) cultural models about the self are inscribed (Street 1995: 141).

Notwithstanding this discursive construction of school as a site of non-violence, school has, as NGOs paradoxically acknowledge, become another site in which children experience violence from their peers and their teachers. Save the Children acknowledges that teachers often use violent methods of discipline in the classroom and Plan acknowledges that sexual harassment and sexual violence by teachers against girls is almost commonplace. Plan cites sexual harassment as one reason why girls leave school early (2012:11, 14) and it notes that teachers are themselves the perpetrators of violence, including sexual harassment and sexual violence against students (boys and girls, although there is little discussion of teacher sexual violence against boys) (2012: 15). It recognises that 'gender-based violence' in school limits girls' access to education (2012: 41, and in more detail pp. 53–4). This disrupts the idea of the school as a zone of peace, the location of modernity and therefore of rationality and discourse. This disruption is managed by attributing the violence in schools to the breaching of the school's boundaries by the culture in which it squats. Violence is not an effect of school itself but is 'driven by deeply entrenched cultural beliefs and attitudes towards children' (2012: 53). This containment of the cause of violence being rooted in cultural attitudes protects the discourse of school itself as a site of peace and a refuge from violence.

Similarly, in Save's report, the chapter on schools as 'sites of conflict or agents of peace' essentially attributes the former (school as a site of conflict) to the incorporation of local political discourses into the school and the latter with the insulation of schools from these discourses. It notes that 'in countries affected by conflict, the national curriculum can become particularly politicised' and yet on the same page that 'the curriculum can be used to promote peace . . . curricula for primary schools [to achieve this] . . . would include human rights, humanitarian law, citizenship and life skills' (2010: 26). This juxtaposition of local politics to global rights entirely erases both the political struggles that generated those rights and that modes of citizenship, and the promotion of peace, are themselves political issues.

Gender equality

Central to the discourse on education as a moral technology is the assertion that it both instantiates gender equality in the classroom and erodes gendered inequalities in the wider society and culture. Although Plan acknowledges in some places that, for example, 'education does not operate in a vacuum and, even if children's education rights can be secured, it does not necessarily follow that wider social change will result' (2012: 26), this caveat is effectively erased by repeated references to the school as a site in which gender equality can be learned and which will 'empower' girls. Early childhood education, for example, will ensure that 'boys and girls grew up with the same values and opportunities' (Plan International 2012: 9).

Indeed, girls are identified as the ideal subject of development in the Plan report. This is much less explicit in *The Future is Now* because of its focus on barriers to school attendance arising from conflict rather than underdevelopment. In *State of the World's Girls*, girls are unencumbered by the benefits of gender inequality that accrue to boys and by the habituation to subjugation that is the lot of adult women who do not resist the transformative potential of education:

> The impact of education can extend beyond the girls who actually get the education. What these girls go on to do, what they achieve, and the example they set, could change attitudes about the roles of women and girls in society over time. As girls become more educated and enter the workforce, families and social structures can become reconfigured and gender roles may shift.
>
> (Plan 2012: 118)

This assumption that through specific approaches to education NGOs can use the school to instantiate gender equality and eradicate gender-based violence has been found in other analyses of NGO work on gender and education (Stromquist 2002; Murphy-Graham 2008; Sharma 2008; Stromquist and Fischman 2009; Dejaeghere and Wiger 2013; Parkes *et al.* 2013). In the name of gender equality girls are represented as blank slates who accept the new inscription of gender relations that NGOs instruct them in. Deeper cultural and indeed political questions about the logics of gender, about what it means to be in transition to a socially recognised gendered adulthood in any specific social and cultural context are bracketed out of the discourse of school as the site for the inculcation of gender equality.

Here again, local cultural practices are entirely set aside. Indeed no recognition is given to the fact that in all cultures there are practices, including the acquisition of knowledge and skills – technical and cultural – that mark and make possible the transition to a socially recognised and gendered adulthood. If individuals are to transgress the borders of local gendered practices/subjectivities this is likely to involve them in conflicts and contestations, sometimes violently so. Deep shifts in gendered identities that challenge hegemonic masculinities and femininities and the sexualities that mark them cannot be accomplished by fiat but require sustained cultural political struggle. None of this is addressed in NGO campaigns.

In development representations in general the absence of boys and men, particularly in representations of Africa, is very noticeable. In these education campaigns in conflict and post-conflict states this elision is even more striking because of the contradiction between insisting on the school as a place in which tolerance and non-violence is learned and the exclusion of boys from the discourse on these beneficial impacts of education. In the Plan report there are a few references to sexual violence/sexual harassment of boys in school by teachers and others. Given the general silence about boys' subjection to sexual violence, the figures cited in Plan's report are surprisingly high, with 73 million boys under 18 experiencing forced sexual intercourse according to the World Health Organization's *World Report on Violence and Health* (2002) – this compares to 150 million girls (Plan International 2012: 53). What is more puzzling is that there is no discussion in the document of how this is to be confronted. Indeed, throughout these documents there is a gap between the clear representation of school as a moral technology in which girls learn how to be better people and the almost total erasure of boys from the space of the classroom. The only discussion of boys in classrooms points to their disaffection from education and their disruption of girls' learning (p. 92). If girls are the ideal subject of development this is partly because they are represented as the mothers of the next generation who will raise their children in more egalitarian ways. The pathways of normative masculinity are not thought to be as damaging to boys as they are to girls. Girls become responsible for protecting themselves from sexual aggression rather than boys being held responsible for their own violence.

The lack of attention to boys in the 2012 report also glosses over boys' lack of social power, despite the widespread recognition that civil wars in sub-Saharan African (e.g. in Sierra Leone and Liberia) were partly reactions of boys or 'junior' men to their exclusion from access to land and other economic resources. Plan's 2011 report, *What about Boys?*, is one of the few reports that focused on the role of boys in the struggle for gender equality. In this report boys and men are often spoken about together, as if the benefits that accrue to men from normative gender regimes accrue equally to boys. There is very little discussion of the violence that boys face at the hands of men (and also often of women) as they are inducted into heteronormative gender regimes. Furthermore, one of the main discourses that the 2011 report deploys is that gender equality and ending violence against girls and women by boys and men involves redefining what it means to be a 'real man', e.g. it reports on an Indian community campaign which uses the slogan 'Real Man Thinks Right' (2011: 17). Elsewhere it cites the comment of a participant that a man is not 'a real man – if he beats women up' (2011: 89, see also p. 123 for the same view from young men in a Balkans study). In this discourse, the underlying gender regime still persists, however it is simply that new tasks get inscribed into the discourse of the 'real man'

The involvement of NGOs in transforming gender in schools aims to change the character of the school as a state apparatus endowing it with radical potential. From a Foucauldian perspective this view misunderstands the fundamental character of contemporary government, that is, as I have argued above, about expanding the right to govern in the name of increasing the health and welfare of the population. It is to this end that schools may expand the scope for a specific type of gender equality, one that is co-present with the expansion of capitalism and a liberal sense of the (gendered self) as radically individual, independent, rational and autonomous; in short with a model of gender that meshes with, indeed forms part of, the reformation of human subjectivity towards the liberal self-governing subject. Whether such a reformation is understood as being liberatory in a broader sense obviously depends on the analysis of the project of expanding capitalist modernity that is at the heart of development.

Conclusion

Childhood is the site on and through which development interventions inscribe new practices, dispositions and attitudes, in short, new subjectivities, that are compatible with the exercise of liberal governmentality, and girls are often the exemplary figure of these interventions. They do this through rationalities and techniques of government that separate out the political from the economic and developmental. *Rewrite the Future* is a campaign to address the education of children in conflict and fragile states, it is inherently a political campaign; *Learning for Life* is a project to expand school education from early years through to young adulthood and to expand opportunities for girls. It is necessarily political. Both campaigns make demands of governments and other agencies. Their right to make these interventions, to press demands on government, is not congruent with the architecture of liberal governance which insists that it rules by and for the people. NGOs do not rest their right to govern childhood on democratic politics but instead on their expertise, their scientific assessment of need and their evidence on the impacts of their interventions. That development means capitalist development and that capitalism is an inescapably unequal regime is never addressed; and in fact is misrepresented through the emphasis placed on the ability of modernity to deliver gender equality while ignoring the persistence of class inequality.

In the discourse analysis presented in this chapter I have shown how scientific discourses of development are used to map the idea of normal adolescent development onto normal economic development, naturalising the idea of capitalist modernity as it does so. In this discourse the school and its technologies are identified as a site of protection so long as it can be separated from the wider cultural context in which it squats. Furthermore, school is understood as a site that teaches tolerance and peaceful co-existence and enables gender equality in contrast to the atavistic and violent cultures that surround it. This discursive construction of the school as a zone of safety and a kind of incubator of modernity is problematic for many reasons, not least because it offers a technical fix to what is essentially a political problem. Political problems, such as violence against girls, require political solutions that involve an understanding of the local and national power dynamics within which violence occurs and is legitimated.

Notes

1 www.savethechildren.org.uk/about-us/what-we-do/education/rewrite-the-future.
2 http://plan-international.org/about-plan/resources/publications/campaigns/
because-i-am-a-girl-learning-for-life-2012/.

References

Agamben, G. (2005). *State of Exception*. Chicago: University of Chicago Press.

Dean, M. (1999). *Governmentality: Power and Rule in Modern Society*. London: Sage.

Dejaeghere, J. and Wiger, N. (2013). 'Gender discourses in an NGO education project: openings toward gender equality in Bangladesh'. *International Journal of Educational Development*, 33 (6), 557–65.

Dercon, S. and Sanchez, A. (2011). *Long-Term Implications of Under-Nutrition on Psychosocial Competencies: Evidence From Four Developing Countries*. Oxford: Young Lives.

Foucault, M. (1978). *The History of Sexuality*. London: Penguin.

Foucault, M. (2003). *Society Must Be Defended: Lectures at the College de France, 1975–76*. New York: Picador.

Foucault, M. (2008). *The Birth of Biopolitics: Lectures at the College de France, 1978–79*. Basingstoke and New York: Palgrave Macmillan.

Gallagher, M. (2008). 'Foucault, power and participation'. *International Journal of Children's Rights*, 16 (3), 395–406.

Garcia-Moreno, C., Jansen, H., Ellsberg, M., Heisse, L. and Watts, C. (2006). 'Prevalence of intimate partner violence: findings from the WHO multi-country study on women's health and domestic violence'. *The Lancet*, 368, 1260–9.

Inda, J. (2005). 'Analytics of the modern: an introduction'. In *Anthropologies of Modernity: Foucault, Governmentality, and Life Politics* (pp. 1–22). Malden: Blackwell.

James, A. and James, A. (eds) (2004). *Constructing Childhood: Theory, Policy, and Social Practice*. Basingstoke: Palgrave Macmillan.

Kamat, S. (2004). 'The privatization of public interest: theorizing NGO discourse in a neoliberal era'. *Review of International Political Economy*, 11 (1), 155–76.

Kress, G. and Jewitt, C. (2005). *Urban Classrooms, Subject English: Multimodal Perspectives on Teaching and Learning*. London: RoutledgeFalmer.

Marshall, D. (2004). 'Children's rights in imperial political cultures: missionary and humanitarian contributions to the Conference on the African Child of 1931'. *The International Journal of Children's Rights*, 12 (3), 273–318.

Murphy-Graham, E. (2008). 'Opening the black box: women's empowerment and innovative secondary education in Honduras'. *Gender and Education*, 20 (1), 31–50.

Parkes, J., Heslop, J., Oando, S., Sabaa, S., Januario, F. and Figue, A. (2013). 'Conceptualizing gender and violence in research: insights from studies in schools and communities in Kenya, Ghana and Mozambique'. *International Journal of Educational Development*, 33 (6), 546–56.

Plan International (2011) *Because I am a Girl: The State of the World's Girls 2011 – So, what about Boys?* Available at: http://plan-international.org/about-plan/resources/publications/campaigns/because-i-am-a-girl-so-what-about-boys/.

Plan International (2012). *Because I am a Girl: The State of the World's Girls 2012: Learning for Life*. London: Plan UK. Available at: https://plan-international.org/about-plan/resources/publications/campaigns/because-i-am-a-girl-learning-for-life-2012.

Salm, J. (1999). 'Coping with globalization: a profile of the northern NGO sector'. *Nonprofit and Voluntary Sector Quarterly*, 28 (4), 87–103.

Save the Children (2009). *Rewrite the Future: Three Years On*. London: Save the Children. Available at: www.savethechildren.org.uk/resources/online-library/rewrite-the-future—-three-years-on.

Save the Children (2010). *The Future is Now: Education for Children in Countries affected by Conflict.* London: Save the Children. Available at: www. savethechildren.org.uk/resources/online-library/the-future-is-now-education-for-children-in-countries-affected-by-conflict.

Sharma, A. (2008). *Logics of Empowerment: Development, Gender, and Governance in Neoliberal India.* Minneapolis: University of Minnesota Press.

Srivastava, S. (1998). *Constructing Post-Colonial India: National Character and the Doon School.* New York: Routledge.

Street, B. (1995). *Social Literacies: Critical Approaches to Literacy in Development, Ethnography, and Education.* London and New York: Longman.

Stromquist, N. (2002). 'Education as a means of empowering women'. In A. Papart, S. Rai and K. Stadut (eds). *Rethinking Empowerment: Gender and Development in a Global/Local World.* London: Routledge.

Stromquist, N. and Fischman, G. (2009). 'Introduction – from denouncing gender inequities to undoing gender in education: practices and programmes toward change in the social relations of gender'. *International Review of Education*, 55 (5–6), 463–82.

Thompson, E. (1967). 'Time, work-discipline and industrial capitalism'. *Past and Present*, 38, 56–97.

Valentine, G. (2004). *Public Space and the Culture of Childhood.* Aldershot: Ashgate.

Wells, K. (2009). *Childhood in a Global Perspective.* Cambridge and Malden: Polity Press.

World Health Organization (2002) *World Report on Violence and Health.* Geneva: WHO.

12 Gender violence, teenage pregnancy and gender equity policy in South Africa

Privileging the voices of women and girls through participatory visual methods

Relebohile Moletsane, Claudia Mitchell and Thandi Lewin

This chapter reflects on two 'epidemics' – gender violence and teenage pregnancy in South Africa – and asks why, despite the impressive rhetoric of change in the country's educational and gender policies, children continue to experience the negative effects of gender inequality in the country. In so doing, we seek to contribute to deepening understanding of ways of moving from policy rhetoric to action. We begin by mapping the issues concerning gender violence and teenage pregnancy in South Africa. This allows us to offer a critical analysis of the legislative and policy framework in the context of various socio-economic barriers to building gender equitable schools. Drawing on our research with girls and women, we suggest ways in which participatory visual methodologies can contribute, not only to understanding the links between gender violence, teenage pregnancy and other manifestations of gender inequality, but also to developing relevant policy interventions.

South Africa is a particularly interesting site to explore these issues since it has a strong commitment to gender equality in political, social and economic life. It is signatory to several regional and global treaties and policy frameworks targeting gender inequality in all spheres of life, including global frameworks such as the Millennium Development Goals (MDGs), the Convention on the Elimination of all Forms of Discrimination against Women (CEDAW) and the Beijing Platform for Action (BPFA),[1] as well as African agreements such as the Southern African Development Community (SADC) Protocol on Gender and Development and the African Union (AU) Second Decade of Action of Education. Guided by principles of the Constitution, with its commitment to equity and human rights, South Africa has developed a strong policy framework for gender equality in education. Yet while the country has made huge strides in enrolling girls in primary education, and has high gender parity indexes at all educational levels, the poor quality of their educational experiences remains an area requiring attention. One of the most pervasive reasons for the poor participation and low success of girls in the schooling system is gender inequality, and in particular, its manifestations in violence against girls and women, and the consequent problems, including high rates of teenage pregnancy and HIV infections. The Human Rights Watch report, *Scared at School* (2001), documented high levels of sexual violence in South African schools. More than a decade later, reports of gender violence in the country and its institutions abound.

Gender violence in South Africa

Amongst the various definitions of gender violence is the Women's Refugee Commission's (2009: 3) conceptualisation as:

> any harm enacted against a person's will that is the result of power imbalances that exploit distinctions between males and females. Violence may be physical, sexual, psychological, economic or socio-cultural. It may be perpetrated in private or public settings. GBV principally affects women and girls. It takes many forms, including sexual abuse, domestic violence, legal discrimination, exploitation, early or forced marriage and female genital mutilation.

South Africa has one of the highest rates of sexual violence in the world (Adar and Stevens 2000), with much of this violence against girls under the age of 18, most of whom are in school (Petersen *et al.* 2005). Studies have found that between 39 per cent (loveLife, cited in CADRE 2003) and 66 per cent (Jewkes *et al.* 2001) of adolescent girls had experienced forced sex. A two-province community-based survey found that 27.6 per cent of men who were interviewed admitted to having committed rape at least once in their lives (Jewkes *et al.* 2009b). A national survey found that while 98 per cent of young men reported that the first time they had sex they did so willingly, only 29 per cent of the young women reported their first sexual encounter as consensual (Pettifor *et al.* 2004). Similarly, in Hallman's (2004) study of poverty and unsafe sexual behaviours among young women and men in South Africa, 55 per cent of the women (compared to 94 per cent of the men) reported that their first sexual encounter was consensual.

Of particular relevance to the education system are findings suggesting that most perpetrators and victims are teenagers. For example, Jewkes *et al.* (2011) found that 75 per cent of men who rape do so as teenagers and that intimate partner violence commonly occurs among teenagers. While the South African Schools Act of 1996 prohibits all forms and origins of violence in schools, a number of studies report that many forms of violence are pervasive in and around schools, including corporal punishment, bullying, assault, and rape, gun violence, stabbings, and other forms of physical and emotional violence. The *General Household Survey 2010* reported that 16.8 per cent of learners experienced corporal punishment, while 15.7 per cent reported being threatened with a weapon, and 27 per cent felt unsafe in school (Statistics South Africa 2011). Morrell (2001) observes that physical punishment can be used to assert teachers' (often male) control over boys who are seen as rivals by adult male teachers. Another recent report on violence in South African schools found that sexual harassment and violence against girls were rampant, with toilets commonly the sites of violence perpetrated by boys against girls (Mncube and Harber 2013).

For many learners, the consequences of violence generally and gender violence in particular on schooling and schooling outcomes are dire. Such violence negatively impacts on girls' learning and attendance, leading to absenteeism, diminished school performance and dropout, as well as health-related outcomes including sexually transmitted infections and unwanted pregnancies (Mncube and Harber 2013: 86).

Teenage pregnancy

In the face of these exceedingly high rates of sexual violence against girls, the links between such physical violence and teenage pregnancy cannot be underestimated, with both having their roots in unequal gender relations. In this regard, Jewkes *et al.* (2009a: 675) contend that 'girls' subordinate position in the gender and social hierarchy constrains their ability to make real choices around pregnancy'. Teenage pregnancy amongst schoolgirls has been a focus of sustained media attention in South Africa in recent years, perhaps because, while the country has the lowest rates of teen fertility in Africa, it has high rates compared to the developed world (Panday *et al.* 2009). The *General Household Survey 2011* found that 4.5 per cent of South African girls aged between 13 and 19 were pregnant; 2 per cent of those aged between seven and 24 who were not attending any educational institution blamed this on pregnancy (Statistics South Africa 2012). Pregnancy rates vary by race, socio-economic status, geography and education (Jewkes *et al.* 2009b), with, according to a study of teenage pregnancy in a South African township, most pregnancies occurring among poor black and coloured[2] teenagers, who report unplanned and unwanted pregnancies as well as unstable relationships in which such pregnancies occur (Mkhwanazi 2010).

Reasons for adolescent pregnancy are multiple and varied (Mchunu *et al.* 2012), and include a sense of male entitlement (Mncube and Harber 2013: 104), 'grade repetition and temporary withdrawals from school' (Grant and Hallman 2008) and social and cultural norms (Mkhwanazi 2010). Once pregnant, most girls tend to drop out of school and even fewer return to school after giving birth. For example, in the KwaZulu-Natal Transition study, Grant and Hallman (2008) found that 74 per cent of girls aged 14–19 years dropped out of school at the time of pregnancy and only 29 per cent returned after giving birth. Their research also suggests that the longer such girls stay out of school after pregnancy, the less likely they are to return to school. They assert that girls who lack social support in their homes and are the primary caregivers for their babies are less likely to return to school.

Policy responses to gender violence and teenage pregnancy

These issues relating to gender violence and teenage pregnancy have long been concerns for policy-makers in South Africa. Since 1994 and the demise of apartheid, South Africa has made significant progress in relation to gender equality in the country's socio-cultural institutions, including schools, partly as an outcome of its intent to address historical inequalities (including gender and race) and its democratic and gender-sensitive policy frameworks. It established a National Gender Machinery aimed at interpreting and localising the various global and regional treaties and protocols of the post-Cold War and post-apartheid era. Through the *National Policy Framework for Women's Empowerment and Gender Equality* (2000), the government set up an extensive network of 'gender focal points' – in other words, units focusing on gender in all government departments. In relation to education, supported by recommendations made in the earlier *Gender Equity Task Team Report* (National Department of Education 1997), each provincial education department was to have a dedicated staff member or members responsible for gender equity issues in the province. At the national level, the then Department of Education[3] established a Gender Equity Directorate (GED) in 2000, tasked with monitoring and coordinating activities and policy development across the system. While gender activists and scholars lauded this government initiative, unfortunately, in 2009, the GED was scrapped and its work integrated into a new directorate: Social Cohesion and Equity in Education. Similarly, at national level, partly in response to criticism from various sectors about the poor performance of both the National Gender Machinery in government and the network of gender focal points (Gouws 2006), in 2009 the new Ministry for Women, Children and Persons with Disabilities was established. However, for many gender and feminist scholars and activists, this was seen as a backlash and a step backward against some of the major strides that had already been made towards gender equality. After the 2014 elections, this Ministry was replaced by a Ministry of Women in the Presidency.

Issues relating to gender inequity and violence have been given prominence in education policies associated with the South African Schools Act (1997). These have included: infrastructural development to improve sanitation and safety in schools; peer education programmes to enable young people to tackle exclusionary practices and learn gender responsive and value-driven behaviour; training, guidelines and support materials for teachers and education officials to identify and respond to gender equity-related problems in schools; and advocacy work to support policy implementation (see for example, Department of Education 2001a; Department of Basic Education 2010; Moletsane 2010). Programmes that protect girls from violence and support their right to education regardless of motherhood status or pregnancy (such as school-based girls' clubs) have been developed, as part of the broad approach of government to address gender equality in all aspects of social life.

In spite of these laudable policies and programmes gender inequality and its manifestations in gender violence and teenage pregnancy in and around schools continue to pose challenges. Reasons for this are complex and varied. First, as Dieltiens *et al.* (2009) note, some of the policies are gender blind or view gender equity as merely about parity between the sexes. The emphasis has been on increasing the number of girls who enrol in school, while neglecting ensuring that the environment in which learning occurs is free of the various socio-cultural barriers such as gender violence. This is evident also in the higher education sector, where gender parity in the participation of women as undergraduate students has been taken to represent an achievement of gender equality overall (Department of Education 2001b). Second, there is evidence of a mismatch between policy intent and policy implementation in a range of ways. This manifests both in a lack of understanding of policies on gender-based violence and gender equality, but also in uneven and inadequate institutional and systemic responses to violence and abuse. A recent report on sexual violence perpetrated by teachers in South African schools shows that systemic problems in enforcing policy result in a lack of accountability on the part of teachers who commit abuse and therefore creates an environment in which abuse can continue (Centre for Applied Legal Studies and Avon Global Center for Women and Justice 2014).

Sometimes it is the laws themselves that generate confusion. For example, sections 15 and 16 of the Criminal Law (Sexual Offences and Related Matters) Amendment Act 32 (2007) made it a criminal offence for adolescents between the ages of 12 and 15 to engage in 'certain consensual sexual activities' (Perumal 2013: 107) and for adults (teachers, doctors, etc.) who are aware of such activities but fail to report them. After much criticism from legal experts, feminist scholars and activists about the damaging impacts of this law on children, who may fear reporting gender violence due to the stigma of a criminal record, the Constitutional Court has recently moved towards repealing the Act. As Lou Haysom (2013: 2) reports:

> On 3rd October 2013, the Constitutional Court . . . unanimously declared sections 15 and 16 of the Sexual Offences Act unconstitutional . . . Adolescents who have been convicted in terms of the defective sections will have their criminal records expunged. The judgment is widely regarded as a breakthrough particularly for girls who have been significantly more affected.

Often the problem lies in the ways in which laws are implemented. The ways in which different understandings about gender, sexuality and violence influence policy implementation are clearly evident in the responses by officials and members of the public, who tend to frame teenage pregnancy as a moral problem, and often call for solutions grounded in morality and ethics (Jewkes *et al.* 2009b). Informed by this view, education officials at all levels view girls as promiscuous, their sexuality as problematic, and blame them for such problems as gender violence, teenage pregnancy and sexually transmitted infections, including HIV (Sathiparsad and Taylor 2006). This morality discourse also underpins responses at the community and school levels, as reflected, for example, in the 'abstain, be faithful, condomise' (ABC) interventions which continue to dominate responses targeting young people in schools and communities. Although strongly opposed by government institutions (Commission for Gender Equality 2005), at community level virginity testing is still practised, which involves a gynaecological examination of girls and unmarried young women between the ages of seven and 26 to establish whether or not their hymen is intact (Law 2005; Panday *et al.* 2009). Originally a strategy for sexual regulation aimed to 'protect the innocence of the youth' (Marcus 2008: 536), virginity testing re-emerged as a traditional cultural practice in the last two decades, particularly in the context of HIV and AIDS. Its proponents claim that it helps to revive traditional ways of life that were decimated by colonialism and apartheid, and in the current context, to uphold female chastity, protect girls against child abuse and sexually transmitted infections, including HIV and teenage pregnancies (see also Moletsane 2011). This example illustrates ways in which official policy implementation is often ignored in favour of a practice that is couched within cultural rights.

To address teenage pregnancy, South Africa has implemented some gender-sensitive and rights-based programming and policies, stipulating that girls remain at school during pregnancy and return after giving birth, including the *Measures for the Prevention and Management of Teenage Pregnancy* (Department of Education 2007). At the same time, this document, intended as support material for schools in preventing and managing schoolgirl pregnancy, created a great deal of confusion about the Department's approach to teenage pregnancy and may actually have led to greater discrimination in some schools (Morrell *et al.* 2012). For example, some school principals and education officials have used the *Measures* to exclude girls who are pregnant or mothers, citing a controversial clause that suggests some girls may need to take up to two years off school after giving birth. This is in spite of findings which suggest that the longer a girl stays out of school after giving birth, the less likely she is to return to school (Panday *et al.* 2009).

Linked to this have been calls by scholars and activists for policy-making and adjudication to be 'conscious' of the effects of structural inequality on girls' education. In response, in order to mitigate the negative impacts of poverty and arguably to facilitate the young mother's return to school, the Department of Social Development, as stipulated in the Act No. 13.2004 Social Assistance Act (2004) provides a Child Social Grant.[4] However, informed by the moral panic linked to the perceived high rates of teenage pregnancy in the country, a frequently expressed view exists in public discourse and amongst those working in the education system that this grant has provided a financial incentive for young people to fall pregnant early. This informs public and official attitudes towards pregnant schoolgirls, who are seen as choosing to fall pregnant and hence as immoral and irresponsible. This is in spite of available research which suggests that these perceptions have no basis in fact (see for example, Makiwane *et al.* 2006) and the fact that there is no evidence that rates of pregnancy and teenage fertility are rising.

The above discussion illustrates how a combination of weak policy communication, moralistic attitudes that blame girls for violence and for falling pregnant without recognising the complex socio-environmental circumstances that affect sexual behaviour, and a tendency for sexist attitudes to shape responses to teenage pregnancy, may hinder the impact of a rights-based policy. The debates will continue amongst scholars and activists, but what remains clear is that attempts to ensure girls' right to education must take into account the complex reasons schoolgirls fall pregnant (Morrell *et al.* 2012), and firmly protect their right to safety from violence.

While the discussion so far has focused on policies created in a top-down way, and the problems of how they are implemented in local situations, an alternative starting point is to listen to local voices, and to influence policy creation from the bottom up. We turn now to an approach we have used to learn about the perspectives of girls and women teachers on issues relating to gender inequality in education and its links to teenage pregnancy and gender violence – that of participatory visual methodologies. We believe that such approaches have rich potential for informing policy development from the bottom up.

Participatory visual methodologies

Over the last decade we have been working with young women in rural areas using visual methodologies. Our work is located within the broad area of participatory research for taking action, focusing in particular on ensuring that girls are both seen and heard in policy dialogue through the use of such visual tools as participatory video (Milne *et al.* 2012) and photo-voice (Mitchell 2011a, 2011b). We have found this approach to have considerable potential for influencing policy, first by generating knowledge to inform policy makers/enactors about the perspectives of women and girls themselves on such issues as teenage pregnancy, gender violence and HIV and AIDS, second, through offering a methodology which could be used in training those tasked with policy enactment for effectively addressing gender inequality in education, and finally, and most critically to support girls themselves in relation to agency in addressing the issues.

The fieldwork that we describe here is from our ongoing work in several rural schools in two provinces, KwaZulu-Natal and the Eastern Cape. As we have described elsewhere (Balfour *et al.* 2008), place is in itself a critical component in understanding issues of gender equality, particularly in the context of rurality. KwaZulu-Natal and Eastern Cape are two largely rural provinces, and while this does not necessarily mean higher rates of gender violence, rurality may be associated with access to fewer government services and at the same time a stronger traditional presence. At the same time, as Balfour *et al.* (2008) argue, rurality can also be associated with stronger community ties and the possibility that community members see each other as resources or assets. While a key aspect of the work is to engage girls themselves in addressing the issues, we have also recognised that women as well can play a critical role as potential allies. Careful to avoid what Kirk (2004) describes as the 'womenandgirls' position of lumping girls and women together, we believe it is important to acknowledge that girls do not necessarily have the same experiences and needs as women and that programmes targeting them must take not only the contextual differences, but also the age and developmental distinctions into consideration.

In an article that we published several years ago, 'What can a woman do with a (video) camera?' (Moletsane *et al.* 2009), we describe a project where female community health care workers, female teachers and young people engaged in examining various social issues in their communities and schools through participatory video production. As part of the findings, we saw that the role of women as cultural producers can be an important feature of engagement and taking action against violence. At the same time, women teachers can also be part of the problem by further victimising girls by blaming them for being sexually active (De Lange *et al.* 2012). There may even be a type of 'covering over' of their own memories and experiences as girls (see Mitchell and Reid-Walsh 2008), a point that calls even more for women to be actively engaged in both 'looking back to look forward' and for ensuring that girls are part of the dialogue. Two examples of participatory film-making that emerged in these workshops, one with women teachers and one with girls, poignantly highlight the place of visual methods, but also the ways in which women are (or are not) allies in helping to address issues of gender inequality, sexual violence and teenage pregnancy.

Example 1: what can a female teacher do with a cellphone? Addressing teenage pregnancy

The use of cellphones to make cellphilms in a rural South African context is an instance of a new set of conditions within which to examine critical issues linked to participatory video and the voice of teachers in creating spaces for dialogue.[5] While the technology for cellphilms is relatively new, it is an increasingly popular medium in South Africa because of the widespread access to mobile phones, with more than 85 per cent of adults having access to a cellphone and close to 100 per cent of South Africa having mobile phone coverage (Dockney and Tomaselli 2009). At school sites in KwaZulu-Natal and Eastern Cape, we conducted a two-day cellphilm workshop. The workshop started with a 'me and my cellphone' plenary where participants had a chance to talk about their own cellphone use. For the actual cellphilm production, the group of teachers in the Eastern Cape worked with the prompt: *Make a cellphilm about the most critical issues around risk and youth in the context of HIV and AIDS.* The teachers in KwaZulu-Natal worked with the prompt: *Make a cellphilm related to the critical issues that affect your school.* In both sites these cellphilms were then screened for the whole group, allowing for deep discussion of the issues at hand, and especially turning attention to the participants' own agency in providing solutions to the problems identified. We focus here on a five-minute cellphilm narrative on *Teenage Pregnancy* dramatised by a group of five women teachers from the school in KwaZulu-Natal.

The video, made by the teachers, opens with a group of 'schoolgirls' (played by the teachers themselves) at a party, dancing and drinking alcohol. The scene changes to the morning after where the main character, Lindiwe, wakes up and wonders what might have happened the night before. She rummages through her bag and it seems as though she is looking to see whether she still has the condom she was carrying around. She is very confident, however, and comments to herself that everything is fine and that she didn't really sleep with anyone. With a 'one month later' change, however, we see Lindiwe feeling unwell. She has missed her period and frantically comments 'Oh God, I can't be pregnant. I don't want to be pregnant'. A home-test pregnancy kit however reveals that she is indeed pregnant. Again she repeats 'Oh God, I can't be pregnant'. In a very distraught state, she goes to see a female teacher, who advises her that she must go to the clinic and get properly tested for the pregnancy but also for HIV. That is all there is to do. The teacher is compassionate in one sense in that she listens to Lindiwe. She is also very matter-of-fact, and the film ends right there, with what might be described as a bleak ending.

There are several messages to be taken from this example. On the one hand the teachers are acknowledging that teenage pregnancy is a critical issue. At the same time, it is somewhat shocking that when they could produce anything they wanted, they produce a film that places responsibility squarely on the girl. It seems that it is clearly Lindiwe who is responsible for getting pregnant (partying, drinking, irresponsibility), and once she realises that she is pregnant, she is basically on her own. Nowhere in the narrative does the male partner appear and the only reference to him is Lindiwe's concern about what she did and with whom the night before. Neither the women teachers who created this production nor those who viewed the video thought of the ending as problematic, or envisaged a role for the teacher in offering further support for the girl who is pregnant. Rather it appears to be a message of blame and one that fits with the moralistic tone that we describe above in terms of the framing of teenage pregnancy in policy discourse . . . the girl is at fault and it is the girl who must pay. The video highlights the ways in which adult women, who are part of the lives of such girls, condone by their silence or by their failure to take action, and in doing so become part of the problem when dealing with teenage sex and family violence perpetrated on girls in South Africa.

Example 2: girls as film-makers: addressing sexual violence

Several years ago in the same rural district of KwaZulu-Natal as above, we organised two one-day participatory video-making workshops with teachers, community health care workers, parents and learners. Participants were invited to produce a video on any issue in their lives, yet most chose to address gender violence, including rape (Moletsane *et al.* 2008), poverty (Mitchell *et al.* 2008), transactional sex (Moletsane *et al.* 2009) and incest (Moletsane *et al.* 2009; Mitchell 2011a). Here we describe *Vikela Abantwana* (Protect the Children – a story about incest) as a way to look at how women teachers and girls visualise women in framing approaches to addressing sexual violence.

Produced by a group of five 14–15-year-old girls, the three-minute video tells the story of Phindeleni, who is found crying in the classroom by her best friend. As she reveals her story, we learn that she has been raped by her father. We also learn that she has tried to tell the various women in her community, but no one is willing to pass the information on to her mother. For example, she confides in the housekeeper, but the housekeeper feels that she cannot directly confront her boss (Phindeleni's mother), and so passes the information on to a neighbour who she hopes will then inform Phindeleni's mother. Phindeleni's story is greeted with disbelief by the women she tells: 'That cannot be. You are lying neighbour', and when her mother is eventually told, her response is initially denial. Eventually, she is taken to a doctor who confirms that the girl has been raped and also that she is pregnant. When the mother hears this, she bursts into tears. When he is confronted, the father advises that this is something that should be kept in the family. The story ends with Phindeleni's father behind bars in a jail.

At one level, this film has a 'happy' ending, somewhat at odds with the reality of what typically happens to perpetrators of gender violence in South Africa. One study for example suggests that only 1 per cent of cases ever result in any prosecution (Banwari 2011). But overall the message is bleak, and one of the clear messages that is told through the medium of the video is that girls in this school feel that adults do not listen to them when they report rape and other sexual abuse. And although Phindeleni has tried to tell so many of the women around her who should care about her welfare, she has in fact been let down by them, as they take no action on her behalf.

Conclusion: an alternative approach to policy

We have focused on the making of *Teenage Pregnancy* and *Vikela Abantwana* because it seems to us that this kind of work suggests a new way of 'doing policy' by bringing together the voices of women teachers and girls through the medium of participatory video and through workshops that build on what we describe elsewhere as the 'pedagogy of screening' (Mitchell and Moletsane 2014). Such an approach is a way to go beyond engagement (through the making of the videos) to policy dialogue. Thus, we envision that the next step in the participatory workshops should be dialogue and discussion: *What is the message that you are trying to get across in this cellphilm? Who should see it? If you could re-do it, what would you do differently? Is the only possible ending a bleak one? What would it take to change the ending? Who can change the ending?* Indeed it is this element of the work that we see as particularly promising in the use of participatory video and cellphilms. The girls who made the video wanted to show it to their teachers. The teachers in their cellphilm workshops wanted their colleagues, school managers, district and provincial managers, police and other service providers to see the video. While they did not specifically suggest that the girls and young women with whom they come in contact everyday should see their productions, it seems clear to us that this is an important part of the process. Such approaches can be regarded as feminist activist tools or resources, that serve to contest some of the prevailing discourses about girls and sexuality and that expand possibilities for reflexivity and policy dialogue.

Despite the policies and interventions implemented since 1994, gender equality in education in South Africa remains elusive as contradictions between a socio-political context informed by a human rights framework and the continuing high levels of gender inequality, which manifest in gender violence in and around schools and teenage pregnancy, continue. We have explored a number of reasons why this might be the case. It seems clear that, in spite of the rights-based policy framework, the voices of those most negatively impacted by gender inequalities in and around schools continue to be marginalised. This is particularly so in the case of girls who are poor, black and are living in rural areas. We suggest that current policy-making may not be working because it is not informed by the real voices of those targeted, particularly women teachers and girls in and around schools. Nor is there sufficient engagement with teachers and officials tasked with policy implementation to enable them to critically reflect on issues of gender, morality and inequality. Our suggested approach to addressing these issues is informed by Panday *et al.*'s (2009) assertion that teenage sexuality and pregnancy cannot be addressed by one sector alone. Rather, a comprehensive and integrated approach that involves various sectors (the home, school, community, health and others) is necessary. In order to contribute to educational policy on gender, sexuality and violence, we argue that careful consideration of the policy landscape is needed, as well as more nuanced understandings of these sensitive and difficult topics that can be elicited through visual methodologies such as participatory video. Ultimately, we propose the idea of what Kapoor and Choudry (2010) refer to as a 'from the ground up' approach to policy dialogue. This involves the use of participatory methodologies, which, with their built-in intention to engage participants as active agents of change in their own lives, aim to engage and mobilise participants. We believe that rather than doing research *about* or *on* teenagers, who tend to bear the brunt of the negative impacts of poverty, pregnancy and violence, participatory visual methodologies will yield more positive fruit by turning their gaze onto the challenges affecting them and working with them to address these. At a time when there is clearly a set of entanglements when it comes to the field of gender, violence, poverty and education, it is clear from the examples above that there is a need to test out participatory methods. Such approaches promote a nuanced understanding of the challenges, help to develop strategies for addressing the issues, and ultimately have the potential to be transformative.

Notes

1 See Table 2.1 in Chapter 2 for further information on global declarations.
2 Here Mkhwanazi uses the designation, originally formulated by the apartheid regime but now used by the current government, of population groups in South Africa, where black referred to black Africans and coloured referred to people of mixed race descent.
3 After the 2009 elections, the Department of Education was split into two: the Department of Basic Education and the Department of Higher Education and Training.
4 A monthly grant from the South African government given to family and/or caregivers of children who are in need of financial support.
5 Cellphilms, as Dockney and Tomaselli (2009: 126) note, are movies 'made with a cellphone, made for a cellphone'. In our participatory visual work, we have used cellphilming as an adaptation to the 'No Editing Required' approach to participatory video (see Mitchell *et al.* in press)

References

Adar, J. and Stevens, M. (2000). 'Women's health'. In A. Ntuli, N. Crisp, E. Clark and P. Barron (eds), *South African Health Review* (pp. 411–27). Durban: Health Systems Trust.

Balfour, R., Mitchell, C. and Moletsane, R. (2008). 'Troubling contexts: toward a generative theory of rurality as education research'. *Journal of Rural and Community Development*, 3 (3), 100–11.

Banwari, M. (2011). 'Poverty, child sexual abuse and HIV in the Transkei region, South Africa'. *African Health Sciences*, 11 (3), 117–21.

Center for AIDS Research, Development and Evaluation (CADRE) (2003). *Gender-Based Violence and HIV/AIDS in South Africa: A Literature Review*. Johannesburg: CADRE.

Centre for Applied Legal Studies and Avon Global Center for Women and Justice (2014). *Sexual Violence by Educators in South African Schools: Gaps in Accountability*. University of the Witwatersrand and Cornell University.

Commission for Gender Equality (2005). *Submission to the Select Committee On Social Services: Children's Bill*. Available at: www.pmg.org.za/docs/2005/051214kotze. htm (accessed 24 May 2014).

De Lange, N., Mitchell, C. and Bhana, D. (2012). 'Voices of women teachers about gender inequalities and gender-based violence in rural South Africa'. *Gender and Education*, 24, 499–514.

Department of Basic Education (2010). *Speak Out: Youth Report Sexual Abuse: A Handbook for Learners on How to Prevent Sexual Abuse in Public Schools*. Pretoria.

Department of Education (2001a). *Opening our Eyes: Addressing Gender-Based Violence in South African Schools: A Manual for Educators*. Pretoria.

Department of Education (2001b). *National Plan for Higher Education*. Pretoria.

Department of Education (2007). *Measures for the Prevention and Management of Learner Pregnancy*. Pretoria. Available at: www.education.gov.za.

Dieltiens, V., Unterhalter, E., Letsatsi, S. and North, A. (2009). 'Gender blind, gender-lite: a critique of gender equity approaches in the South African Department of Education'. *Perspectives in Education*, 27 (4), 365–74.

Dockney, J. and Tomaselli, K. (2009). 'Fit for the small(er) screen: films, mobile TV and the new individual television experience'. *Journal of African Cinema*, 1 (1), 126–32.

Gouws, A. (2006). 'The state of the national gender machinery: structural problems and personalised politics'. In S. Buhlungu (ed.), *State of the Nation: South Africa, 2005–2006* (pp. 143–66). Pretoria: HSRC Press.

Grant, M.J. and Hallman, K.K. (2008). 'Pregnancy-related school dropout and prior school performance in KwaZulu-Natal, South Africa'. *Studies in Family Planning*, 39, 369–82.

Hallman, K. (2004). 'Socioeconomic disadvantage and unsafe sexual behaviors of young women and men in South Africa'. Policy Research Division Working Paper No. 190, New York: Population Council.

Haysom, L. (2013). 'Sex, gender and childhood. Editorial'. *Agenda*, 97 (3), 1–3.

Human Rights Watch (2001). *Scared at School: Sexual Violence in South African Schools*. New York: Human Rights Watch.

Jewkes, R., Morrell, R. and Christofides, N. (2009a). 'Empowering teenagers to prevent pregnancy: lessons from South Africa'. *Culture, Health and Sexuality*, 11 (7), 675–88.

Jewkes, R., Skweyiya, Y., Morrell, R. and Dunkel, K. (2009b). *Understanding Men's Health and Use of Violence: Interface of Rape and HIV in South Africa*. Pretoria: Medical Research Council.

Jewkes, R., Sikweyiya, Y., Morrell, R. and Dunkle, K. (2011) 'Gender inequitable masculinity and sexual entitlement in rape perpetration South Africa: findings of a cross-sectional study'. PLoS ONE 6 (9): e24256. doi:10.1371/journal.pone.0024256.

Jewkes, R., Vundule, C., Maforah, F. and Jordaan, E. (2001). 'Relationship dynamics and teenage pregnancy in South Africa'. *Social Science and Medicine*, 52 (5), 733–44.

Kapoor, D. and Choudry, A. (2010). *Learning from the Ground Up: Global Perspectives on Social Movements and Knowledge Production*. New York: Macmillan.

Kirk, J. (2004). *Reflexivity and Working with Teachers in a Development Context* (unpublished doctoral thesis). McGill University, Montreal, Canada.

Law, L. (2005). 'Virginity testing: in the best interest of the child?' (Briefing Paper 145). Catholic Parliamentary Liaison Office. Available at: www.cplo.co.za.

Makiwane, M., Desmond, C., Richter, L. and Udjo, E. (2006). 'Is the Child Support Grant associated with an increase in teenage fertility in South Africa? Evidence from national surveys and administrative data'. *Human Sciences Research Council (HSRC) Report*. Pretoria: HSRC.

Marcus, T. (2008). 'Virginity testing: a backward-looking response to sexual regulation in the HIV/AIDS crisis'. In B. Carton, J. Laband and J. Sithole (eds), *Zulu Identities: Being Zulu, Past and Present* (pp. 536–44). Scottsville. University of KwaZulu-Natal Press.

Mchunu, G., Peltzer, K., Tutshana, B. and Seutlwadi, L. (2012). 'Adolescent pregnancy and associated factors in South African youth'. *African Health Sciences*, 12 (4), 426–34.

Milne, E.-J., Mitchell, C. and De Lange, N. (eds) (2012). *Handbook on Participatory Video*. Lanham: Alta Mira Press.

Mitchell, C. (2011a). 'What's participation got to do with it? Visual methodologies in "girl-method" to address gender based violence in the time of AIDS'. *Global Studies of Childhood*, 1 (1), 51–9.

Mitchell, C. (2011b). *Doing Visual Research*. London and New York: Sage

Mitchell, C. and Moletsane, R. (2014) 'Seeing is believing, but who's looking? Addressing some tensions in "from the ground up" policy dialogue in relation to sexual violence'. American Educational Research Association, Philadelphia, 4–7 April.

Mitchell, C. and Reid-Walsh. J. (2008). 'Girl method: placing girl-centred research methodologies on the map of Girlhood Studies'. In J. Klaehn (ed.), *Roadblocks to Equality: Women Challenging Boundaries* (pp. 214–33). Montreal: Black Rose Books.

Mitchell, C., de Lange, N. and Moletsane, R. (in press). 'Me and my cellphone: constructing change from the inside through cellphilms and participatory video in a rural community'. *AREA*.

Mitchell, C., de Lange, N. and Nguyen, X. (2008). '"Let's just not leave this problem": exploring inclusive education in rural South Africa'. *Prospects*, 38 (1), 99–112.

Mkhwanazi, N (2010). 'Understanding teenage pregnancy in a post-apartheid South African township'. *Culture, Health and Sexuality: An International Journal for Research, Intervention and Care*, 12 (4), 347–58.

Mncube,V. and Harber, C. (2013). *The Dynamics of Violence in South African Schools: Report*. Pretoria: University of South Africa.

Moletsane, R. (2010). *Gender Review in South African Basic Education*. UNICEF and Department of Basic Education.

Moletsane, R. (2011). 'Culture, nostalgia, and sexuality education in the age of AIDS in South Africa'. In C. Mitchell, T. Strong-Wilson, K. Pithouse and S. Allnutt (eds), *Memory and Pedagogy* (pp. 193–208). London: Routledge.

Moletsane, R., Mitchell, C., Smith, A. and Chisholm, L. (2008). *Mapping a Southern African Girlhood*. Rotterdam: Sense.

Moletsane, R., Mitchell, C., De Lange, N. Stuart, J., Buthelezi, T. and Taylor, M. (2009). 'What can a woman do with a camera? Turning the female gaze on poverty and HIV/AIDS in rural South Africa'. *International Journal of Qualitative Studies in Education*, 22 (3), 315–31.

Morrell, R. (2001). 'Corporal punishment and masculinity in South African schools'. *Men and Masculinities*, 4 (2), 140–57.

Morrell, R., Bhana, D. and Shefer, T. (2012). 'Pregnancy and parenthood in South African schools'. In R. Morrell, D. Bhana and T. Shefer (eds), *Books and Babies: Pregnancy and Young Parents in Schools* (pp. 1–30). Cape Town: HSRC Press.

National Department of Education (1997). *Gender Equity Task Team Report*. Pretoria.

Panday, S., Makiwane, M., Ranchod, C. and Letsoalo, T. (2009). *Teenage Pregnancy in South Africa – with a Focus on School-Going Learners*. Pretoria: Department of Basic Education.

Perumal, D. (2013). 'Misguided reform: regulating consensual sexual activity between adolescents in South African law from a gender perspective'. *Agenda*, 97 (3), 107–17.

Petersen, I., Bhana, A. and Mackay, M. (2005). 'Sexual violence and youth in South Africa: the need for community-based prevention interventions'. *Child Abuse and Neglect*, 29, 1233–48.

Pettifor, A., Rees, H., Steffenson, A., Hlongwa-Madikizela, L., MacPhail, C., Vermaak, K. and Kleinschmidt, I. (2004). 'HIV and sexual behaviour among young South Africans: a national survey of 15–24 year olds'. Johannesburg: Reproductive Health Research Unit, University of the Witwatersrand.

Sathiparsad, R. and Taylor, M. (2006). '"Diseases come from girls": perspectives of male learners in rural KwaZulu-Natal on HIV infection and AIDS'. *Journal of Education*, 38, 117–37.

Statistics South Africa (2011). *General Household Survey 2010*. Pretoria: Statistics South Africa. Available at: www.statssa.gov.za/publications/P0318/P0318June2010.pdf.

Statistics South Africa (2012). *General Household Survey 2011*. Pretoria: Statistics South Africa. Available at: www.statssa.gov.za/publications/P0318/P0318April2012.pdf.

Women's Refugee Commission (2009). *Peril or Protection: The Link Between Livelihoods and Gender-based Violence in Displacement Settings*. New York: Women's Refugee Commission.

13 Conclusion

Emerging themes for the field of gender, violence, poverty and education

Jenny Parkes

This final chapter draws together strands of discussion running through the book to reflect on emerging dimensions of the new field of academic research, policy and practice in gender violence, poverty and education. In grappling with the original aims posed in Chapter 1, the authors have brought rich insights as well as raising some difficult questions for those wanting to tackle this area of scholarship, those engaging at community, school, family or individual level in preventing gender violence, and those who want major changes in policy approaches whether national or international. In this chapter I discuss how the authors answer the questions posed in the introduction concerning theoretical insights into the nature of violence, demonstrations of how young people living in poverty contexts engage with and resist violence, and mediators and mechanisms to counter violence.

The book urges researchers, practitioners and policy-makers to think in a multi-dimensional way. This is a huge shift for those working on the ground, and for scholars of gender and women's studies, requiring simultaneous attention to a complex range of behaviours, forms of regulation, normative models of social relations and intersecting inequalities. There are tensions between on the one hand being able to recognise violence in its complex forms and, on the other, understanding how children and youth, whilst at school, whilst in school, whilst around adults, have to resist, respond and play safe when they encounter violence. Violence can be a coinage, a form of capital, a means to an end. Those living in poverty often live with poverty and violence simultaneously. These themes are explored below.

Theorising multi-dimensional violence

In seeking explanations for how violence becomes normalised in schools, homes, communities and societies, the book contributors have been inspired by theoretical work from several disciplines. The philosophical and sociological works of Foucault (Chapters 5 and 11) and Bourdieu (Chapters 1, 2, 4, 7, 8 and 9) have provided insights into the regulatory processes of structures and institutions, and how structural violence becomes incorporated in minds and bodies through symbolic violence. Feminist theorists, including Young (Chapter 2), Risley (Chapter 10) and Connell (Chapters 2 and 7) have deepened understandings of the ways in which oppressive gender regimes and norms aggravate violence. In this work, and especially the work on masculinity and violence, we see the continuing legacy of radical feminist writing on women's bodies, male sexual prowess, lust and dominance, that is perhaps underplayed nowadays but still resonates in the lives of girls and women discussed in several chapters. Post-structural feminists, particularly Butler (Chapter 2), have generated insights into how violence emerges at the borders of gender discourse, where those who threaten the fragile boundaries by transgressing gender and sexual norms are excluded and denigrated. Theories from poverty studies and development studies, particularly the Capability Approach, and the work of Sen and Stewart (Chapters 2 and 6) have been used creatively to shed light on how different forms of inequalities constrain human flourishing and produce violence. Ideas from Childhood Studies have been used to consider how violence can serve to mould socially constructed childhoods, and to illuminate children's resilience (Chapters 4, 5 and 11). The authors build on and adapt these approaches in their quests to understand how violence affects young people's lives in poverty contexts. Drawing on these analyses, I have constructed a model of how violence is produced and perpetuated (see Figure 13.1).

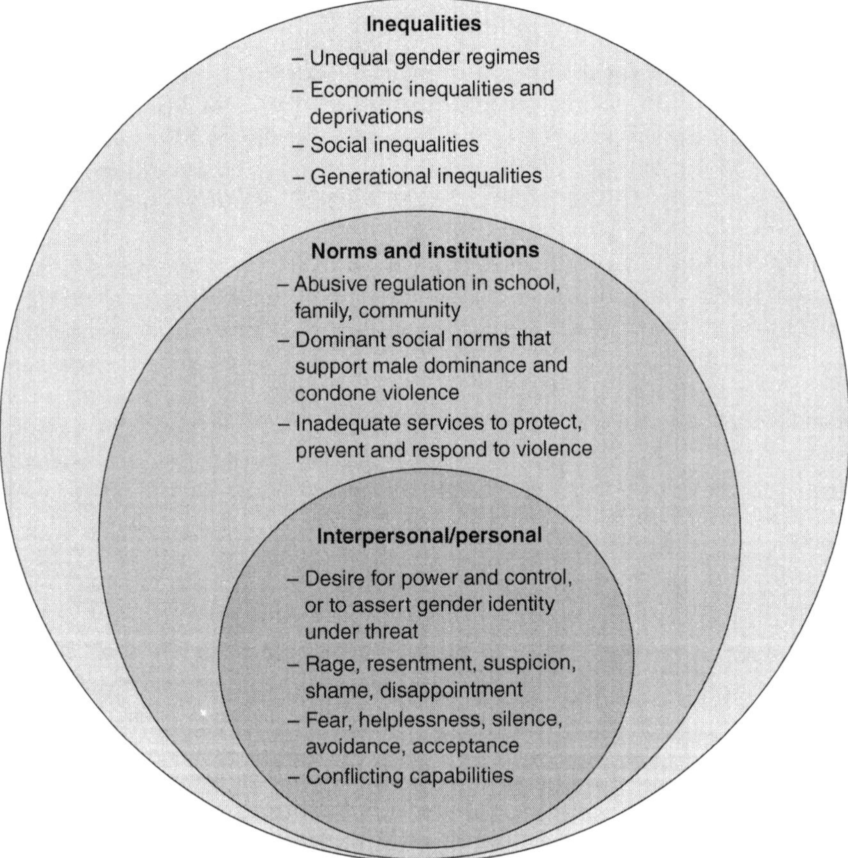

Figure 13.1 The production and perpetuation of violence

The outer ring depicts inequalities at the macro-level that create the conditions for violence. A key insight of many of the chapters (see especially Parkes and Unterhalter, Chapter 2) is that violence is not caused by poverty in any simple linear way, but that mundane, everyday acts of violence take place in contexts of intersecting social, political and economic inequalities. These inequalities generate the structural violence of norms and institutions depicted in the middle ring, as described for example in Buller's account of the legacy of corruption in the police, justice and school systems in a socially excluded neighbourhood of Peru (Chapter 8). The inner ring shows the interpersonal and personal effects of structural violence. Some chapters discuss these in terms of symbolic violence, as in Heslop *et al.*'s discussion (Chapter 9) of how norms about gender and sexuality in rural communities of Kenya, Ghana and Mozambique constrain girls' agency and choice – and also the recognition that there may be choice – in sexual relationships. Helplessness, silence, collusion and acceptance are common responses to violence identified in several chapters, serving to perpetuate violence (e.g. Chapters 4, 5 and 6), But in these and other chapters (e.g. Chapters 7 and 8), the authors also identify other emotional responses – rage, resentment, shame and the urge to establish control – that indicate that young people are often well aware of the injustices in their lives. For some young people, like the boys living in gang neighbourhoods discussed by Parkes and Unterhalter (Chapter 2), and the Tanzanian teachers described by Tao (Chapter 6), forms of structural violence create conflicting identities, or, in Tao's terms, capability conflicts, with everyday violence used in the (conscious or unconscious) attempt to resolve these conflicts. For example, in a context where there are very large, poorly resourced classes, valuing 'being able to help students learn' might be in tension with 'being in control of a class', with corporal punishments both gaining a constrained form of control and expressing frustration about the irreconcilability with creating a safe, violence-free context for learning.

Everyday acts of violence, in this multi-dimensional framing, are produced by and reproduce particular subjectivities, norms and institutions, and broader inequalities. We are only just beginning to understand the links between structural and personal violence, and a key implication for researchers, practitioners and policy-makers is the need to look critically not just at violence but at anti-violence strategies – at the ways in which education, the environment, the culture and the economy create violent lives.

Countering violence

There is another way of looking at these issues, through the lens of young people themselves. A particular strength of the book is the way authors capture the voices of the violated, those who have to work, live and respond to violence in intimate relationship to them, and on a daily basis. We are only just beginning to recognise and value resilience, solidarity and resourcefulness as capabilities that can be developed. While the model discussed so far may help to explain the perpetuation of violence, several chapters discuss exceptions, when young people counter violence. Buller, for example, points out that the very conditions that produce violence can also generate a sense of solidarity and resourcefulness that may help some young people in an urban settlement in Peru to resist the violence of street gangs (Chapter 8). Similarly, Pells *et al.* (Chapter 4) give instances of young people in Vietnam who respond to witnessing their fathers' domestic violence through forms of care and support. Such exceptional cases hint at ways of countering violence that could inform education initiatives. Building on the research discussed in this book, Figure 13.2 extends the model presented above (Figure 13.1) to illuminate possible mediators and mechanisms for countering violence.

The inner ring depicts the personal and interpersonal resources that enable young people to resist violence, including for example having the knowledge, capacity and confidence to reflect on and take action against inequitable norms. Such reflexive awareness needs to be supported by belonging to social networks,

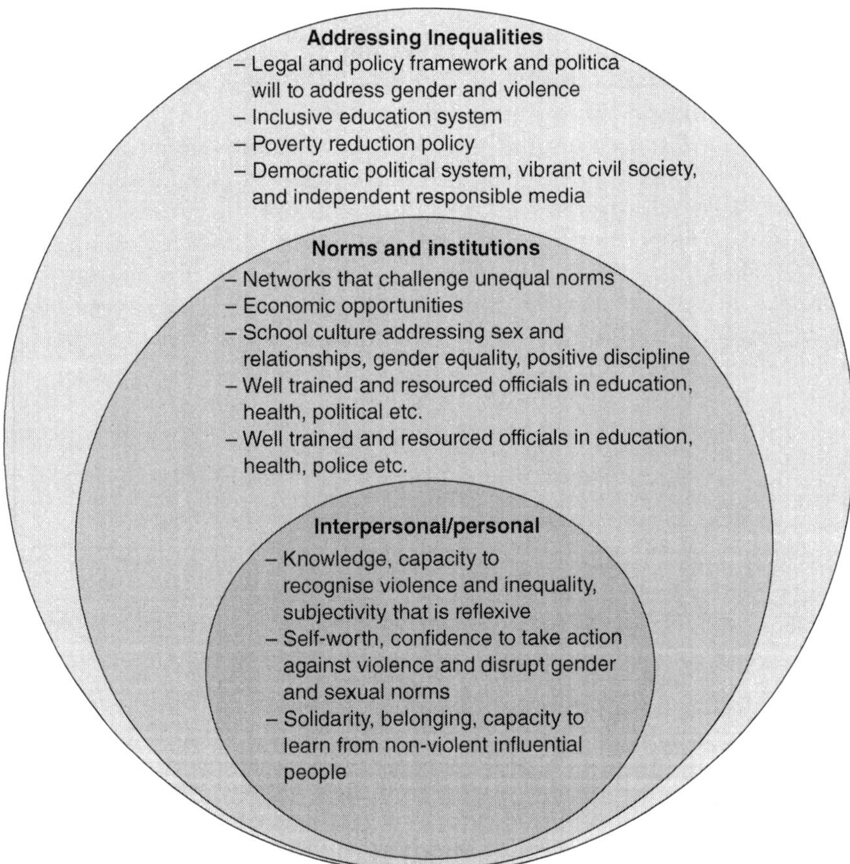

Figure 13.2 Mediators/mechanisms for countering violence

being able to learn from admired and influential people who counter violence, labour market opportunities, and supportive and inclusive school cultures. Somewhat depressingly, in the case studies presented in this book schools do not seem currently to be promising sites for contesting gender violence, and the personal/interpersonal mediators appear to be influenced mainly by factors unconnected with schooling. Religion, long-term relationships with girlfriends and boyfriends, getting a job, or becoming a parent steer young men away from violent lifestyles through providing better economic prospects, an alternative moral code, sense of purpose and social network (Chapters 7 and 8). Instances of girls and boys learning how to challenge violence take place in community programmes or in girls' clubs run by NGOs, that may be on the school premises but remain separate from the formal curriculum (Chapters 9 and 10). However, several chapters propose ways in which schools can enable young people to counter violence, through for example building school cultures that use positive discipline (Chapters 5 and 6), teaching about sex and relationships, and gender equality (Chapters 4 and 9), and offering a varied and relevant curriculum (Chapter 7). These approaches depart from narrowly focused inputs that focus just on acts of physical, sexual and emotional violence, which tend to have little impact (Leach *et al.* 2014), at best acting as sticking plasters. Indeed there is some evidence that such inputs can sometimes be harmful, as in the case of classroom assistants employed to address sexual violence in refugee camps in Sierra Leone, who were found to reinforce prevailing gender discourses that place the onus on girls to change and whose emphasis on punitive approaches led to hostility of teachers, who viewed them as 'sex police' (Kirk 2007). Rather than focusing on single issues, like corporal punishment or bullying, it may be more productive to develop multi-dimensional interventions targeting school cultures. For example, in Chapter 6 Tao concludes that working with Tanzanian teachers and school management on protocols and duty-bound activities, and on their own beliefs about child rearing, gender and pedagogy, could help to reduce the constraints on teachers' capabilities to teach without violence.

Authors also discuss the importance of 'holistic' approaches, combining education with other spheres, as in the community projects in Brazil discussed by Wilding (Chapter 10), which offered an alternative sense of belonging to young men than that generated by gang membership, along with opportunities to explore social expectations around masculinity and femininity, and at the same time offered practical help with employment and food parcels. Such approaches recognise and address the multi-dimensional nature of violence.

However, despite the multi-dimensional awareness of the project designs, in their enactments, several of the interventions discussed in this book seem to have limited effectiveness in challenging inequitable gender relations. Girls in the projects with urban youth in Brazil for example are seen by project workers as a counterpoint to male aggression, reiterating rather than challenging gender norms and sidelining girls' concerns (Chapter 10). Girls' clubs in Kenya, Ghana and Mozambique enable girls to speak out against violence, but avoid disrupting norms about sex and sexuality through teaching about safe sex (Chapter 9).

Rap music in urban Peru, and boxing in urban Brazil, are viewed as useful outlets for boys to express rage, thus sublimating violence, but these activities are highly gendered, reinforcing normative masculinities around toughness (Chapters 8 and 10). In Chapter 8, Buller reflects on the potential for 'pragmatic trade-offs', which might make an intervention more palatable to young people or to potentially hostile community members (see also Nussbaum 2005; Aikman 2010). In addition, staff running such programmes need to be well trained to recognise and address the many dimensions of violence. Unterhalter (2012) has pointed out the importance of working with the 'missing middle' – including officials in education, health, welfare, the police and NGO workers – often forgotten in work on translating policy into action in schools.

The outer ring of Figure 13.2 depicts approaches to counter violence at the macro-level. In recent years, there has been a plethora of legislative and policy development on violence, gender and education at national and international levels, but several reviews lament the lack of progress in reducing levels of violence (United Nations 2011; Leach *et al.* 2014). In part this may be due to the lack of a sufficiently multi-dimensional approach. For example, in the case of South Africa discussed by Moletsane *et al.* (Chapter 12), policy actors at national level have created strong human rights legal and policy frameworks and national machinery intended to mainstream gender and tackle violence within education, but the failure to address intersecting inequalities and a morality discourse around teenage sexuality circulate at national, provincial and local levels of policy enactment, thus hindering the impact of rights-based policy to gender violence.

Often too, international and national policy plans are insensitive to local norms and belief systems, with policy actors tending to 'blame the poor' (Unterhalter *et al.* 2012). Isobelle Gunning (1991) discusses the arrogance of moves to ban the practice of female genital mutilation that do not consider the intricacies of the practice within local social, economic and cultural contexts, arguing that law enforcement may serve to strengthen the practice locally, as a form of defiance against outside cultural imposition. Some similar criticisms have been directed towards INGOs, as articulated in Wells' critique of NGO practice as the imposition of a neo-colonial system of domination (Chapter 11). These analyses point to the need for policy-makers and NGOs to build more responsiveness to local perspectives.

While Figure 13.2 combines approaches from various chapters, evident across the collection is the importance of interventions to operate at multiple levels to counter violence. A multi-dimensional approach can operate within each level of the model (e.g. at the macro level, including poverty reduction, health and social welfare, as well as inclusive education systems, and laws and policies on violence) and between levels, in direct interventions with young people, alongside working with institutions and national level systems. Together, Figures 13.1 and 13.2 offer a multi-dimensional theory of change for gender violence and education in poverty contexts.

A research agenda

This multi-dimensional framework for understanding and countering gender violence is only a start, and there is much work to be done to build this new field of knowledge, in order better to inform policy and practice. Thus, I want to end by drawing together theoretical, empirical and methodological ideas for future research gleaned from chapters of this book.

As discussed by Parkes and Unterhalter in Chapter 2, more work is needed to understand the connections between the many dimensions of violence, poverty and inequality, and the linkages with education. We have found it productive to work with theoretical approaches from across different disciplines, and think that as we become more adept at this, our analyses will become more sophisticated. For example, the insights of Bourdieu and others on structural and symbolic violence have shed light on the relationship between inequalities, norms and identities in the (re)production of violence, but current theoretical tools are less effective at helping to understand how violence is interrupted. Here I think post-structural feminism and capabilities theory may both offer scope to enrich our analyses. For example, feminist post-structural ideas about marginality, exclusion and discourse (see Chapter 2 for work inspired by Butler 1999), and Tao's work on capability conflicts (Chapter 6) seem to me to have much potential to enrich our insights into how conflicts at a subjective level may operate to counter violence in poverty contexts.

At an empirical level, there remain many gaps in our knowledge. For example, much more research is needed in poverty contexts to examine issues still shrouded in silence around sex and sexuality, including homophobic violence, sexual violence against boys, the effects on children of intimate partner violence and the expression of sexual desire by girls and young women. More research is also needed on processes of change. Leach *et al.* (2014) lament the lack of evidence about school characteristics that challenge gender violence. While they describe as 'promising' whole-school approaches that include teacher training, curriculum revisions, classroom pedagogies, school governance and ethos, financial and infrastructural support, more robust evidence is needed on how these approaches create and sustain change.

As discussed in detail by Leach (Chapter 3), researching gender violence with children is replete with ethical and methodological challenges, and the researchers contributing to the book offer valuable insights from their experiences. Creative, sensitive and participatory approaches to information gathering have been discussed, as in the example of video production and cellphilms (Chapter 12), in which South African girls and teachers use their cell phones to make and then discuss short films about issues that concern them in their schools and communities. In order for research to better inform policy and practice, closer collaboration in the design and conduct of research on gender, violence and education is needed between research, policy and practice (Dejaeghere *et al.* 2013). Some chapters discuss programmes led by NGOs that combine research and action, like ActionAid's Stop Violence Against Girls in School project discussed in Chapter 9 and the NGOs in Brazil discussed by Wilding (Chapter 10), and the Young Lives project, discussed in Chapters 4 and 5, conducts research with a strong emphasis on informing policy on childhood poverty. These research–policy–practice relationships also entail critical self-reflection, and engagement across boundaries of academic, professional and practical knowledge. Countering criticisms about the limited scope and lack of rigour of many evaluations of gender violence interventions (Ricardo *et al.* 2011; Leach *et al.* 2012; Lundgren 2013), they tend to use mixed methodologies, attempting to gather robust, reliable evidence using baseline and endline studies, and some of them are longitudinal, enabling them to examine in depth processes of change (Chapters 4, 5 and 9). Leach *et al.* (2014) point out that it is technically easier to measure change in narrowly focused programmes, through for example, measuring rates of corporal punishment before and after a training programme, than in multi-dimensional interventions. There are, however, some promising developments in multi-dimensional measures, with for example CARE's Common Indicators Framework synthesising four dimensions for assessing change in projects on gender and schooling: attainment (access, progression, completion, achievement), equality (gender sensitivity in perceptions of teachers, children, communities), quality (physical learning environment, educational content, pedagogies) and empowerment (girls' agency, supportive strategic relations, structural environment) (Miske *et al.* 2010). ActionAid's Stop Violence Against Girls in School project (Chapter 11), more specifically concerned with violence, has built measurement of these dimensions along with measures of levels of violence, girls' responses to violence, outcomes of reporting and of informal and formal justice systems at community, district and national level (Parkes and Heslop 2013). As well as gender and violence, a multi-dimensional methodology needs to include measures of horizontal and vertical inequality/poverty (Stewart 2002; Alkire and Sumner 2013).

These multi-dimensional measures, often developed in research–policy–practice partnerships, may be fruitful in building the evidence base, but they are fraught with difficulties. For example, measuring changes in levels of violence over the course of ActionAid's Stop Violence project proved of limited value, since the intervention led to an increase in girls' confidence to speak about the violence they experienced. Apparent increases, therefore, in levels of sexual violence could be viewed as a failure in programming, but were more likely to demonstrate the programme's success in enabling girls to speak out (Parkes and Heslop 2013). The complexity of the multi-dimensional relationships does not lend itself easily to reductiveness of quantitative research, and qualitative data has been vital in interpreting the quantitative evidence (see also data from Young Lives discussed in Chapter 5). It is the qualitative data that offers insights to why and how change has happened or not.

Conclusion

In this concluding chapter, I have begun to construct a theory of change, drawing on the rich data and analyses discussed throughout the book to set out the current parameters of this new field of research into gender, violence, poverty and education. The book offers insights to violence scholars, gender scholars, poverty scholars, and also to policy-makers and practitioners trying to reduce conflict and violence, and help those confronted with gender violence: girls, women, boys and men. The studies we have presented highlight the importance when researching gender violence in poverty contexts of trying to understand the myriad ways in which violence in its many guises shatters young people's lives – their dreams, their learning, their physical and emotional well-being. They draw out the complex relationships between violence and poverty, raising questions about whether we should privilege the reduction of poverty first in order to remove structural violence, or should we pursue anti-violence strategies to reduce the harmful effects of violence. Of course the answer is both – we need to address the links between gender violence and economic disadvantage; and we need to focus on masculinity, and the ways in which patriarchy perpetuates violence against young people (as in teacher–pupil violence) and by young people (as in the case of young men enacting violent masculinities as a form of resistance to their marginalisation). The educational challenge is slowly, painstakingly to support young people's quests to re-stitch the violated fragments, weaving the threads in ways that learn from but try not to repeat past inequities and violations, to struggle towards safer futures.

References

Aikman, S. (2010), 'Marching to different rhythms: international NGO collaboration with the state in Tanzania'. *Development in Practice*, 20 (4–5), 498–510.

Alkire, S. and Sumner, A. (2013), 'Multidimensional poverty and the post-2015 MDGs'. *Development*, 56 (1), 46–51.

Butler, J. (1999), *Gender Trouble: Feminism and the Subversion of Identity*. London and New York: Routledge.

Dejaeghere, J., Parkes, J. and Unterhalter, E. (2013), 'Gender justice and education: linking theory, policy and practice'. *International Journal of Educational Development*, 33 (6), 539–45.

Gunning, I. (1991), 'Arrogant perception, world travelling and multicultural feminism: the case of female genital surgeries'. *Columbia Human Rights Law Review*, 23, 189–248.

Kirk, J. (2007), 'Gender-based violence in and around schools in conflict and humanitarian contexts'. In G. Terry and J. Hoare (eds), *Gender-Based Violence* (pp. 121–32). Oxford: Oxfam.

Leach, F., Dunne, M. and Salvi, F. (2014), *A Global Review of Current Issues and Approaches in Policy, Programming and Implementation Responses to School-Related Gender-Based Violence (SRGBV)*. Paris: UNESCO Education Sector.

Leach, F., Slade, E. and Dunne, M. (2012), *Desk Review for Concern: Promising Practice in School Related Gender Based Violence Prevention and Response Programming Globally*. Dublin: Concern Worldwide.

Lundgren, R. (2013), 'Intimate partner and sexual violence among adolescents: reviewing the evidence and identifying the way forward'. Paper for Expert Group Meeting on Adolescent Sexual and Reproductive Health, 4–6 February.

Miske, S., Meagher, M. and DeJaeghere, J. (2010), 'Gender mainstreaming in education at the level of field operations: the case of CARE USA's indicator framework'. *Compare: A Journal of Comparative and International Education*, 40 (4), 441–58.

Nussbaum, M. (2005), 'Women's bodies: violence, security, capabilities'. *Journal of Human Development*, 6 (2), 167–83.

Parkes, J. and Heslop, J. (2013), *Stop Violence Against Girls in School: A Cross-Country Analysis of Change in Kenya, Ghana and Mozambique*. London: ActionAid International.

Ricardo, C., Eades, M. and Barker, G. (2011), *Engaging Boys and Young Men in the Prevention of Sexual Violence: A Systematic and Global Review of Evaluated Interventions*. Sexual Violence Research Initiative (hosted by the Medical Research Council, South Africa) for the Oak Foundation.

Stewart, F. (2002), *Horizontal Inequalities: A Neglected Dimension of Development*. Oxford: QEH Working Paper 81.

United Nations (2011), *Five Years On: A Global Update on Violence against Children. Report from the NGO Advisory Council for follow-up to the UN Secretary-General's Study on Violence Against Children*. New York: UN.

Unterhalter, E. (2012), 'Silences, stereotypes and local selection: negotiating policy and practice to implement the MDGs and EFA'. In A. Verger, H. Kosar Atinyelken and M. Novelli (eds), *Global Education Policy and International Development: New Agendas, Issues and Policies* (pp. 79–100). London: Bloomsbury.

Unterhalter, E., Yates, C., Makinda, H. and North, A. (2012), 'Blaming the poor: constructions of marginality and poverty in the Kenyan education sector'. *Compare: A Journal of Comparative Education*, 42 (2), 213–33.

Index

ACASI *see* audio computer-assisted self-interviewing
ActionAid 138–9, 144–6, 148n1, 203, 204
adolescent development 172–3
advocacy 144, 146, 148n6, 186
Africa: audio computer-assisted self-interviewing 38; ethical issues in research 41; intimate partner violence 17; NGO reports 176, 178; school violence 30–1, 33, 34; sex education 136; sexuality in 138–46; war and conflict 16, 18, 179
Agamben, G. 171
agency 5, 63; corporal punishment 85, 90, 95; girls' sexuality 143, 144, 147; structural violence 137; young Black men in South Africa 114n2
Alderson, P. 40
alternative masculinities 103, 113, 165
anger 126, 129, 130
anonymity 41–2
apartheid 104, 188
Archer, L. 22
Asia: corporal punishment 68; intimate partner violence 17; school violence 33, 34; war and conflict 18
audio computer-assisted self-interviewing (ACASI) 38
avoidance strategies 59, 62, 128–9

Balagopalan, S. 70
Balfour, R. 189
Barker, G. 132
Because I am a Girl: Learning for Life (Plan International) 168, 171–80
behaviour, teaching good 93, 95, 96

Beijing Declaration and Platform for Action (1995) 13, 183
belonging 105, 132
Bernault, F. 85
bio-politics 168–9
bodies: commodification of female 4, 32; sexualisation of female 135
Botswana 33, 35, 37, 85, 136
Bourdieu, Pierre 15, 52, 60, 106, 113, 119, 132n1, 197, 203
Bourgois, Philippe 12–15, 23, 52
boxing academy 157, 161, 202
boys: children's ideal masculinities 140; contemporary masculinities 22–4; corporal punishment 67, 68, 70, 72–7, 80, 93–4, 97n1; domestic violence 63; encouraged into violence by girls 162; essentialisation of 15; gangs in Brazil 154, 157, 159, 160, 161, 164; methodological challenges 36; NGO reports 178–9; over-reporting of sexuality activity 35; Peru 125; prevalence of sexual violence against 17, 179; sexual abuse in schools 34; sexuality 135, 140–1, 144, 145–6; South Africa 184, *see also* masculinity
Brazil 8, 38, 153–67, 201, 202, 203
bribery 123
Buller, Ana Maria 7, 118–34, 199, 200, 202
bullying 5, 30, 33, 184
Butler, Judith 21, 198

Cambodia 176
Capability Approach 7, 86, 87–8, 90–5, 198, 203
capital 106

capitalism 179–80
CARE 204
Caribbean 31, 33
caste 31–2, 67, 69–70, 78, 80
CATs *see* Community Advocacy Teams
CEDAW *see* Convention on the
   Elimination of All Forms of
   Discrimination Violence Against
   Women
cellphones 190–1, 193n5, 203
Chambers, Robert 36
chastity 140, 145, 147
Chege, F. 43–4, 95
childhood 169–70, 171, 173, 174, 180,
   198
children: corporal punishment 7, 67–83,
   84–99; domestic violence in Vietnam
   7, 51–66; ethical issues in research
   38–42; methodological issues 35–6,
   37; UN Report on Violence Against
   Children 12, 14; war and conflict
   20–1; *see also* boys; girls; UN
   Convention on the Rights of the
   Child
Chilisa, B. 32, 37, 41, 136
Choudry, A. 193
Christianity 138, 140
Clacherty, G. 42
class: Brazil 155; corporal punishment
   79, 80; India 67; intersectionality
   31–2; NGO reports 173;
   reproduction of 106, 113; youth
   projects in Rio de Janeiro 164
classroom management 97
coercion 3, 7–8, 136, 137, 142–4,
   146–7
colonial schooling 69–70, 170
commodification of female bodies 4, 32
Common Indicators Framework 204
Community Advocacy Teams (CATs)
   148n3, 148n7
community interventions 131–2
confidentiality 38, 39, 41–2
conflict 16, 18–21, 30, 179
Confucianism 53–4
Connell, Raewyn 19, 94, 197
consent: informed consent in research
   39–40; sexual consent 136, 147
contraception 136, 141

Convention on the Elimination of All
   Forms of Discrimination Violence
   Against Women (CEDAW) 13, 183
Convention on the Rights of the
   Child (CRC) 13, 38, 169; corporal
   punishment 70, 79, 81n2, 84;
   participatory research 36; research
   principles 43
conversion factors 87
'co-operative conflict' 87–8, 90
corporal punishment 5, 30, 199;
   Capability Approach 86, 87–8;
   definition of 81n2; effects of 84; India
   7, 67–83; international research 68–9;
   local support for 32; parents' views on
   77–9, 94; Peru 124; poverty linked
   to 75–7; prevalence 72, 73–4; reasons
   for using 85–6; research methods and
   ethics 71–2, 88; South Africa 184;
   Tanzania 7, 84–99
corruption 123, 199
CRC *see* Convention on the Rights of
   the Child
'crisis of youth' 153
cultural capital 106, 114
culture: corporal punishment 97; female
   genital mutilation 202; NGO reports
   177, 178; research challenges 32;
   virginity testing 188
curriculum 177, 201
cyber-bullying 21, 30

Dakar Framework on Action on
   Education for All (2000) 13
Darwall, S. 91
dating violence 30
De Berry, Joanne 20
De Lannoy, Ariane 7, 103–17
Declaration on the Elimination of
   Violence Against Women (DEVAW)
   12, 13
denial 33, 34
denigration 5
DEVAW *see* Declaration on the
   Elimination of Violence Against
   Women
development discourses 172, 174, 180
Dieltiens, V. 186
discipline 69, 79

discrimination 12, 118; multi-layered 31–2; Peru 20; pregnant girls 141
dispositions 119, 132n1
Dockney, J. 193n5
domestic violence: children's experiences of 56–9; children's responses to 59–61, 62–3; corporal punishment linked to 86; definition of 51; influence on schooling 61–2; Peru 124, 126, 128; protection of research participants 40; research methodology 52–3; strengthening girls' capacity to challenge 145; Vietnam 7, 51–66, 200; *see also* intimate partner violence
Donald, D. 42
Dowdney, Luke 160, 161, 162, 163
drawing activities 37
dress 135, 140, 141
drugs 22, 23, 112, 128, 131, 157
drunkenness 56–7, 60, 124, 128
Dunne, M. 68, 69, 98n1

economic capital 106, 113
economic growth 55, 63
education 3, 15, 16, 24, 203; Brazil 153; countering violence 200; NGO reports 171, 174, 175, 176–8, 180; Peru 121, 131, 132; right to 169; sex education 136, 140–1, 147, 201; South Africa 114, 183, 186–7; war and conflict 20–1; youth employment projects 156; *see also* schools
Egypt 97n1
El Agustino 118–34
employment: Brazil 153, 156; Peru 121; Vietnam 55
Ending Violence Against Women: From Words to Action (2006) 14
EPOCH 72
essentialism 15, 19
ethical issues 38, 42, 43, 72
ethnicity 31–2, 53
Europe 30
everyday violence 5, 15, 118–19, 199; in the home 63; inequalities 21; Peru 7, 124–6; role of education 24
'eviction jobs' 127
exchange sex 4, 5, 94, 136, 137, 142–3, 144

exclusion 5, 32, 132, 155
explicit gender violence 68

family honour 33
family roles 54
Farmer, P. 118
favelas 153, 155–6, 157–8, 165n1
female genital mutilation 202
femininity: children's ideal femininities 140; discourses on 8; female teachers 91; hegemonic 178; India 70; Vietnam 54–5, 61; youth projects in Brazil 160–1; *see also* girls
feminism 17, 18, 32, 165, 192, 197–8, 203
field, concept of 119
financial security 143
football violence 123–4, 125, 127, 131
forced marriage 5
Foucault, Michel 69, 80, 168–9, 197
free will 137
Freire, Paulo 148n5
FRELIMO 20
The Future is Now (Save the Children) 168, 171–80

Gallagher, M. 38
Gandhi, Mahatma 16
gang-rape 3, 67
gangs 15, 23–4, 30, 199; Brazil 8, 153–4, 155, 156–64, 201; Peru 123, 125, 129, 200; South Africa 7, 105, 108, 109–10, 111, 112, 113
Gavey, N. 137, 142, 146
gender 5–6; corporal punishment 68–9, 77, 80–1, 86, 89, 91, 93–5, 97n1; feminist theorising 197–8; gangs in Brazil 154–6, 159–61; gender equality and NGO reports 177–80; 'gender gap' in research 153, 155; hegemonic masculinity 19, 21; hierarchies 53, 60, 63; norms 21; performativity 21; Peru 119, 125, 132; sexual norms 139–41; as social construct 31–2; teacher identities 96; Vietnam 53–4; *see also* femininity; masculinity
gender violence, conceptualisations of 5–6, 31–2, 184; *see also* violence

genital mutilation 202
Ghana 8, 35, 41, 44, 94, 138–46, 176,
     199, 201
Giddens, A. 106, 113
Gilbert, J. 165
girls: ActionAid project 204; Africa
     30–1; children's ideal femininities
     140; commodification of girls' bodies
     4, 32; corporal punishment 67, 68,
     70, 72–5, 76–7, 80, 93–4; domestic
     violence 63; essentialisation of 15;
     gangs in Brazil 154, 155–6, 157,
     158–65, 201; gender violence and
     teenage pregnancy in South Africa
     183–96; girlhood 21–2; girl-on-
     girl violence 30; methodological
     challenges 35, 36; NGO campaigns
     168, 171, 172–80; prevalence of
     sexual violence against 17, 179; sexual
     harassment 33, 34; sexuality 35,
     135–50, 199; *see also* femininity
girls' clubs 144, 145, 148n6, 201
governmentality 168–70, 179–80
Grant, M.J. 185
Guinea 19
Gunning, Isobelle 202

habitus 52, 60, 62, 63, 119, 131, 132n1
Hallman, K. 184, 185
Harber, C. 69
harmony 55, 58–9, 60, 63
Hart, R.A. 37
Haysom, Lou 187
Heaney, Seamus 25
hegemonic masculinity 19, 21, 23, 24,
     103–4, 105, 113, 178
Henderson, P.C. 106–7, 113, 114n2
Heslop, Jo 7–8, 135–50, 199
Hess, Tim 135–50
heterosexuality 22–3, 34, 136
hierarchies: gender 53, 60, 63;
     masculine 61, 132
higher education 186–7
hip hop music 129–30, 131, 132
HIV/AIDS 3, 136, 174; Kenya 38;
     Mozambique 138; participatory visual
     methodologies 189, 190, 191; school
     violence 30, 31; South Africa 187,
     188; Uganda 20
holistic approaches 153–4, 164, 201

homophobia 5, 22, 30, 34, 203
hopelessness 131
Horton, P. 61
human rights 17, 169, 202; corporal
     punishment 32; NGO reports 171,
     177; sexual harassment 32–3; South
     Africa 183, 192
Human Rights Watch 184
humiliation 5
Humphreys, S. 85, 91, 93–4, 96

identity 19, 106, 113; gangs 163; teacher
     identities 96–7; young Black men in
     South Africa 105, 109, 110, 113–14
Ikasi style 104–5, 108–9, 112
implicit gender violence 68
incest 191–2
India 3, 7, 20, 67–83, 179
individualism 22, 24
inequalities 4, 9, 11, 24, 203; ActionAid
     project 138; countering violence
     200; definitions of violence 12–15;
     domestic violence 52; everyday
     violence 21; global 16; habitus 52;
     intersecting 5, 32, 146, 164, 165,
     197, 199; model of violence 198–9;
     Peru 131; school violence 31; sexual
     coercion 136, 137; South Africa 104,
     185–6, 188, 202; structural violence
     7; vertical and horizontal 15, 16, 24,
     25; Vietnam 56, 58; war and conflict
     18, 20; youth projects in Rio de
     Janeiro 164
informed consent 39–40
institutional violence 122–3, 155
international non-governmental
     organizations (INGOs) 168, 170–80,
     202
intersectionality 5, 31–2, 146, 164, 165,
     197, 199
interventions 131–2, 144–6, 147, 168,
     201, 202
interviews 35, 36, 38; corporal
     punishment 71, 88; Peru 120–1;
     Vietnam 52; young Black men in
     South Africa 105–6
intimate partner violence (IPV) 5,
     16–17, 124, 137, 176, 203; *see also*
     domestic violence
Islam 135, 138, 140

Januario, Francisco 135–50
Jeffrey, C. 67
Jewkes, R. 184, 185
Jolly, Susie 135

Kapoor, D. 193
Kenya 3, 8, 38, 43–4, 94, 95, 138–46,
    199, 201
King, Martin Luther 16
Kirk, J. 189
Kleinman, A. 118
Kumar, K. 70

Latin America: gender parity in
    education 176; high levels of violence
    118; school violence 31, 33
Leach, Fiona 5, 6, 30–47, 97n1, 203,
    204
Learning for Life (Plan International)
    168, 171–80
Lewin, Thandi 183–96
Liberia 176, 179
Link, B. 131
literacy 177
local context 32, 43
love 143
Luta pela Paz (LPP) 156–7, 159,
    160–1, 162

Machakanja, P. 97n1
Machel, Graca 18
Malawi 176
Mandela, Nelson 16
marginalisation 4, 15, 40, 155, 157,
    193, 205
marriage 143, 147
masculinity 22–4, 205; age-related
    shifts 128; alternative masculinities
    103, 113, 165; children's ideal
    masculinities 140; corporal
    punishment 68, 85, 89, 91, 96;
    discourses on 8; gang identity 163–4;
    hegemonic 19, 21, 23, 24, 103–4,
    105, 113, 178; India 70; normative
    179; Peru 128, 130, 131, 132; school
    violence 33; Vietnam 61; young Black
    men in South Africa 7, 103, 104,
    105, 109, 110, 113; youth projects in
    Brazil 160–1, 163; *see also* boys
McRobbie, A. 22

measurement issues 204
Mediterranean 17
Merry, S.E. 53
methodological issues 35–8, 203–4;
    corporal punishment 71–2, 88; Peru
    120–1; sexuality 138–9; South Africa
    105–6; Vietnam 52–3
Middle East 16, 18, 33
Millennium Development Goals 14, 67,
    81n1, 183
misrecognition 119, 131
Mitchell, Claudia 5, 183–96
modernity 17, 21, 180
Moletsane, Relebohile 8, 183–96, 202
Moore, Henrietta 19
morality, sexual 135, 141, 187, 188,
    191, 202
Morrell, Robert 22–3, 68, 85, 104, 184
Morrow, Virginia 7, 38, 40, 67–83,
    98n1
Mozambique 8, 20, 94, 138–45, 199,
    201
Mullins, C. 130
music 129–30, 131, 132, 202

NGOs *see* non-governmental
    organizations
Nguyen Thi Thu Hang 7, 51–66
Nigeria 176
non-governmental organizations
    (NGOs) 8, 12, 201; Brazil 155, 157,
    158, 164, 203; critiques of 202; Save
    the Children/Plan International
    reports 168, 170–80
normalisation of violence 126, 130
norms 21, 202; corporal punishment
    67, 85, 95; countering violence 200;
    'gender regime' of schools 32; model
    of violence 198, 199; school as site of
    governance 174; sexual 139–41, 147
North Africa 33
Ntseane, G. 32, 37, 41

Oando, Samwel 135–50
Observatório de Favelas 157, 160
oppression 7, 15, 16, 24, 118, 122, 131
Owen, S. 85

Pakistan 3, 9n1, 34, 173
Panday, S. 193

parents: ActionAid project 145;
domestic violence in Vietnam 56–62,
63; informed consent 39–40; views
on corporal punishment 77–9, 94;
violent parents in Peru 124, 127–8,
131
Parkes, Jenny 3–10, 11–29, 135–50,
197–206
participatory research 36–7; ethical
issues 38, 40; participatory visual
methodologies 8, 37, 183, 189–92,
193, 203
patriarchy 19, 34, 37, 67, 205
payment of research participants 36, 42
Pearce, J. 164
pedagogy 174
Pells, Kirrily 7, 51–66, 200
performativity 19, 21
Peru 7, 19–20, 69, 118–34, 199, 200,
202
Phelan, J. 131
Philippines 176
Pickett, K. 17
Pinheiro, P.S. 81
Pinker, Steven 17–18
Pitts, John 23
Plan International 168, 170–80
police 122, 155
policy: Brazil 153; countering violence
200; domestic violence 63–4; global
policy-making 18; informed by
research 44; South Africa 8, 183,
185–9, 192–3, 202; Vietnam 55
political violence 122
Population Council 43
Posel, D. 103
positive reinforcement 96
post-structuralism 198, 203
poverty 4, 6, 9, 11, 24, 197, 203,
205; ActionAid project 138; Brazil
155; corporal punishment 72, 73–4,
75–7, 80; countering violence 200;
definitions of violence 12–15, 32;
India 7; oppressions associated with
15; payment of research participants
42; Peru 120, 121–3, 131; policies
64; poverty line 15; school violence
31; sexuality and 135, 142, 144, 147;
shame 62; South Africa 104, 108,

188, 191; trap or net 15–16; Vietnam
55; war and conflict 18
Powell, M.A. 38, 43
power 3, 5, 12, 130–1; corporal
punishment 68, 69, 89; Foucault
on 168–9; inclusion of girls in anti-
violence projects 164; model of
violence 198; research issues 43;
sexual coercion 136; teacher-pupil
relationships 144; Vietnam 54
pregnancy 141, 142, 146; *see also*
teenage pregnancy
privacy 38
protection of research participants 39,
40–1
public/private spheres 154–5

questionnaires 35, 38, 88

race: apartheid in South Africa 104;
governance of childhood 170;
intersectionality 31–2; youth projects
in Rio de Janeiro 164
racism 23, 104
Ramphele, M. 114n3
rape 17, 23, 136, 137, 142; definition of
sexual violence 33; India 3, 67; police
perpetrators 155; school violence 31;
sentences for 3; South Africa 184,
191–2; war and conflict 18, 19–20
Ratele, K. 104
refugees 19
religion 31–2, 140, 201
Renold, Emma 22
reproductive role of women 54, 56
research: agenda for 202–4; challenges
31–4; corporal punishment 68–9;
ethical issues 38–42, 43; 'gender
gap' in 153, 155; methodological
challenges 35–8, 203–4; participatory
visual methodologies 8, 37, 183,
189–92, 193, 203; recommendations
42–4; school violence 6, 30–47;
violence in Brazil 157–8; young Black
men in South Africa 105–7; *see also*
methodological issues
resentment 126, 198, 199
resilience 61, 62, 63, 199
respect 91

revenge 126, 130
Rewrite the Future (Save the Children)
    171–80
rights discourse 169
Rio de Janeiro 153–67
Ripoll-Núñez, K. 68
'risk societies' 21
risk-taking 23, 173
Risley, A. 153, 155, 164, 197
Rivers, C.R. 33
Rohner, R.P. 68
Rojas, V. 69
Rossetti, S. 33
Rotas de Fuga 156–7, 158–9, 160–1,
    163
rural areas: corporal punishment 72,
    73–4, 76; Peru 120; South Africa
    189, 193
Rwanda 20, 176
Rydstrom, H. 54, 55, 61

Sabaa, Susan 135–50
Saunders, P. 25n1
Save the Children 43, 53, 68, 168,
    170–80
Scheper-Hughes, N. 52
schools 3, 5, 30–47, 170; ActionAid
    project 138; corporal punishment 67,
    68, 69–81, 84–99, 199; countering
    violence 200, 201, domestic
    violence influence on schooling
    61–2; ethical issues 38–42, 43; India
    69–70; methodological challenges
    35–8; NGO reports 8, 172–80; Peru
    122–3, 125; research challenges
    31–4; research recommendations
    42–4; resilience boosted by school
    experience 63; sex education 136,
    140–1, 147, 201; South Africa
    109, 110–11, 184, 186, 187, 188;
    whole-school approaches 203, *see also*
    education
Sen, Amartya 7, 87, 198
Sen, Atreyee 20
sex 7–8, 135–6, 203; corporal
    punishment for sexual relationships
    94; criminalisation of 146;
    methodological challenges facing
    researchers 35; South Africa 184,

187; transactional sex 32, 191; *see also*
    sexuality
sex education 136, 140–1, 147, 201
'sexting' 21
sexual abuse 22, 31, 44n1; definition of
    32; protection of research participants
    41; school violence 34; *see also* sexual
    violence
sexual exchange 4, 5, 94, 136, 137,
    142–3, 144
sexual harassment 5, 30, 32–3, 41, 174,
    177
sexual violence 17, 136, 137, 138;
    definition of 33; measurement
    issues 204; NGO reports 177, 179;
    Peru 125; in schools 30–1, 33, 34,
    41; secrecy and denial around 33,
    34; South Africa 184, 187, 191–2;
    strengthening girls' capacity to
    challenge 147; war and conflict 18,
    19–20, 30; *see also* rape; sexual abuse
sexuality 31–2, 135–50, 173, 199,
    203; ActionAid intervention 144–6;
    coercion 136, 137, 142–4, 146–7;
    research methods 138–9; sexual
    norms 139–41; social construction of
    137; South Africa 187–8, 193, 202;
    see also sex
shame 198, 199; poor children 62;
    pregnancy 141; teachers 91, 93
Shiv Sena movement 20
Sierra Leone 19, 179, 201
silence 34
Singh, Renu 7, 67–83
single mothers 20
social capital 106, 114, 131, 156
social justice 37
social networks 200–1
social structures 95
social support 60, 111–12, 164, 185
Socialism 53, 54, 55
son preference 54, 58
South Africa: corporal punishment 68,
    85, 98n1; gender violence in 8,
    183–96, 202; masculinities 23;
    research methodology 105–6; sports
    training 25n2; teenage pregnancy
    183–4, 185, 186–8, 190–1, 192–3;
    young Black men in 7, 103–17

South Asia 34
sovereign power 168–9
The Spirit Level (Wilkinson and Pickett)
    11, 25n1
sports training 25n2, 157, 160, 161
Stewart, Frances 15, 198
stigma 141
Straus, M. 85, 86
street violence 124–5, 154
structural violence 4, 7, 24–5, 118, 146,
    203; as cause of domestic violence
    52; coercion 137, 147; definition of
    12–15; everyday violence 118–19;
    interpersonal and personal effects
    of 199; Peru 119–20, 121–4, 131;
    poverty 15–16, 205
subjectification 24
subjectivity 5, 61, 62, 173
sublimation mechanisms 129–30, 202
Subramanian, R. 70
surveys 30, 35, 36, 53, 55, 71
Swartz, Sharlene 7, 103–17
symbolic capital 106
symbolic violence 5, 8, 15, 24–5, 119,
    199, 203; coercion 137, 147; habitus
    52; poverty 15–16; Vietnam 58, 60

taboos, sexual 33, 136, 144, 145
Tanzania 7, 84–99, 136, 176, 199, 201
Tao, Sharon 7, 84–99, 199, 201, 203
Taoism 53, 55
teachers: attitudes and experiences of
    43–4; constraints on capabilities
    90–5, 201; corporal punishment
    7, 67, 70–1, 74–9, 84–97, 184;
    following protocol 92–3, 95–6;
    India 70; informed consent 39;
    NGO reports 175, 177; Peru 122–3;
    sexual harassment by 33, 41; sexual
    relationships with 143–4; sexual
    violence by 31, 34, 41; South Africa
    184, 187, 190–1, 193
teenage pregnancy: Africa 30;
    punishment of pregnant girls 146; Rio
    de Janeiro 162; sexual coercion 142;
    shame 141; South Africa 183–4, 185,
    186–8, 190–1, 192–3
Teni-Atinga, G. 44
terminology 32–3

terrorism 120, 122
'tit-for-tat' logic 126, 130, 132
Tomaselli, K. 193n5
training: teachers 96–7, 175; youth
    employment projects 156
transactional sex 32, 191; *see also* sexual
    exchange

Uganda 20, 176
UN Convention on the Rights of
    the Child (UNCRC) 13, 38, 169;
    corporal punishment 70, 79, 81n2,
    84; participatory research 36; research
    principles 43
unemployment 104, 107, 156
United Kingdom (UK) 17, 21, 22, 23
United Nations (UN): Declaration on
    the Elimination of Violence Against
    Women 12, 13; High-Level Panel
    Goals 80; Report on Violence Against
    Children 12, 14; Security Council 14;
    see also UN Convention on the Rights
    of the Child
United States (US) 17, 23, 30, 68, 85
Unterhalter, Elaine 6, 11–29, 199, 202,
    203
urban areas 72, 73–4, 118, 120

Vavrus, F. 136
verbal abuse 74–5, 94
video projects 37, 189, 190–2
Vienna Declaration (1993) 13
Vietnam 7, 51–66, 200
violence 3–4; countering 199–202;
    definition of 4, 12–15; differing
    conceptualisations of 31–2; female
    perpetrators 21–2, 30; gangs in Brazil
    153, 154–6, 157–65; implicit and
    explicit gender violence 68; increase
    in 16–18; intergenerational cycle of
    119; multi-dimensionality 8, 18,
    197–9, 202; NGO reports 175–7,
    178, 179; normalisation of 126, 130;
    Peru 118, 122–32; political solutions
    180; poverty and 4, 6, 9, 11, 205;
    research agenda 202–4; in schools
    30–47; South Africa 103, 104,
    183–96, 202; strengthening girls'
    capacity to challenge 145, 147;

terminology 32–3; Vietnam 51–66; 'violence continuum' 52, 119; *see also* structural violence; symbolic violence
virginity testing 187–8
visual methods 8, 37, 183, 189–92, 193, 203

Wagner, K. 85
Walby, Sylvia 17
Walker, L. 113
war and conflict 16, 18–21, 30, 40, 179
well-being 86, 87
Wells, Karen 8, 168–82, 202
WHO *see* World Health Organization
Wilding, Polly 8, 153–67, 201, 203
Wilkinson, R. 17
Wilson, Emma 7, 51–66
witchcraft 144

womanhood 54
World Health Organization (WHO) 16–17, 40, 118, 179

Xu, X. 85

Young, Iris Marion 15, 197
Young Lives 6–7, 9n2, 64n1, 203; ethical issues 42; India 67, 71, 76; methodological challenges 35–6; Vietnam 52–3
Yousafzai, Malala 9n1
Youssef, R. 97n1
youth, crisis of 153
youth projects 156–7, 158–65

Zambia 176
Zimbabwe 35, 98n1, 176